Global Macro

Global Macro

Theory and Practice

Andrew Rozanov

Risk books

Published by Risk Books, a Division of Incisive Media Investments Ltd

Incisive Media
32–34 Broadwick Street
London W1A 2HG
Tel: +44(0) 20 7316 9000
E-mail: books@incisivemedia.com
Sites: www.riskbooks.com
www.incisivemedia.com

ISBN 978 1 906348 90 8

British Library Cataloguing in Publication Data
A catalogue record for this book is available from the British Library

Publisher: Nick Carver
Commissioning Editor: Sarah Hastings
Managing Editor: Lewis O'Sullivan

Designer: Lisa Ling
Copy-edited by Laurie Donaldson

Typeset by Mark Heslington Ltd, Scarborough, North Yorkshire
Printed and bound in the UK by Berforts Group Ltd

Endorsements and praise for *Global Macro: Theory and Practice*

Congratulations to Permal for organizing a marvelous contribution to understanding global macro investing – a must read! Often I am asked to recommend a book so that one can better understand this approach – and Permal has provided such insight with a diverse, articulate group of professionals.

M. Elaine Crocker, President, Moore Capital Management, and former Executive Vice President of Trading Administration, Commodities Corporation

Unprecedented levels of uncertainty, a risk on / risk off roller-coaster, "basket cases" in need of structural reform now to be found not so much in emerging markets, but in the developed world – this is indeed a time for investors to "think the unthinkable and not to expect normal rules to apply," as ably put by one of the contributors to this book. In an environment like this, it is particularly gratifying to welcome this timely initiative by Permal that provides a thoughtful look at one of the main investment styles in alternatives – global macro, making a strong case for its long-term investing value. I have no doubt it will help investors immensely in navigating the challenges of portfolio construction.

Arminio Fraga, Chairman and Chief Investment Officer, Gávea Investimentos, and former Governor of the Central Bank of Brazil

"Global Macro: Theory and Practice" is an important primer for institutions seeking to understand macro from two sides of the looking glass: the view of practitioners like myself and the view of investors. The broad range of topics covered – discretionary versus systematic approaches, the role of risk management in macro, the role of policy analysis and prediction in macro, among others – will draw institutional investors into the stimulating world I have lived and breathed for three decades.

Paul Tudor Jones II, Co-Chairman and Chief Investment Officer, Tudor Investment Corporation

This is a fascinating book which covers an important and all too commonly misunderstood strategy. Macro investing has a long and illustrious history which is entertainingly described. At the same time the book provides a comprehensive overview of how this strategy differs so much from other investment approaches. The engaging writing style makes it an appealing read for anyone interested in broadening their understanding of investing and a compulsory read for investors who want to fully understand the different styles, strategies and challenges of macro.

Colm O'Shea, Founder and Chief Investment Officer, COMAC Capital LLP

A well-conceived and superbly executed volume that is a must read for anyone interested in portfolio management. The nature and role of global macro is sufficiently poorly understood to evoke the fable of the blind men and the elephant. The comprehensive treatment here, offered by an array of insightful practitioners engaged in its various facets, explicates the full global macro elephant in highly readable fashion. The central takeaway: a properly constructed and sized allocation to global macro managers will improve the expected risk-adjusted returns of any investment portfolio.

F. Helmut Weymar, Founding Chairman and Chief Executive Officer, Commodities Corporation

Contents

About the Editor

Andrew Rozanov is managing director and head of institutional portfolio advisory at Permal Group, responsible for advising sovereign wealth funds and other long-term institutional investors on various aspects of asset allocation, portfolio construction, risk management and alternative investments. Before joining Permal, he worked at State Street, where he was managing director and head of sovereign advisory, and in various other roles at State Street Corporation, as well as working at UBS Investment Bank. Andrew is well known in the industry for having introduced the term "sovereign wealth funds", and is a Chartered Financial Analyst (CFA), Financial Risk Manager (FRM) and Chartered Alternative Investment Analyst (CAIA). He holds a master's equivalent degree in Asian and African Studies from Moscow State University.

About the Authors

Barry Bausano is president of Deutsche Bank Securities and global co-head of market prime finance, and previously served as head of equities Americas and global head of hedge funds. He is on the board of Deutsche Bank Securities, the Equities Global Executive Committee and the Americas Corporate Banking and Securities Executive Committee. Barry has previously been a macro hedge fund manager at Tiger Management, Steinhardt Partners, Moore Capital Management and Red Wolf Capital, after beginning his career at Kidder Peabody. He graduated from Harvard College with a degree in economics, and is on the board of directors of the Managed Funds Association.

Arjan Berkelaar is head of investment strategy and risk management at KAUST Investment Management Company, the sole advisor to the King Abdullah University of Science and Technology Endowment in Saudi Arabia. He was previously a principal investment officer and head of multi-asset class investment strategies at the World Bank Treasury, where he was responsible for developing investment strategies and advising internal and external clients on asset allocation and related policy matters. Arjan has also advised central banks on reserve management issues and sovereign wealth funds, including oil funds and national pension reserve funds, on asset allocation and investment strategies. He holds a PhD in finance from the Erasmus University Rotterdam and an MSc in mathematics from the Delft University of Technology, and is a CFA and CAIA charterholder.

John Casano is a managing member and co-founder of Financial Diligence Networks, LLC, and has been allocating to hedge funds since 2001. He was previously employed as a senior hedge fund research consultant at NEPC, LLC, where he was involved in hedge fund research and due diligence activities, and has provided consulting services for allocations to non-traditional asset classes made by various public, corporate, Taft–Hartley and endowment/foundation clients. Prior to joining NEPC, John was employed at Cambridge Associates, and since 2001 has also held hedge fund research and risk management related functions at many fund of hedge funds in New York. He has a BS in finance from Villanova University and is CAIA accredited.

Gerlof de Vrij is CEO/CIO at Blenheim Capital Management BV. Before joining Blenheim, he held roles as managing director, absolute return strategies, at APG Asset Management, head of strategy and research at PGGM Investments and head of strategy and research at the Philips Pension Fund. Gerlof has previously worked at ABN Amro, progressing to head of international bond research. He is a member of the expert panel of the Norwegian Government Pension Fund Global and a member of the investment committee of the Heineken Pension Fund, and has been a keynote speaker at many international conferences. Gerlof graduated in monetary economics from Tilburg University, and was assistant professor at Radboud University Nijmegen.

Simon Fox, director of macro, currency and commodity research at Mercer, is responsible for developing the firm's intellectual capital and global manager research coverage with respect to global macro hedge funds, currency and commodity strategies, having been with Mercer since 2003. He is also chair of the macro ratings review committee as well as a member of Mercer's Alternatives Investment Committee. Simon works with a broad range of clients, advising on manager selection and portfolio construction. He has a degree in mathematics from Oxford University and a masters in European politics and policy from the London School of Economics, and is a CFA charterholder.

Gene Frieda has served as a senior global strategist for Moore Capital since May 2007, focusing on global macro policy issues. Prior to joining Moore Europe, he served as the global head of emerging markets research and strategy and as a proprietary trader at RBS, based in London. Between 1995 and 2002, at various times Gene ran global emerging markets research, Asian research and Latin

American research for IDEAGlobal and 4Cast from bases in New York, London and Singapore. He received an MSc in economics from the London School of Economics and BA degrees in political science and economics from the University of Oklahoma.

Roy Hoevenaars is portfolio manager at Blenheim Capital Management BV. Before joining them in 2012, he worked at APG Asset Management, where his last role was as senior portfolio manager for the GTAA fund. His responsibilities included development and portfolio management of cross-asset systematic absolute return strategies, as well as focusing on volatility and correlation markets for equities and currencies. Prior to that, Roy held several other roles within APG. He has also held part-time academic positions at Maastricht University, where he obtained a PhD in financial econometrics and an MSc degree in econometrics and operations research, and is a lecturer in derivatives and asset allocation at postgraduate courses.

Omar Kodmani is president of the Permal Group, managing all day-to-day aspects of the business. He was previously senior executive officer, responsible for monitoring Permal's international investment activities as well as asset-gathering initiatives. Before joining Permal in 2000, Omar worked at Scudder Investments in London and New York, where he developed the firm's international mutual fund business. Prior to that, he worked at Equitable Capital (now part of Alliance Bernstein). Omar holds the CFA designation, an MBA in finance from New York University Stern School of Business, a BA in economics from Columbia University and a GC certificate from the London School of Economics.

David Murrin is chairman of Emergent Asset Management. After starting his career in the oil exploration business, he has spent the last 25 years in the financial markets, first at JP Morgan on their internal MBA equivalent finance programme, then trading FX, bonds, equities and commodities, before founding and managing their European market analysis group. David founded Apollo Asset Management in 1993, and co-founded Emergent Asset Management in 1997 and Emvest in 2008. He published the book *Breaking the Code of History* in 2011, and speaks widely on it as a keynote speaker on television and company boards. In 2012, David also co-founded Spartent Global Solutions. He has an honours degree in geophysics from Exeter University.

Barry Schachter has led the risk management function at five hedge funds, including the global macro funds, Caxton Associates and Moore Capital, and worked in risk management at Chase. He was also involved in derivatives regulation and bank supervision at the CFTC and the US Comptroller of the Currency, and has been a board member of PRMIA and IAFE. Barry is a fellow of the program in mathematics of finance at the Courant Institute of NYU and a research associate at the EDHEC Business School. Among his publications, he edited *Intelligent Hedge Fund Investing*. Barry is a speaker and blogger on risk management issues, and has a PhD and MA in economics from Cornell University and a BS from Bentley University.

Isaac Souede is chairman, chief executive officer and chief investment strategist for the Permal Group. He is also director of Permal Group Inc, a role he has held since 1987. Isaac was appointed chairman, chief executive officer and director of Permal Asset Management Inc in 2003, and director of Permal Group Ltd in 2005. He serves as a director of the Steinhardt Fund as well as other funds within the Permal Family of Funds. Isaac holds an MBA from the University of Michigan and a BS from the State University of New York at Stony Brook, and is a licensed CPA in the State of New York.

Menachem Sternberg is the chairman of the board and CEO of Eagle Trading Systems. He started his career in the global financial markets in 1979 with Commodities Corporation (USA), and held a senior position with Caxton Corporation prior to joining Eagle in 1997. Menachem has advised governmental and corporate clients as an economic consultant, and has also served on the faculty of Ben Gurion University and as a visiting scholar at Princeton University. He is a member of the NFA and received a BA from Tel Aviv University and a PhD in economics from Princeton University, with his doctoral dissertation dealing with theoretical issues concerning hedging and market behaviour.

Kenneth Tropin is chairman, founder and a principal of Graham Capital Management, as well as being chairman of their executive and investment committees, a member of the risk committee and responsible for managing the strategic investment of the firm's proprietary capital. Prior to founding Graham in 1994, Kenneth worked in the alternative investment industry, including as president and chief executive officer of John W. Henry & Company, and senior vice president and director of managed futures at Dean Witter Reynolds. He has also served as chairman of the Managed Funds Association and its predecessor organisation, which he was instrumental in founding during the 1980s.

Pieter Jelle van der Sluis is CIO quantitative strategies at Blenheim Capital Management. Before joining Blenheim in 2012, he worked at APG Asset Management, having senior roles within the research and equity departments, before becoming head of systematic strategies with responsibility for the internal systematic strategies portfolios, which he initiated and developed. He has also been a part-time assistant professor at VU University Amsterdam, and held full-time academic positions at the University of Amsterdam and at Tilburg University. He received a PhD in economics and econometrics from the University of Amsterdam and the Tinbergen Institute, and an MSc in econometrics from VU University Amsterdam.

Grant Wilson is the CIO and founder of Civic Capital, an independent macro advisor and emerging manager that provides an advisory service to hedge funds, proprietary trading desks, sovereign wealth funds and central banks. He started as an investment analyst and portfolio manager at Bankers Trust Australia in 1996, before joining the Government of Singapore Investment Corporation in 2001, where he was promoted to global head of macro and currencies. Grant then worked at Moore Capital in New York as a portfolio manager before launching Civic Capital in 2010. He has a BComm/LLB from the Australian National University and an MScIPE from the London School of Economics.

Igor Yelnik is the former head of portfolio management at IPM Informed Portfolio Management AB (Sweden), where he led the development of their core investment strategy, GTAA. IPM and its

GTAA fund have won a number of industry awards, including Hedge Fund Manager of the Year 2011 and Quant Provider of the Year 2010 from *Global Pensions* and Best Macro Fund Over US$1 billion 2011 from *HFM*. Prior to joining IPM, he co-founded St. Petersburg Capital, an asset management firm specialising in the Russian securities market, and Unibase Invest, a managed futures business based in Tel Aviv. Igor graduated from Leningrad Polytechnic Institute, where he obtained a masters degree in computer science in 1986.

Introduction

Isaac Souede

Permal Group

On behalf of Permal Group, I am very pleased to introduce this book on global macro, which I believe is the first of its kind in the industry. For a hedge fund strategy with such a long and storied tradition, it is most surprising how little information has been available to an interested reader over the years. While there have been several excellent collections of interviews with individual macro managers, offering helpful insights into their thinking, this book represents the first edited volume with contributions by a cross-section of experienced macro practitioners, and which is intended as a wide-ranging and in-depth introduction to this unique family of investment strategies.

Global macro has always been one of the core specialities of our firm since its founding in 1973. In 2013, as we celebrate Permal's 40th anniversary, we are re-confirming our commitment to this strategy, which has attracted renewed institutional interest since the global financial crisis of 2007–09. Permal Group runs one of the oldest and largest funds of global macro funds in the industry, which – together with separately managed accounts and other portfolios of global macro funds – constitute approximately US$8 billion, or 40% of our total assets under management (as of September 2012).

In the 20 years since its launch in 1992, our flagship fund of global macro funds has grown and evolved dramatically. During its first decade, it grew from just a handful of managers to 16 macro funds, both discretionary and systematic, with US$700 million in assets. Over the following 10 years, the number of managers increased to nearly 50, with core discretionary and systematic allocations being complemented by two sub-allocations: natural resources and relative value. Assets under management also grew to around US$5 billion during that time. In addition, a major portion of the fund is now invested through Permal's managed accounts with the underlying managers, which offer full transparency, increased liquidity, superior governance and the ability to engineer tailor-made exposures.

The idea for this book came out of multiple discussions with large institutional investors, who felt the need to learn more about the various aspects of global macro but had a difficult time finding comprehensive and in-depth analysis of institutional quality on the subject. With Permal's roots and reputation as a global macro specialist, we have often been asked by such investors for recommendations about useful reference materials or authoritative guides to this particular segment of the hedge fund industry. As there were no books that we felt met their needs, we decided to produce one instead.

We designed *Global Macro* to offer a representative cross-section of the views of different market practitioners, all operating in different segments of financial markets, yet all involved – in some important way – with global macro. Among the contributors there are discretionary and systematic managers, global macro strategists, a risk manager, a prime brokerage specialist, investment consultants, fund of funds managers and institutional investors. Each contributor was asked to focus on one particular aspect of global macro which they knew well and which, when combined with the other insights, would offer a panoramic yet nuanced view of the current state of play in the global macro industry.

The opening chapter, by my colleague Andrew Rozanov, provides the historical context for the book, tracing the origins and history of global macro, but also mapping out three important developments that are likely to shape the industry going forward. In the next chapter, Kenneth Tropin offers a unique perspective on the various issues and challenges involved in setting up and running a successful discretionary macro firm, while in Chapter 3 Menachem Sternberg introduces systematic macro, describing in some detail what makes for a successful quantitative approach to global macro. In Chapter 4, Igor Yelnik compares and contrasts different approaches, with a particular focus on the two streams that make up systematic macro: global tactical asset allocation (GTAA) and commodity trading advisors (CTAs).

In Chapter 5, Grant Wilson describes in some detail the unique role of a global macro strategist and the various issues and challenges involved in carrying out the job successfully; he includes a practical case study of how two strategists with very different methodological backgrounds would have handled a particular analytical challenge. In Chapter 6, Gene Frieda provides a tour de force of emerging market analysis as practiced by a global macro strategist, illustrating exactly how one could translate top-down macroeconomic scenarios into specific trade recommendations.

In Chapter 7, Barry Schachter elaborates on the key risk management principles as they apply to global macro, and reviews the challenges and limitations of using value-at-risk (VaR), stress testing and other risk management tools in the specific context of a global macro firm. Chapter 8, by David Murrin, focuses on one particular aspect of risk in global macro that is rarely discussed in detail: geopolitics. His chapter presents a unique analytical framework for thinking about geopolitical risk both logically and consistently.

In Chapter 9, Barry Bausano offers the unique perspective of a prime broker with a strong franchise of global macro clients who, in his previous professional life, also used to be a global macro practitioner that worked for three legendary macro managers. The next chapter, by John Casano, looks at sourcing and applying leverage in global macro strategies and how it is different from leverage in other hedge fund strategies – specifically in equity long/short funds.

In the next chapter, Simon Fox considers the role of global macro in institutional portfolios from an investment consultant's perspective, which is followed by a different perspective, that of a fund of hedge funds practitioner, as explained in Chapter 12 by Omar Kodmani and Andrew Rozanov.

Finally, the last two chapters consider global macro strategies from the perspective of a large institutional investor with a long-term investment horizon – a public or private pension plan, an endowment, a foundation or a sovereign wealth fund. In Chapter 13, Arjan Berkelaar walks the reader through the logic and process of allocating to discretionary and systematic macro strategies, run by external managers, in the context of a multi-asset class institutional portfolio. In Chapter 14, Gerlof de Vrij, Roy Hoevenaars and Pieter Jelle van der Sluis explain how a large and sophisticated asset owner with strong in-house management capabilities and infrastructure can design and operate a global macro programme, consisting of in-house discretionary and systematic components, as well as an external manager component.

On behalf of Permal Group, I would like to thank all the contributors for their time and effort in helping to bring this ambitious project to fruition and producing a truly outstanding book. I believe we are breaking new ground and filling a void in the hedge fund literature. It is my hope that this book will help investors achieve a better understanding of global macro strategies and what they can do for their portfolios.

1

Global Macro: Origins, History, Prospects

Andrew Rozanov

Permal Group

The purpose of this chapter is to set the stage and to provide an appropriate historical context for the rest of the book. All the other contributors were asked to focus on one particular aspect of global macro which they know well and which, when combined with the other insights, would offer a panoramic yet nuanced view of the current state of play in the global macro industry. This chapter, on the other hand, will look to the past, tracing the origins and history of global macro, but also look to the future, outlining three major developments that are likely to shape the industry going forward.

But, first, we must define our terms. While there is no universally accepted definition of "global macro," typically most market practitioners will agree on the types of strategies covered by this term. As with most hedge funds, global macro managers strive to generate attractive risk-adjusted absolute returns in all market conditions, but they go about it in a very distinct and unique way. Specifically, all global macro funds usually share the following five characteristics:

1. global scope (ie, risk taking across different geographies);
2. multi-asset coverage (ie, risk taking across different asset classes);
3. top-down approach (ie, positioning for broad market and asset class re-pricings);
4. focus on liquidity (ie, operating in the most liquid markets and instruments); and

5. asymmetric trade construction (ie, limited downside and unlimited upside).

Global macro is sometimes referred to as a "go anywhere" strategy, meaning that the manager is free to roam the world and to participate in different markets and asset classes in search of opportunities. While in other hedge fund strategies "style drift" is usually equated with "mission creep" and is seriously frowned upon, in global macro it is built into the mandate. When defined in such broad terms, global macro will necessarily cover multiple different styles and approaches. Indeed, throughout this book, there are constant references to sub-strategies that can be mapped along the following three dimensions:

1. discretionary versus systematic;
2. fundamental versus technical; and
3. trend following (momentum) versus relative value (mean-reversion).

For example, *systematic fundamental* managers typically base their investment decisions on macroeconomic and financial data (eg, growth, inflation, fiscal and monetary policy, company earnings, bond yields, etc), which are analysed quantitatively and which result in computer-generated trading signals and positions. Historically, this approach has been characteristic of global tactical asset allocation (GTAA) firms, which tend to focus more on relative value opportunities and mean-reversion trades. On the other hand, *systematic technical* managers usually base their investment decisions on price trends and patterns, which are also processed quantitatively and often result in trend-following or momentum-based trades. This is typical of commodity trading advisors (CTAs) or managed futures programmes.

A *discretionary fundamental* approach is usually centred on an individual risk taker, who analyses a broad range of economic and financial data, formulates an investment thesis and implements the trade. While certain quantitative tools and technical charts can be used to support the analysis, they do not constitute the defining core part of the investment process. In contrast, a *discretionary technical* approach would have charting techniques at its core, but as a global macro discipline it is relatively rare. Although most discretionary managers can put on both trend-following and relative value trades, their proportion and frequency will depend on specific market conditions and the idiosyncrasies of individual firms.

This chapter is structured in three parts. First, we will explore the improbable origins of global macro by looking at one particular aspect of the fascinating and multi-faceted career of John Maynard Keynes – namely, his evolution from a global macro trader to a value equity investor. We ponder the reasons for this transformation from the point of view of a modern-day macro practitioner. In the second part, we briefly review the history of global macro from the early 1970s onwards, focusing on those aspects that, in this author's opinion, have not been sufficiently emphasised in the existing hedge fund literature.[1] In the third part, and concluding the chapter, we will consider three major developments that are likely to shape the global macro industry through the 2010s.

THE TRANSFORMATION OF J. M. KEYNES[2]

Many global macro practitioners acknowledge the tremendous intellectual influence and inspiration they found in the work of one of their most illustrious predecessors – John Maynard Keynes.[3] While he was a man of many talents – a brilliant macroeconomist, a dazzling intellectual, a compelling writer and an influential statesman – he was also a very successful investor. His most impressive track record was built over the 22 years during which he managed the King's College endowment funds at Cambridge University, which was all the more remarkable for having been achieved over a period that included the financial crash of 1929, the Great Depression and World War Two.[4]

The history of Keynes's trading and investment activity is fairly well documented. He started speculating in financial markets before World War One in order to supplement his academic salary. By 1915, just under a third of his annual income was derived from investments. By 1919, Keynes had joined forces with a friend who was a partner in a stockbroking firm and a former colleague at the Treasury, to launch a trading syndicate set up to take advantage of the floating currencies that followed the war. Today, their enterprise would be considered a classic discretionary fundamental global macro hedge fund.

The fund started operations on January 1, 1920, launched with money from family and friends. Initially, Keynes went long the US dollar and short the German mark, the French franc and the Italian lira, betting that currencies of the economies devastated by the war would soon collapse as inflation took hold. By the end of February he was up more than 20%. In the following months, however, the gains on his positions were offset by a short bet on the pound sterling against the US dollar: the Bank of England unexpectedly raised interest rates, resulting in losses for the syndicate. Then, as financial markets became temporarily optimistic about the prospects of the Continental economies, European currencies rallied against the pound sterling and, although the rally was short-lived, it lasted long enough to wipe out the capital in Keynes's highly leveraged fund.

This was the first time in his investment career that Keynes blew up as a fund manager. He was lucky that his friends and family stood by him and did not redeem, with some even providing a critical bridge loan that enabled him to continue operations. Undeterred and confident in his analysis, Keynes persisted with his short forward positions in the three European currencies. Eventually, his view was vindicated: the positions moved decisively in his favour, and by the end of 1920 he had repaid his new borrowings and had a small profit. In two years, he cleared all of his debts to friends and family and had a decent profit to show for his trading in currencies and commodities.

Throughout the 1920s, Keynes followed a distinct investment approach that today would be described as global macro. He considered himself a "scientific gambler," putting on highly leveraged positions to speculate on currencies, commodities, bonds and equities. In 1921, on the day of his appointment as chairman of the board of a major British life insurance company, he proclaimed his central investment thesis for managing the firm's assets: "[We] ought to have only one investment and it should be changed every day."[5] His "active investment policy" combined investing in real assets with constant switching between short-dated and long-dated bonds, based on predictions for interest rate changes.[6] Keynes followed what he called a "credit cycle" investment strategy, based on indicators developed at the London School of Economics and the Economic Research Department at Harvard University, which claimed to predict changes in relative prices of different assets over the business cycle.[7] His approach at the time was all about market timing and forecasting short-term fluctuations.

However, after losing his second fortune in commodities in 1928 and in the stock market crash of 1929, Keynes embarked on a radical overhaul of his investment beliefs and his overall approach to financial markets: he made a decisive and conscious shift away from the top-down, credit cycle driven, global macro trading approach to a bottom-up, contrarian, relative value investment approach. While Lord Skidelsky, his famous biographer, likens Keynes simultaneously to George Soros and Warren Buffett, it may be more accurate to say that throughout his investment career Keynes underwent a transformation from a George Soros-type macro trader to a Warren Buffett-type equity investor. His new approach was based on: a long-term investment horizon; a large allocation to equity; a concentrated portfolio of carefully selected value stocks; and a strong contrarian bent (ie, buying, not selling, in a falling market). It was this approach that largely accounted for his remarkable 22-year track record at the King's College endowment funds.

While the above narrative describing the evolution of Keynes's investment philosophy is well established and documented, for a student of global macro one question remains unanswered: what was the main underlying reason that forced Keynes to switch from being a top-down macro trader to a bottom-up equity investor? After all, he appeared to possess many of the character traits and skills that should make for a highly successful global macro manager: a sharp and curious analytical mind; an ability to think creatively "outside the box"; a thorough understanding of macroeconomics; an appreciation for how irrational human emotions can drive market prices away from fundamentals; and the ability to change his mind whenever the facts changed.

Below we propose three possible explanations, which are not mutually exclusive. First, his brilliance as a macroeconomist and financial analyst notwithstanding, it is entirely possible – in fact, it is quite likely – that Keynes was a terrible risk manager. As modern-day macro practitioners will attest, when managing a highly leveraged fund in volatile and uncertain markets, very precise risk controls become absolutely critical – not just to the success, but to the survival of the fund. These risk controls include, among other things, appropriate position sizing, exposure limits, stop-loss levels and exit strategies, as well as the discipline to implement them unflinchingly. While a macro manager needs to be sufficiently independent-minded, they cannot afford to become overconfident and stubborn – they must accept that there will be numerous occasions when the market proves them wrong. A manager also needs to be fully focused and hands-on in their approach to risk management – in other words, they cannot afford to be distracted by other interests and pursuits. Finally, while no risk management system will ever be 100% fail-proof, a good macro manager always learns from their failures.

Keynes appears to have failed on all accounts. As one of his biographers noted, he "was extremely stubborn during short-term market fluctuations."[8] He may have changed his views whenever the facts changed, but sudden and unexplained market moves apparently did not qualify. Keynes was also constantly distracted by the multiple activities and commitments of his busy academic and public life, as well as his private affairs. Finally, he never seemed to learn from his blow-ups and "near-death" financial experiences. He was wiped out due to excessive leverage *three* times: in 1920–21, 1928–29 and 1937–38. The final episode is the most telling: even after he had switched to the highly successful approach of bottom-up value equity investing, which was producing solid results for the endowment funds, in his personal accounts Keynes yet again failed miserably due to excessive leverage and overtrading.

Another possible explanation for Keynes's decision to abandon his original top-down macro approach may have to do with his personality and temperament as an investor. Some investors just seem to be more naturally predisposed, as part of their "professional DNA," to be contrarian, to seek out relative value opportunities, and to earn size, value and illiquidity risk premia. This inclination often sits very uncomfortably in the context of a highly leveraged, short-term-oriented hedge fund. But once it is placed in a different context – that of an unleveraged and unconstrained long-term investment vehicle – often the same contrarian investor would flourish and begin to deliver spectacular returns.

In one of his works, Keynes wrote: "It may often profit the wisest [market operator] to anticipate mob psychology rather than the real trend of events [and] to anticipate the basis of conventional valuation a few months hence, rather than the prospective yield of an invest-

ment over a long term of years."[9] In other words, he clearly understood what was required to succeed as a trend-following or momentum-based trader, but must have decided he was neither inclined nor necessarily well suited to this style of investing. It is also important to note that his investment philosophy developed in parallel with his increasing theoretical emphasis on the social need for stabilising investment: Keynes now firmly believed that both governments and investors must fight the mania for liquidity.

Finally, a third possible explanation for the change in Keynes's investing style may have to do with the breakdown of the international trade and monetary system in the 1930s. Global macro investing works best in a globalised world of floating exchange rates, free trade and free cross-border capital movement. It also relies heavily on a predictable, transparent and well-functioning system of government regulation and liquidity provision by monetary authorities, implemented in a consistent and internationally coordinated way. Unfortunately, during the Great Depression there was a strong move globally towards greater nationalism and protectionism. The US adopted the Hawley–Smoot Tariff Act in 1930, which restricted global trade and accelerated the fall in commodity prices, while Britain departed from the gold standard in 1931, which disorganised the world's monetary system. As the US was not willing and the UK was not able to stabilise the global trade and financial system, the prospects for global macro trading were becoming increasingly dim. In that kind of environment, it would have been logical for US and UK investors to refocus on their respective stock markets.

Towards the end of his life, Keynes's crowning achievement as a global statesman was the establishment of a new post-war economic and financial world order – the Bretton Woods system of fixed exchange rates and closed capital accounts, overseen and administered by the International Monetary Fund and the World Bank. From a macro practitioner's perspective, however, it was highly ironic that the same man who started out his investing career trading free-floating currencies and commodities would effectively render global macro trading obsolete by fixing exchange rates and restricting capital flows. As a result, the global macro style of investing disappeared from the financial markets for almost three decades.

A BRIEF HISTORY OF (MODERN) GLOBAL MACRO

After World War Two, much of the Old World either ended up behind the Iron Curtain or lay in ruins. For a long time there were no meaningful trading or investing opportunities outside the US. But even as Western Europe and Japan gradually started to rebuild and grow, the Bretton Woods system effectively prevented the global macro style of trading from re-emerging in any shape or form. Unsurprisingly, the modern hedge fund industry takes its roots in long/short equity investing, pioneered by Alfred Winslow Jones in 1949.[10] For two decades after that, most hedge fund operators were traditional stock pickers – including those who decades later would reinvent themselves as global macro managers (George Soros, Michael Steinhardt, etc).

Things started changing rapidly when President Nixon took the US off the gold standard in August 1971, effectively ringing the death knell for the Bretton Woods system of fixed exchange rates. OPEC's oil embargo in 1973 led to skyrocketing oil prices, high inflation and extreme volatility, which in turn introduced new risks for many market participants. The financial industry responded by providing new hedging instruments, such as listed financial futures, which were highly liquid and easily tradable. All of a sudden, there were multiple new opportunities for profitable global macro trading, which were immediately seized by those who were best positioned to capitalise on them: specialist commodity traders.

While it is widely acknowledged that modern-day global macro investing developed out of two separate streams – the equity stream and the commodity stream – it is nonetheless important to set the record straight in terms of the actual chronological sequence of events. The commodity specialists came first and shaped the global macro industry for 15 years.[11] This was the first stage – growth and development – that was effectively dominated by a single firm: the legendary Commodities Corporation.

The second stage – which we shall refer to as the "golden age" of global macro – began around 1987 and lasted until 2000. During this period, the global macro style of investing matured and came into its own, becoming a widely accepted and closely followed segment of the hedge fund industry. While global macro traders with commodity backgrounds continued to do very well, this period was dominated by two charismatic macro traders who evolved from the equity stream: George Soros of Soros Fund Management and Julian Robertson of Tiger Management.

The third stage, which accounted for the first decade of this century, was a difficult time for global macro managers. First, when Tiger shut down and Soros restructured in 2000, there were widespread concerns that the strategy had hit the proverbial brick wall. Then, when it recovered and started growing again, it was increasingly eclipsed by other hedge fund strategies: this was the period of early institutionalisation of hedge funds, and institutions showed clear preferences for long/short equity and various arbitrage-type strategies. However, in the wake of the global financial crisis of 2007–09, when discretionary and systematic macro strategies outperformed with flying colours, institutional investors showed renewed interest in macro. This was the beginning of the current stage: broadening acceptance and integration of global macro in institutional portfolios. We shall now look at some of the highlights that characterised each individual stage.

Commodities Corporation[12]

The company was established in 1970 by F. Helmut Weymar, based in Princeton, New Jersey, with the objective of applying top-level scientific minds and cutting-edge computing technology to trading commodity markets.[13] This was one of the earliest examples of hardcore quants (or "rocket scientists") coming together to develop profitable trading models to manage money. For purposes of this chapter, we will highlight just three key developments commonly attributed to Commodities Corporation and which effectively laid the foundation of the modern-day global macro industry.

First, it was within the confines of Commodities Corporation that the concept of a *generalist* discretionary macro trader – someone taking positions across all geographies and asset classes, based on both fundamental and technical analysis – was first developed. Two legendary traders in particular, Michael Marcus and Bruce Kovner, were responsible for developing and fine-tuning this approach. A whole cohort of highly successful discretionary macro managers, also hired or seeded by Commodities Corporation, followed in their footsteps, eventually striking out on their own. The first among these global macro stars to go fully independent was Bruce Kovner himself, who in 1983 set up Caxton Corporation, which has since become one of the premier discretionary macro firms. Two other industry legends soon followed: Paul Tudor Jones with Tudor Investment Corporation and Louis Bacon with Moore Capital Management.

Second, Commodities Corporation was also responsible for developing one of the very first trend-following computer trading systems, which proved highly successful and spawned a whole new industry of CTAs. The computer model it deployed was called the Technical Computer System (TCS), and was first developed by Frank Vannerson in 1970 and refined over the years. It is ironic that the Commodities Corporation, which was originally established to develop a systematic fundamental approach to trading, instead became hugely successful in two other disciplines: discretionary fundamental and systematic technical. Success in the originally targeted discipline eluded the company, but was achieved much later by other firms in the industry.[14]

Finally, Commodities Corporation developed and refined a unique risk control and risk management system, which still survives, albeit in different forms, in practically all global macro firms, both discretionary and systematic. Essentially, each individual trader or trading module is treated as an independent profit and loss centre, managing its share of the overall capital allocation. Over time, the allocation increases with good performance and decreases with bad performance. If half of the allocated capital has been lost, all positions are closed and a mandatory cooling period is instituted. During this time, the trader responsible for the loss must write a memo to the management explaining what happened and what lessons have been learned to avoid a similar loss in the future. Invariably, the Commodities Corporation alumni who went on to manage their own highly successful funds instituted similar risk control and management systems at their own firms, thus making it part of the DNA of modern global macro.

Soros versus Tiger

Although George Soros and Julian Robertson initially launched their fund management careers as long/short equity specialists in the mould of A. W. Jones, both will likely be remembered as iconic global macro managers of the late 1980s and 1990s. While he may not have been aware of it at the time, George Soros ushered in the golden age of global macro in 1987, when he published his bestselling book *The Alchemy of Finance*, in which he described his philosophy and approach to macro trading.[15] When the book came out, suddenly everyone in the financial industry discovered global macro.

Then, five years later, when Soros succeeded in his massive speculation against the British pound – effectively ejecting it out of the Exchange Rate Mechanism and making a cool US$1 billion profit, thereby earning the dubious title of the "Man Who Broke the Bank of England" – it was not just the financial circles that were abuzz.[16] Suddenly, everyone with an interest in current affairs became obsessed with macro funds. And while he may have evolved into a full-fledged macro trader much later in the game than his commodity trading peers, George Soros deserves full credit for putting global macro on the map in such a determined and influential way.

With his spectacularly profitable currency trades, Soros proved that a talented hedge fund manager with a long/short equity background can be every bit as successful as the best currency traders. Julian Robertson proved the same point in the commodities markets. In 1994–95, based on in-depth and painstaking research, the Tiger team built up a massive short position in copper, which proved extremely volatile. Although their fundamental research unambiguously pointed in one direction – copper had nowhere to go but down – the price action throughout the period was very challenging: often prices would go up for no apparent reason, resulting in painful unrealised losses for Tiger. While many other hedge fund managers with short copper positions were squeezed out, Robertson held on and even added to his positions, believing firmly in the superiority of his research. Then, in the spring of 1996, a scandal broke out involving a rogue copper trader at a Japanese trading house and his failed attempts to support prices. The resulting price collapse was swift and brutal, vindicating Robertson and resulting in a tremendous profit for Tiger.[17]

As hedge fund managers, Soros and Robertson had a lot in common: both were strong, independent-minded individuals with larger-than-life personalities; both had been very successful long/short equity managers; both engaged in macro trading fairly late in their investing careers; and both had the ambition to be at the top of the hedge fund game, running the largest and best-performing fund in the industry.[18] But, in terms of investment philosophy and style, they could not have been more different.

One of George Soros's famous principles was to "invest first, investigate later." A large unexplained market move could be an inflection point, the beginning of a new trend or, more importantly, a harbinger of a major change in the "rules of the game."[19] A macro trader could spend a lot of time and effort researching the rationale, but by the time they were ready to put on a full-fledged position, the opportunity could be gone. Alternatively, they could formulate a tentative thesis and put on a small position immediately, treating it as an experiment or a hypothesis test. If subsequent investigation provided a clear explanation for the move and the trade was making money, the trader would increase position size aggressively to reflect the strength of their growing conviction. Otherwise, if the position was losing money and the hypothesis was wrong, they would close out early to limit their losses. It was also imperative to "listen to the market," but not because it was always right: Soros believed it was mostly wrong, but it could still be powerful and lasting enough to overwhelm any leveraged contrarian investor.

In contrast, at Tiger, investing was all about extensive, in-depth fundamental research; it would have been unthinkable for Robertson and his team to put on a trading position without first going through an exhaustive process of uncovering and evaluating everything there was to know about the situation, whether a stock investment opportunity in the long/short equity book or a commodity trading opportunity in the macro book.[20] It was all about the underlying fundamental story, which had to be well researched and well understood by the Tiger team. Then, and only then, a position would be put on in size, reflecting the strength of Tiger's conviction. If the market moved against it, not only would it *not* be a sign to get out, it would often present an opportunity to add to the original position. Robertson did not believe in listening to the market: in his view, there was no *market* as such, just a collection of individual stocks, currencies and commodities an investor could buy or sell.[21]

This is not to suggest that Robertson was inflexible: if the facts changed, just like Keynes, he could be quick to change his opinion. But a large unexplained market move was not the same as a change in the underlying fundamentals: if he still believed in the story, he would stick to his positions and maybe even add to them. Soros, on the other hand, would feel vulnerable and insecure:[22] a large unexplained market move could be signalling a change in fundamentals that was not yet visible; worse still, according to his *reflexivity* method, such a move could by itself affect fundamentals.[23]

Soros and Tiger represented two very distinct approaches to global macro. Although it would be an oversimplification to classify George Soros as a pure trend follower or momentum investor, his method was certainly much closer to the discretionary macro traders of the Commodities Corporation tradition. In contrast, Julian Robertson was more of a contrarian relative value investor, who sought to apply rigorous fundamental research to macro markets. We will briefly return to this important distinction in the final section, when we ponder the future of global macro investing.

From global macro to multi-strategy (and back)

When institutional investors began making sizable allocations to hedge funds in the late 1990s and early 2000s, global macro managers found themselves at a disadvantage. First, many macro funds were built around a single risk taker, who was typically the owner and founder of the firm, and who made all the critical decisions. In addition to the key-man risk and a lack of transparency around decision-making, to some institutions this suggested an investment process that was not particularly well defined or structured. Second, global macro was very difficult to pin down in terms of asset allocation: unlike most other hedge funds, there was no asset class or risk premium that could be used to anchor the allocation decision. Finally, many institutions had misgivings about global macro being a particularly risky strategy: compared to other hedge funds, volatility tended to be higher and Sharpe ratios lower, especially among systematic managers;[24] also, many institutions had a preconceived notion of macro managers applying excessive amounts of leverage.[25]

It also did not help that both Soros and Tiger were having trouble trading the irrational markets of the Internet mania. Eventually, just before the bubble burst, Robertson shut down the fund, while Soros restructured his operation and dialled down risk after Stanley Druckenmiller, his top lieutenant, resigned.[26] This prompted some observers to hastily pronounce that global macro was dead. Against this backdrop, and with a cool reception from institutional investors, the relative weight of global macro steadily declined, reaching an all-time low of 15% of hedge fund assets in 2007.[27]

During this early institutionalisation stage, many global macro managers realised that they had to evolve in order to capture their fair share of institutional flows: they invested heavily in state-of-the-art risk management infrastructure; upgraded their middle- and back-office operations; developed institutional-quality reporting and compliance systems; hired professional investor relations specialists; and introduced detailed succession and disaster recovery plans. Gradually, they acquired the look and feel of sophisticated, large-scale institutional asset managers.

More importantly, they increasingly made changes to the traditional single-manager, single-strategy business model. First, they hired more traders and portfolio managers – who were allocated capital alongside the main principal risk taker. While the latter often continued to manage the largest allocation, a team of macro traders with different and complementary styles contributed to a more diversified and stable return profile. Some firms actually made it a core part of their investment philosophy to operate broadly diversified multi-manager global macro funds, spanning the full spectrum of discretionary and systematic styles.

Second – and, in hindsight, much more controversially – some macro managers started to evolve not just into multi-manager, but multi-strategy firms. In fairness, this was not an entirely new development: just as Soros and Tiger, having evolved from the equity stream, traded both equity long/short and macro books, some of the macro managers from the commodity stream had also hired dedicated teams to manage equity investments alongside their traditional macro strategies.[28] However, since the turn of the century, this trend had accelerated and broadened in scope to include other strategies (credit trading, event-driven, statistical arbitrage, asset-backed securities, etc). Some of the larger macro funds even had small allocations to illiquid private equity-type investments.

For managers keen to attract institutional money, the logic of such evolution was compelling. Unlike macro, most trading books of a multi-strategy firm tended to have lower volatility and higher Sharpe ratios. Also, combining all of these different strategies with the original macro portfolio held the promise of a more diversified and stable return stream. Finally, since most strategies in a typical multi-strategy fund focused on a specific asset class or instrument type and exploited an easily identifiable risk premium, they were an easier fit within an institutional portfolio.

However, the global financial crisis of 2007–09 revealed the main flaw in this approach: strategies that appeared low risk and uncorrelated during normal times, actually carried massive left-tail risks and became highly correlated in abnormal times. Worse still, many underlying markets became so illiquid that it was impossible to exit positions at any price. As a result, some managers found themselves in an impossible situation: even as their core macro strategy outperformed dramatically, their overall returns were dragged down by massive losses in other strategies. Some of these managers, who had prided themselves on their ability to turn on a dime and change their positions at a moment's notice, were bogged down in illiquid markets, forced to restrict investor redemptions by introducing gates and side pockets.

As a result, a major rethinking of the multi-strategy format followed, with many global macro managers making a conscious decision to return to their roots by refocusing on their core strategy.[29] And for institutional investors, this change of direction could not have come a day too soon: discretionary and systematic macro were the only two hedge fund strategies that offered genuine decorrelation and diversification when it really mattered, while at the same time providing a positive expected return over the long term.[30]

THE FUTURE OF GLOBAL MACRO

With global macro being back in favour and gaining widespread acceptance among institutional investors, it is interesting to ponder what the future may hold. There are at least three major exogenous developments that can be expected to have a material impact on these strategies in coming years.

First, there is the all-pervading concern about the nature of the macroeconomic environment in the aftermath of the global financial crisis. All macro practitioners – not just hedge fund managers, but also central bankers and economic policymakers – are navigating through uncharted waters of massive and persistent deleveraging in the private sector, rock-bottom interest rates, unorthodox monetary policy, public and private debt overhang, high unemployment and anaemic growth.

Is the global economy on the mend or is it in the middle of its first "lost decade"? Is the unusual market behaviour of the early 2010s (ie, a succession of risk-on/risk-off regimes and high cross-asset correlations) a temporary aberration or the new norm? Are Treasuries at ultra-low interest rates a screaming sell or a screaming buy? Are global equities undervalued or overvalued? To answer these questions, a macro manager will need to work harder than ever before: the predictable pattern of normal business cycles and policy reactions has broken down, the level of uncertainty is extremely high and the cost of making the wrong call is higher than ever. If the world is indeed in the early stages of a protracted Japan-like scenario, then global macro managers will need to adapt.[31]

The second major impact on the future of global macro will come from the continuing development of emerging market economies. When George Soros first published his book in 1987, these markets were not really part of the standard macro trading universe. During the next 10 years, however, macro funds became a major presence in emerging markets – initially trading Brady bonds in the early 1990s, then successfully challenging unsustainable currency pegs in Asia and Latin America. But, even as these markets became more liquid and tradable, offering new opportunities for global macro funds, they were still just a sideshow: it was not critical for macro managers to understand what was going on in emerging market economies to be able to analyse and trade G10 markets successfully.

By the time of the global financial crisis this situation had changed dramatically: having a well-informed view on the macroeconomic situation and an accurate reading of the exchange rate, monetary and fiscal policies in emerging markets generally, and in China in particular, was now critical to formulating an accurate view on the G10 markets. Yet, most global macro firms still do not appear to have the same level of in-depth expertise and local presence in China and elsewhere in the emerging world that they traditionally have in the developed world. Given widespread concerns about the availability and reliability of data, having such local presence and expertise already commands a significant premium. The importance of being able to access and analyse data coming out of China and other emerging market economies over the next few years will become even more critical to success.

Finally, through the 2010s and beyond, global macro investing will likely undergo yet another important transformation, as the process of institutionalisation enters its next phase. Unlike all the other hedge fund strategies, global macro has the unique potential to be linked directly into top-down institutional decision-making: strategic and tactical asset allocation, portfolio construction and risk management. There is no reason why the role and place of global macro in institutional portfolios should be limited to the alternatives allocation. But what happens when the unique analytical apparatus and skill-set associated with global macro is transported from a short-term leveraged fund to a long-term, unleveraged and unconstrained institutional investor?

Many cash-rich institutional investors with inter-generational investment horizons are beginning to realise that they have a competitive advantage in taking on certain types of risk. For example, in a speech in 2010, David Denison, President and Chief Executive Officer of the Canada Pension Plan Investment Board (CPPIB), made the following observation: "Our view is that the vast majority of the considerable intellectual capital devoted to the investment industry is actually focused on a 0–24 month time horizon. [As a long-term investor], we quite simply believe there is a better opportunity for us to capture value-added returns by focusing on the long horizon end of the spectrum where there are far fewer participants and far less competition."[32]

As a result, the distinction between short-term macro *trading* and long-term macro *investing* will likely become more pronounced. The former will continue to be an important part of an institution's hedge fund allocation; it will also be increasingly linked into short-term portfolio positioning and tactical asset allocation. The latter, however, will be a fairly new development; due to its longer investment horizon and the liability profiles of institutions adopting this approach, it will have certain distinguishing features: it will be contrarian in nature; it will be based on extensive research; it will be focused much more on relative value and much less on liquidity; and it will require a longer time horizon for the investment positions to come to fruition. In other words, while global macro trading will continue to resemble the timeless approach of George Soros and the legendary macro traders of the commodity stream, global macro investing will be more reminiscent of John Maynard Keynes's and Julian Robertson's fundamental approach to financial markets.

1 In the interests of brevity, this chapter intentionally omits the discussion of some of the key events in the history of global macro (eg, the crash of 1987, the ERM crisis of 1992, the Asian financial crisis of 1997 and the Russia/LTCM crisis of 1998), which is available elsewhere; for an excellent summary of the global macro historical timeline, see Drobny (2006); for a more detailed narrative, see Mallaby (2010).
2 This section is based on the historical accounts of J. M. Keynes's trading and investment activity as presented in the following sources: Skidelsky (2003), Biggs (2006), Skidelsky (2009), Chambers and Dimson (2012), Davis (2012).
3 Of all the famous economists, J. M. Keynes is by far the most frequently mentioned and quoted in the various interviews with global macro managers (see Schwager, 1989, Schwager, 1992, Drobny, 2006, Drobny, 2010, Schwager, 2012). Milton Friedman is a distant second, with no economist from the Austrian school mentioned or quoted once. At least two modern-day macro managers, Sushil Wadhwani and Colm O'Shea, name Keynes as their favourite economist who had tremendous influence on their thinking (see Drobny, 2006, and Schwager, 2012, respectively).
4 For a detailed and painstaking reconstruction of Keynes's track record managing the King's College endowment funds, as well as various statistical tests to ascertain his investment preferences and style, see Chambers and Dimson (2012).
5 Skidelsky (2003).
6 Ibid.
7 Skidelsky (2009).
8 D. E. Moggridge (1992), as quoted by Davis (2012).
9 Skidelsky (2009), quoting from J. M. Keynes's *A Treatise on Money*.
10 For an excellent historical account of the post war origins of the hedge fund industry and the A. W. Jones long/short equity model, see Mallaby (2010).
11 While it is true that Michael Steinhardt and George Soros started their hedge fund careers several years earlier in the late 1960s, at the time they focused exclusively on the equity market. They did not evolve into full-fledged global macro managers until the mid- to late 1980s.
12 This sub-section draws on the history of Commodities Corporation in Mallaby (2010).
13 The other partners involved in setting up and running the company were Amos Hostetter, Frank Vannerson, and Paul Samuelson – the Nobel prize-winning economist and the original venture investor in Commodities Corporation.
14 Many successful GTAA models are based on a systematic fundamental approach to global macro. Another firm that has been particularly successful in this approach at the time of writing is Bridgewater, the largest hedge fund firm with US$120 billion under management (as of December 2011); for more information on Bridgewater, see Ray Dalio's interview with Jack Schwager (Schwager, 2012)).
15 See Soros (1987).
16 For a detailed and colourful account of this defining episode in global macro history, see Mallaby (2010); see also the HBS case study by Ferguson and Schlefer (2009).
17 For a detailed description of this episode, see Strachman (2004).
18 At their peak in the late 1990s, Soros and Tiger each managed in excess of US$20 billion, which was the largest-ever hedge fund size at the time.
19 One of Soros's most oft-repeated quotes is: "I do not play according to a given set of rules; I look for changes in the rules of the game." (Soros, 1995).
20 One of the more telling episodes involves a proposal by a Tiger analyst to short the shares of a Korean auto company due to reported engine problems with one of its cars. Robertson, not satisfied with the "second-hand" nature of the report, insisted that he and the analyst actually purchase two cars in question and test them independently to verify the report. They found the problem and subsequently shorted the stock (Strachman, 2004).
21 Strachman (2004).

22 Soros once semi-jokingly said: "I am not a professional security analyst. I would rather call myself an insecurity analyst." (Soros, 1995).

23 Throughout his career, Soros developed his own unique method of approaching financial markets (and other social phenomena), which he refers to as the "theory of reflexivity." The basic idea is that whenever thinking agents with imperfect knowledge interact with each other, their subjective biases and misconceptions – if they become self-reinforcing – can affect the underlying fundamentals and alter the objective reality.

24 For a more detailed discussion of how global macro strategies compare to other hedge funds on various risk measures, see Chapter 12 of this book.

25 For a more detailed discussion of how to analyse and interpret leverage in global macro strategies, see Chapter 10 of this book.

26 For a more detailed discussion of this episode in global macro history, see Mallaby (2010).

27 Sources: Hedge Fund Research, Dow Jones Credit Suisse.

28 For example, Paul Jones hired Jim Pallotta in 1993 to run Tudor's equity book; Bruce Kovner hired Kurt Feuerman in 1998 to run Caxton's equity book (see Taub, 2010, and Taub, 2012).

29 See Taub (2010) and Taub (2012) for specific examples of changes instituted at Tudor and Caxton after the global financial crisis.

30 According to the Dow Jones Credit Suisse Hedge Fund Index data, there were three strategies that delivered meaningful positive returns during the global financial crisis of 2007–09: dedicated short bias (DSB), managed futures (MF) and global macro (GM). However, DSB is a strategy with a negative long-term expected return: it has lost more than half of its value since inception in January 1994. Therefore, MF and GM (ie, systematic and discretionary macro) were the only two hedge fund strategies that delivered positive returns in the crisis *and* a long-term positive return overall. For a more detailed discussion of this point, see Chapter 12.

31 There are indications that global macro managers are thinking long and hard about the unusual nature of the post-crisis macroeconomic environment. For example, Wadhwani and Dicks (2011) put forward the hypothesis that the potential growth rate in the US may have decreased dangerously close to stall speed, making the economy vulnerable to minor shocks and dramatically shortening investors' risk appetite cycles, which in turn results in intermittent "risk-on/risk-off" cycles. In another example, Brookes and Daoud (2012) propose the concept of "disaster risk" as the main explanation behind the abnormally low yields and structural breaks in the pricing relationship between government bonds and equities.

32 Denison (2010); it is important to emphasise that this philosophy does not preclude long-term investors from making allocations to shorter-term global macro opportunities: for example, CPPIB also runs what it calls a "short horizon alpha" group, which focuses on the development and implementation of scalable shorter horizon active management strategies.

REFERENCES

Biggs, B., 2006, *Hedge Hogging* (Hoboken, NJ: Wiley).

Brookes, M. and Z. Daoud, 2012, "Disastrous Bond Yields," Fulcrum Research Paper, July.

Chambers, D. and E. Dimson, 2012, "Keynes the Stock Market Investor," working paper, March 5.

Davies, G., 2012, "Keynes, the Hedge Fund Pioneer," *Financial Times*, August 22.

Denison, D., 2010, "What it means to be a Long-Term Investor," notes for remarks, Conference Board of Canada and Towers Watson, Summit on the Future of Pensions, April 13.

Drobny, S., 2006, *Inside the House of Money: Top Hedge Fund Traders on Profiting in the Global Markets* (Hoboken, NJ: Wiley).

Drobny, S., 2010, *The Invisible Hands: Hedge Funds Off-the-record – Rethinking Real Money* (Hoboken, NJ: Wiley).

Ferguson, N. and J. Schlefer, 2009, "Who Broke the Bank of England?" Harvard Business School Case Study (9–709–026).

Mallaby, S., 2010, *More Money than God: Hedge Funds and the Making of a New Elite* (New York: Penguin Press).

Schwager, J. D., 1989, *Market Wizards: Interviews with Top Traders* (New York, NY: New York Institute of Finance, 1989

Schwager, J. D., 1992, *The New Market Wizards: Conversations with America's Top Traders* (New York, NY: Wiley).

Schwager, J. D., 2012, *Hedge Fund Market Wizards: How Winning Traders Win* (Hoboken, NJ: Wiley)

Skidelsky, R., 2003, *John Maynard Keynes, 1883–1946: Economist, Philosopher, Statesman* (New York, NY: Penguin Books).

Skidelsky, R., 2009, *Keynes: The Return of the Master* (New York, NY: PublicAffairs).

Soros, G., 1987, *The Alchemy of Finance: Reading the Mind of the Market* (New York, NY: Simon & Schuster).

Soros, G., 1995, *Soros on Soros: Staying Ahead of the Curve* (New York, NY: John Wiley).

Strachman, D., 2004, *Julian Robertson: A Tiger in the Land of Bulls and Bears* (Hoboken, NJ: Wiley).

Taub, S., 2010, "Tudor Returns to Its Roots," *AR Magazine*, **2**(1), September.

Taub, S., 2012, "Caxton's Law," *AR Magazine*, **3**(5), February.

Wadhwani, S. B. and M. Dicks, 2011, "Risk On/Risk Off: A Phase or a New Paradigm?" working paper, November 16.

2

Discretionary Global Macro: A Manager's Perspective

Kenneth G. Tropin

Graham Capital Management, L.P.

While global macro is one of the "original" hedge fund strategy types, it has generally evolved alongside the industry – from single managers trading a portfolio to more complex multi-manager, multi-asset class portfolios. Managing a discretionary global macro fund is therefore a complex and expensive venture. Many macro funds are still dominated by a founder or key risk taker who tends to concentrate a fund's risk profile, but the majority of large macro funds now have multiple portfolio managers trading a portion of the fund. The typical macro fund trades a broad variety of asset classes, geographic regions and instrument types, necessitating a robust investment platform and an equally robust operational backbone. The increasingly institutional nature of hedge fund investors also reinforces this need for robust systems, processes and reporting, both internally and externally. Successful funds should have a well-defined business model, top calibre trading talent, a disciplined investment process, robust risk management and a sophisticated operational infrastructure.

While there is no single methodology for successfully running a discretionary global macro fund, this chapter will focus on various investment and operational considerations from one investment manager's perspective. It is critical to acknowledge that the industry – including both trading and management – evolves over time, whether due to regulation, paradigm shifts in global markets or other exogenous factors. Because of this, investment managers should evaluate their individual processes on an ongoing basis in order to remain potentially effective. Therefore, this chapter will present a topical perspective with the understanding that the process for running a discretionary macro fund will undoubtedly continue to evolve over time.

As with any strategy, the starting point for a discretionary macro fund is the "raw talent." A successful global macro fund should strive to attract and retain the most talented discretionary portfolio managers available, and build substantial infrastructure in order to adequately support these portfolio managers and minimise non-market related distractions, while also meeting the due diligence needs of the firm's clients. Given the importance of creating a structure that identifies and fosters successful portfolio managers, much of this chapter will emphasise the portfolio management aspects of managing a discretionary macro fund in the current market environment.

Historically, one of the key attributes of global macro strategies is that they tend to display low correlations to a broad variety of traditional indexes as well as to other hedge fund strategies, such as long/short equities, relative value and credit strategies. As a result of these low correlations, global macro strategies tend to add true diversification to an investment portfolio, and tend to provide performance when broad markets or other strategies are under duress. The 2007–09 credit crisis – when macro funds broadly outperformed other strategies – was perhaps the best litmus test for this assertion.

Other areas of this book delve into the portfolio benefits of macro strategies, so this will not be a specific area of focus for the chapter. However, it is worth noting some of the attributes of macro strategies that historically have led to their low correlation, as it provides context for managing a macro fund. These differentiating factors include the emphasis in macro strategies on liquid markets, which makes it more likely a manager will actually be able to sell when markets are under duress, as well as the ability of macro practitioners to trade multiple market sectors, rather than being constrained to any one market or asset class. Additionally, the lack of an embedded long or "value" bias relative to other strategies enables macro funds to have positive or negative beta depending on the market opportunity set. Further, macro strategies tend to capture divergence, or directional breakouts in markets, rather than focusing on mean reverting or convergence-type strategies, which can suffer significant losses if markets move far from a historic mean during periods of duress.

Finally, it is worth noting that the term "global macro" often encompasses a broad umbrella of strategies, and there are many subsets of macro investing. The most basic dichotomy is between discretionary macro trading and systematic macro trading. In discretionary macro, portfolio managers trade global markets based on a view of fundamental macro drivers across economies. In systematic macro (also referred to as "managed futures" or "CTAs"), trading algorithms implement positions based on market trends or price dynamics, and in some cases on other factors such as fundamental macroeconomic data. Both of these strategies tend to trade liquid global stock, bond, currency and commodity markets. CTAs traditionally trade listed futures and foreign exchange, whereas discretionary macro funds typically trade futures and foreign exchange as well as cash and derivative markets. While the author's firm has a significant presence in both discretionary and systematic macro trading, the primary focus of this chapter is on the issues and considerations related to managing a discretionary macro business.

ESTABLISHING A WELL-DEFINED BUSINESS MODEL

As mentioned earlier, two major styles of global macro strategies have emerged over time. In systematic macro trading, an individual or quantitative research team develops a computerised algorithm to identify market and price movements, and the algorithm (or "model") then makes the decisions as to when to buy or sell based on a variety of proprietary indicators that generate trading signals. Success is determined by the robustness of the concept and the research process behind the trading model, as well as the establishment of an equally robust technology and trading infrastructure to execute a model's trading signals. Risk management is integrated into the model, and there is little or no discretionary intervention once the model has been developed – hence the term "systematic."

In discretionary global macro trading, a portfolio manager (or managers) determines when to buy and sell various instruments based on a range of fundamental and technical inputs. While there are many styles of discretionary macro trading, the starting point for trading tends to be the establishment of a framework or "themes" based on a portfolio manager's analysis of key macroeconomic factors. This analysis often spans a range of global economies and asset classes, and may include a high-level analysis of key macroeconomic indicators such as growth rates, inflation rates and monetary policy in key economies, or may be more micro in nature and include an analysis of how specific legislation or policy action will impact segments of the yield curve or other asset markets.

As themes are developed, they act as a road map or compass for the portfolio manager as to the presumed directionality of asset markets; if market prices deviate from the portfolio manager's compass, this may provide the opportunity to implement a trade. Portfolio managers may establish a forward-looking view for the general directionality of markets, and implement a trade expecting the market to "catch up" with this view over time. For instance, a portfolio manager may believe that an economy is beginning to display signs of a "virtuous cycle" as low interest rates feed into consumer and business demand driving employment and spending higher and thereby leading to further growth; in such a world, equity and commodity prices should drift higher while yield curves should be steep as low interest rates and the growth environment may feed into inflation or higher rates further down the road. On the other hand, portfolio managers may look for opportunities "after the fact", where they believe markets are mispricing currently available macroeconomic data. For instance, a key piece of data may be released which drives market prices, but the portfolio manager may believe that the data point has been misinterpreted and asset prices have moved too far as a result, and they may look to "fade" or trade against that move.

In discretionary trading, the breadth of instruments traded is generally very wide, and risk management is implemented by the portfolio manager during trade construction and typically via a risk management team that carefully monitors the portfolio's exposure after a trade has been established. Again, there are many styles of discretionary macro trading, but in its purest form, discretionary macro managers tend to focus on the most liquid global markets and instruments. Managers may trade listed global futures and foreign exchange, as well as cash and derivative markets. While some macro funds may trade structured products and less liquid markets, these positions tend to be a small part of a macro manager's portfolio, albeit with the caveat that liquidity in any market is a constantly moving target.

For any investment manager and their clients, it is important to establish a clearly defined business model when structuring a macro business. A typical distinction between discretionary macro funds is whether they are single manager funds or multi-manager funds. Single manager discretionary portfolios tend to emphasise the expertise and trading of one individual risk taker, typically the founder or Chief Investment Officer (CIO). Many single manager funds actually employ multiple portfolio managers, but nonetheless the founder or CIO plays a central role as the largest risk taker, and may also "size up" or concentrate the positions of other portfolio managers if there is a theme the principal would like to emphasise in the portfolio. At the very least, the founder or CIO often brings moral suasion to bear, and other portfolio managers tend to know the key thoughts or positions of the principal, making it somewhat difficult to establish opposing views. This style of trading is well established in the macro community, and many of the largest funds in the space have been founded and continue to be run by a central risk taker.

At the other end of the spectrum, discretionary macro funds may employ a true multi-manager style of trading. In this framework, multiple portfolio managers trade a specific allocation of capital. Each portfolio manager is provided with trading rules and risk factors (described further below) to which they agree to adhere, and formulate positions based on the portfolio manager's independent market views. Ideally, the component strategies would utilise a variety of discretionary trading methodologies and disciplines and participate in a wide breadth of global markets, thereby fostering low correlations among the portfolio management teams. When these function as planned, the benefit to the manager and to investors is a diversified portfolio comprised of a broad array of markets and trading methodologies, and a portfolio which can potentially capitalise on a variety of market environments.

There is no one "right" way to trade a discretionary macro portfolio. The author's own firm employs a multi-manager macro portfolio, and historically has developed a portfolio of truly low or non-correlated macro strategies where at any one time a specific strategy or asset class may have driven returns, but where over time returns have been derived from multiple alpha streams. But regardless of the business model chosen, it is important that a manager establish a clearly defined strategy where portfolio managers – and investors – understand how capital is allocated in the portfolio, the instrument types and style in which that capital can be traded, and the risk constraints that exist at the individual portfolio manager and aggregate portfolio level. Portfolio construction and risk management will be discussed later in this chapter, but the key takeaway should be that a clearly defined business model and trading and risk parameters are key inputs for the potential success of a macro platform.

IDENTIFYING, ATTRACTING AND RETAINING TRADING TALENT

A central ingredient of running a successful discretionary global macro fund is finding, attracting and retaining the most talented portfolio managers in the industry. Hedge funds must constantly compete for stand-out talent in order to build the strongest team possible and to have the highest probability of success. Due to the competitive landscape, recruiting has become increasingly expensive, as funds compete for individual talent by providing attractive payouts and substantial initial capital for portfolio managers to trade.

In assessing potential recruits, an investment manager should consider multiple factors, including the following.

- ❑ Does a portfolio manager have a substantial track record, both in terms of longevity and the quality of returns? This track record should be based on a consistent and replicable strategy that has demonstrated an edge over time, and any signs of style drift should be minimal – or at least the result of gradual style evolution over time.
- ❑ Does a portfolio manager have appropriate professional credentials, and does the portfolio manager display a history of moving from firm to firm? Clearly, a portfolio manager should have the requisite professional credentials, and any history of excessive job switching may indicate management and/or profitability concerns.
- ❑ Is the portfolio manager's edge derived from a robust, well-defined and well-articulated trading methodology? The

portfolio manager should be able to explain in detail the way in which they develop themes, establish trades, determine instrument selection, implement trading stops and take profits.

- Does a portfolio manager have a detailed and well-constructed view of current market dynamics, and are these macro views represented in trading positions that reflect these views? Experienced portfolio managers have a 1:1 mapping of views and positions; less experienced managers tend to have more superficial market views and less coherent and more difficult to defend positions.
- Do a portfolio manager's returns display beta to various market indexes or instruments? While macro managers will at times have high beta to markets, this beta should be episodic and not a consistent presence over time.
- Has a portfolio manager traded substantial capital? A 1.2 Sharpe ratio on US$5 million in capital is very different from a 1.2 Sharpe on US$200 million.
- Has the portfolio manager navigated a variety of market cycles? Seasoned portfolio managers may come from other hedge funds, their own hedge fund or proprietary trading desks at banks. Depending on the background of the individual, it may not be possible to furnish a complete track record for analysis, but a history of weathering a variety of market environments should be established.
- Is a portfolio manager's trading style and instruments traded consistent with or adaptable to a firm's risk culture, volatility tolerance, liquidity constraints and operational and trade processing infrastructure? A portfolio manager should typically be a "fit" for a firm's trading style, and the firm should of course have the ability to trade, process and clear the types of instruments traded.

With respect to a multi-manager macro portfolio, a final consideration is whether a potential portfolio manager's trading style and return history is correlated to other existing managers in the fund. As noted earlier in this chapter, a key benefit of a well-constructed multi-manager fund is the presence of a truly diversified portfolio with unique and disparate potential return streams. While two or more managers may focus on the same markets, it is helpful if they have different styles or timeframes for expressing their trade ideas. Or at the very least, if two or more portfolio managers are correlated, this should be factored in to capital allocation decisions.

Once an appropriate candidate has been identified, the campaign then begins first to recruit the portfolio manager to the firm, and then to retain the most successful talent over time. Just as a firm has multiple criteria for identifying talent, portfolio managers decide to join a particular firm based on a variety of factors. Many of these factors are obvious, and include the size of the capital to be allocated to the portfolio manager and the payout on that capital. Other factors relate to the firm's franchise, culture or manner of operation, and may include factors such as:

- does the firm have a successful track record and, correspondingly, a stable and ideally growing client base, so capital allocations are consistent and have the scope to grow over time?
- does the firm have significant proprietary capital, providing an even more stable capital base?
- is a portfolio manager's payout impacted by the performance of other managers – ie, if an individual portfolio manager is profitable but the fund is not, will that portfolio manager be paid?
- is the firm well managed and capable of providing the infrastructure, counterparty relationships, technology and operational resources so that the portfolio manager can focus on trading without unnecessary distractions?
- does the firm provide a culture of open information and interaction, and will the portfolio manager be surrounded by other bright and talented managers from whom they can glean market insights and unique perspectives?
- is the firm reasonably committed to a portfolio manager's strategy and does it have an adequate degree of patience, providing the portfolio manager the "runway" to become successful?

Beyond these factors, experience shows that a final element in recruitment and retention is providing portfolio managers with a clearly defined mandate and risk framework to trade within, thereby lending clarity for how allocation and risk decisions are made that will impact their trading. Portfolio managers do not want to be derisked or de-allocated for opaque or inconsistent reasons, and need a coherent framework in which they can work and be successful. Some firms believe in ultimate clarity in these factors, and include risk limits and performance and volatility targets in the portfolio manager's employment contract. This management style assures that there is no confusion as to what is expected of the individual trader. On the other end of the spectrum, some hedge fund managers approach boundaries in a less defined manner, which generally leads to more interference over time from management as the "rules of the game" change. This interference can cause potential frustration for experienced portfolio managers who prefer distinct boundaries within which they can freely express their market views. Potential frustration like this can cause turnover among portfolio managers as a result of dissatisfaction with the firm's culture.

Hand-in-hand with a clear framework, portfolio managers must often decide whether they prefer the single manager or multi-manager model described earlier in this chapter. At times, portfolio managers may feel they can "learn" under the auspices of a legendary macro trader, but the trade-off may be that they have less autonomy than they would otherwise. Although the author has a vested interest in the multi-manager model, he has found that experienced portfolio managers often like the rules-based and transparent nature of a multi-manager platform. Regardless, whether in a single manager or multi-manager framework, providing portfolio managers with freedom of thought and intellectual space tends to foster lower correlation between individual portfolio managers and ideally more consistent returns over time for clients.

All of the above factors and considerations should permeate a firm's culture to ensure the success of portfolio managers – and all employees – throughout the firm. The firm's culture is not accidental, and most often is defined at the ownership or leadership level. The founder and senior management create a style, work environment and philosophy upon which the firm is built. For portfolio managers and employees more broadly, a key differentiating feature of culture that varies between hedge fund managers is to what degree is freedom of thought encouraged?

Other key elements of firm culture are more environmental. Is the work atmosphere casual or formal? What is the dynamic on the trading floor? Does the firm tolerate abrasive behaviour by profitable portfolio managers on the trading floor, or is a more collaborative environment established? Some firms may encourage open dialogue between traders, while other firms may isolate different trading teams and discourage the sharing of information between managers. These details contribute to the daily atmosphere of the firm, and the firm has to take responsibility for finding managers who fit into its individual culture. Different portfolio managers prefer different environments, and it is mutually important during the recruiting process for a portfolio manager to understand the firm's culture prior to committing to the firm, otherwise it is unlikely that the portfolio manager will remain at the firm over the long term.

Discretionary trading is very difficult, challenging and stressful, a fact that cannot be underestimated by the management team of any firm that wants to run a successful discretionary macro fund. Trading is an exceptionally challenging endeavour over the long term, which is why profitable portfolio managers are compensated generously for their abilities. Global markets evolve over time, and traders need to capitalise on these changes and maintain their edge. There is a tremendous amount of pressure on portfolio managers due to the responsibility they carry – they manage large sums of capital for clients, themselves and usually for their senior management team. How a management team supports their traders is an integral part of the firm's overall culture. It is important to utilise an individualised approach when coaching and supporting traders. Some portfolio managers do not need much attention, while others need to build confidence and require frequent guidance or reinforcement. Regardless of which coaching style works for an individual portfolio manager, it is important that the trader can identify with the management team and feel that the management team is committed to their success.

THE ASSET ALLOCATION PROCESS

For multi-manager macro platforms in particular, it is important that the firm be committed to a disciplined and repeatable investment process for both trading and allocating capital. Generally, this investment process is managed by an investment committee (or a similar senior management group) that oversees portfolio managers and manages matters relating to portfolio construction, asset allocation and the selection of new strategies. In a multi-manager portfolio, one of the greatest challenges is how to allocate capital over time to individual strategies.

There are two basic models in asset allocation. First, an investment committee may allocate capital based heavily on a discretionary view of market opportunities and an assessment of the likely success of individual portfolio managers to capitalise on the forecasted environment. For instance, the investment committee may believe that commodity trading will provide the most fertile opportunities over the short-to-medium term, and therefore may emphasise allocations in this space. While this might be possible in a fund comprised of only a few underlying strategies, it becomes tedious and less realistic once there are many underlying strategies. Additionally, this method obviously relies on human judgement, which may ultimately lead to biased decision-making or inopportune market timing.

The alternative method is a quantitatively based portfolio construction process, which systematically guides allocation decisions within multi-manager portfolios. A portfolio allocation model may seek to optimise portfolio construction based upon a multitude of quantitative parameters, including returns, volatility and downside volatility, drawdowns, strategy cross-correlations and portfolio manager tenure. This methodology provides decision-makers with data and tools to guide their allocation changes based on quantifiable statistics as opposed to subjective market views.

Some macro firms may employ one or both of these methodologies in determining allocations. At the author's firm, a quantitative approach is emphasised, with the investment committee utilising a quantitative model overlaid with qualitative judgement to steer allocation decisions. Once again, there is no one correct methodology and market circumstances may warrant more or less discretion at any given time, but the use of a quantitative model confines risk taking to the portfolio managers' trading books, and taking a market view in asset allocation may add an additional layer of risk taking to a portfolio.

RISK MANAGEMENT CONSIDERATIONS

Risk management and capital preservation should be the cornerstone of every hedge fund's business – whether discretionary macro, systematic macro or any other style.

The preservation of investment capital during periods of adverse market behaviour is imperative to long-term trading success, as risk is inherent in all investment strategies that have the ability to offer returns in excess of risk-free rates. While even the most robust risk management process may be susceptible to unforeseen "black swan" events, a steadfast commitment to a rigorous and comprehensive risk management process is a necessary precondition to strategically managing risk during both favourable and unfavourable market environments.

The first step in risk management relies on the portfolio managers themselves. Each portfolio manager should have established risk measures and parameters. These generally include measures of first-order sensitivities to the most relevant risk factors for a given book (for example, dollar value of a basis point in the case of interest rate products), measurement of stress loss in extreme market events and the use of explicit stop-loss points. Beyond this first step, however, risk management must be monitored by the firm, which requires an experienced and knowledgeable risk management team as well as sophisticated technological capabilities.

Every portfolio manager should have clear drawdown limits that are monitored and enforced by the risk department or risk committee. These drawdown limits are likely to vary across hedge funds given that every firm has different return and volatility targets. Drawdown limits should be directly related to the intended volatility of each strategy and the overall portfolio. In addition, portfolio managers and the firm should monitor the liquidity of market positions on a regular basis, to ensure that a manager may be able to liquidate positions with little slippage from prior position valuation. This involves a regular review of positions and the expected cost to trade out of these positions in a normal and a stressed market environment. Any liquidity cost assessments are inherently assumptions, and should be reviewed on a regular basis.

Risk monitoring for most discretionary strategies requires the use of both internal and industry-recognised standards to ensure compliance with risk policies and limits established at the portfolio level.

These processes require state-of-the-art technology that is constantly evolving. Value-at-risk (VaR) analysis often provides a useful measure for the risk in directional trading strategies, but one must understand its limitations. For instance, VaR tends to break down for non-linear instruments such as options, or for relative-value trading where the relationship between two instruments can diverge much further than expected. In such cases, stress-test scenarios may provide a better measure of the potential loss from a position. Further, VaR is unlikely to capture unforeseen or extreme market moves, where losses may be much greater than anticipated. Clearly, it is important to establish the appropriate risk measures for each strategy and instrument type, and to apply a holistic approach to risk monitoring combining both quantitative and qualitative considerations.

A discretionary macro fund also has to carefully manage counterparty risk. Counterparties should be chosen from a group of companies renowned for their expertise in the particular market for which they provide a service. Due diligence should be performed on counterparties prior to commencing a relationship, and – as an ongoing process – the exposures and market conditions surrounding current or potential counterparties should be reviewed on a regular basis. The firm should handle counterparty risk in a manner that allows it to react to adverse situations with reasonably little disruption to its business. Typically, this means having back-up counterparties when available or possible for various product types. Once again, however, in extreme, adverse market conditions, a planned back-up counterparty may fail to materialise.

Over time, clients have demanded an increasingly high level of transparency in terms of risk exposure. Investors should gain a fundamental understanding of the strategy as well as the opportunities and risks inherent in it. Most firms provide regular risk reporting, but it varies tremendously from firm to firm. Standards are constantly evolving, but many funds provide frequent risk reporting to clients, including exposure data, VaR, stress-test scenarios, performance attribution, counterparty exposure and, potentially, lagged position data. Regulatory scrutiny regarding selective disclosure is a concern for many hedge fund managers, so it is important to provide adequate and consistent reporting to all clients.

At the author's firm, a key aspect of risk management includes a risk committee that is comprised of senior members of the firm's management, risk, trading and operations teams. The committee meets daily to review position-level information and related risks for each of the firm's strategies within the context of prevailing market conditions. It also discusses how market conditions may be impacting trading counterparties, to guard against a surprise collapse of counterparties who may hold fund collateral. This process is designed to inform members of the firm's senior management team of the various risks to which the firm is exposed and, if appropriate, the risk committee will effect a reduction in risk within a particular strategy or across a specific portfolio of strategies. While this approach has proven effective historically, any firm should evaluate their process on an ongoing basis and evolve it over time as needed or as market conditions dictate.

In the event that a fund must reduce risk to a given market exposure, some funds may run a separate hedging book to attempt to hedge out this risk. Other funds may simply ask a portfolio manager to cut a position to a lower level or to eliminate the position entirely. The author's firm has historically employed the latter approach, and the firm's risk committee has the authority to instruct portfolio managers to cut positions. Philosophically, this approach is based on the belief that the most efficient way to reduce a risk is to eliminate entirely or reduce a position. A hedging book may not effectively eliminate a risk if markets behave differently than expected (so-called "basis risk"). Another issue is that a hedging book is akin to a separate trading portfolio, but without a clear "owner" responsible for its profit and loss. On the other hand, it would be difficult to constantly tell portfolio managers to cut positions if their individual position is adequately sized, but the aggregate fund risk is too high. Portfolio managers do not want to be told to cut a position if they think it will be profitable. Thus, having a low-correlated multi-manager portfolio becomes important once again, because the low correlation tends to lessen somewhat the risk or frequency of position concentration at the fund level.

REQUISITE FIRM INFRASTRUCTURE

Infrastructure is a key factor in the management of any hedge fund, including discretionary macro funds. The infrastructure necessary to successfully run any type of hedge fund is significant. It would be possible to write several chapters on the requisite operational, accounting, legal, compliance and investor relations infrastructure required to run a modern hedge fund, but in the interest of space this section will be brief.

Discretionary macro portfolio managers vary tremendously in terms of style and instruments traded, but maintain one commonality: they need robust support at the firm level so that any distractions from the markets and trading are minimised to the fullest extent possible. This support is created through overall firm infrastructure.

The investment management industry has witnessed unprecedented change since the early 2000s as seemingly endless advances in technology have altered the speed with which information is disseminated, the means by which such information is processed and the manner in which markets are traded. Hedge fund managers should embrace these developments. State-of-the-art technology and systems are of critical importance to the development of innovative alternative investment strategies. The effective use of technology materially enhances a firm's trading and risk-monitoring abilities while also creating operational and reporting capabilities that enable the firm to provide increased transparency and improved communication internally and with clients. Portfolio managers need market data, hardware, efficient trading platforms and overall technical support. State-of-the-art technology is a moving target, and hedge fund managers should stay on top of the latest, leading technology infrastructure to support discretionary portfolio managers in order to maximise their potential to make money and successfully execute trading ideas.

The variety of global markets traded by many discretionary portfolio managers requires extensive support by the back office of a hedge fund. The middle office, meanwhile, often must be equipped to handle trading volume 24 hours per day. Sophisticated accounting teams are also necessary in order to accurately price the book. It is essential to have deep infrastructure built around the valuation process, with multiple layers of redundancy such as pricing by a third-party administrator with regular reconciliation of all positions.

In order for a portfolio manager to focus solely on developing their trading ideas and executing them in the marketplace, it is imperative that they face as few distractions as possible. With respect to the marketing efforts of the fund, management must strike a healthy balance between servicing clients and providing adequate transparency while allowing portfolio managers to do what they do best: trade. It is therefore important that hedge funds maintain a strong marketing and investor relations team that is knowledgeable about the individual discretionary strategies. Additionally, members of senior management should be available to investors to discuss individual strategies and market views. This provides investors with confidence that the firm is being transparent but also allows portfolio managers to focus on trading. This member of senior management might vary depending on the structure of the firm, but is likely to comprise some combination of the chief investment officer, chief operating officer and chief risk officer.

Overall, a firm needs to build a platform where the traders can focus on the markets, and non-market infrastructure is managed for them. Infrastructure is not to be minimised in importance, but should be handled by respective members of management rather than by the portfolio manager.

CONCLUSIONS

As noted at the start of this chapter, macro strategies have demonstrated unique portfolio benefits due to their history of robust absolute returns and low correlation to both traditional and other alternative investments. Of course, realising these benefits ultimately comes down to selecting the right managers – ie, those managers who successfully manage risk and generate positive returns over time. All investors should recognise that generating alpha from macro trading is a demanding and challenging endeavour. Accordingly, in selecting a fund, investors should pay careful attention to the clarity of the investment manager's business model, investment process and operational infrastructure.

While it is likely that other investment managers might have different perspectives and methods, this chapter has delineated some of the key ingredients – gleaned through one investment manager's experience – in running a successful discretionary global macro fund. An investment firm is a complex organisation that will continue to evolve over time. Having an exceptionally talented team of discretionary portfolio managers is of significant importance, but the hedge fund manager should also construct a robust business infrastructure around these portfolio managers to help enable their success. A business model that sets clear parameters for trading, risk control and capital allocation provides a coherent framework for portfolio managers. Establishing an appropriate culture and operational infrastructure for the portfolio managers further solidifies their ability to succeed. Ultimately, trading comes down to percentages – the percentage of successful trades determines the number of profitable trading days, weeks, months and years. A small shift in the percentage of winning trades can have an exponential impact on returns. While a discretionary macro manager cannot control global markets, anticipate "black swan" events or make an unprofitable trader into a profitable one, the manager can create an environment and support structure that provide the potential for success.

3

Systematic Strategies: A Quantitative Approach to Global Macro

Menachem Sternberg

Eagle Trading Systems, Inc

Quantitative trading strategies were underutilised by the investment community for many years, being both unpopular and misunderstood. Many asset allocators and investors shied away from such strategies, labeling them "black box" to indicate that they did not understand them and thus deliberately avoided them. As is often the case with these new and developing areas, myths and a lack of knowledge were characteristic, and led to the inclusion in the same investment bucket of many trading strategies that were very different from each other, sometimes to the point of having almost nothing in common.

In this chapter, we will focus on the quantitative approach to global macro, describing the aim of these strategies, addressing the misconceptions that still surround them and analysing the factors behind their new-found attraction as effective investment strategies and portfolio diversifiers for asset allocators and institutional investors.

DEFINING SYSTEMATIC MACRO

Systematic strategies have been available for many years, utilising vast mathematical models to analyse and participate in market opportunities. Such strategies encompass a wide range of investment styles (arbitrage, relative value, directional, mean reversion, etc), with the common thread being that the trigger to invest always relies on a quantitative formulation of the behaviour of a market and, in some cases, its relationship to other markets and asset classes.

Quantitative strategies are very focused and disciplined in their objective and the path they take to achieve it. Their success depends on the ability to analyse diverse market environments and to identify, in the context of time and market structure, situations requiring price adjustment on which they are able to capitalise.

Systematic macro strategies are designed to identify the need of global markets in a range of sectors (eg, commodities, currencies, fixed income, equities) to adjust to changes in the macroeconomic environment, monetary and fiscal policies, political landscapes, supply/demand imbalances, liquidity situation and market sentiment, or any other factor likely to affect the need of markets to re-price themselves. Historically, their major input and analytical focus used to be market behaviour itself, as well as the dynamic path of price behaviour of each market or its relationship to other markets. Based on such analysis, which in some cases involves other inputs – such as fundamental factors, market diagnostics (eg, trading volumes) and derivative pricing (eg, option pricing) – systematic macro attempts to identify, guide participation and capitalise on markets which show tendencies to adjust to new price levels. The main premise behind systematic strategies is that price behaviour encompasses the effect of a large body of information, a variety of factors and a diverse group of participants (eg, traders, hedgers, investors, speculators), each operating with different objectives, timeframes and constraints. By analysing the dynamic path of price behaviour, one can extract valuable information regarding the market's comfort levels and need to adjust to a new price level.

Over the years, the number of markets that lent themselves to quantitative analysis and trading kept rising, providing additional inputs and opportunities for application by systematic managers. Furthermore, as the availability and quality of information also improved and a growing number of market participants entered the field, the transmission mechanism from information to price effect became more efficient and apparent. However, this process is not always simple or straightforward: sometimes market price behaviour fails to register new information, which may trigger action by some market participants, while being ignored by others. Or it may react with considerable time delay to various developments. While some strategies attempt to be predictive, others try to be successful by reacting to changes as they occur.

Systematic macro strategies have a strong focus on volatility-based risk controls, and money and position management, by rigorously screening, sizing and dynamically adjusting over time each individual position as well as the entire portfolio. Volatility plays a particularly important role in this process: when it is elevated, it usually results in lower participation. Dynamic developments in price behaviour can also provide profit-taking opportunities. However, the most important aspect of position sizing is the risk limit placed on every position by assigning a predetermined stop-loss, which can adjust and tighten over time, to limit losses in trades that do not develop as expected. Thus, in marked contrast to many value-driven equity strategies, rather than increase positions when the market goes against them, systematic macro strategies tend to cut exposures and acknowledge that they are wrong. This combination of disciplined screening of market behaviour together with dynamic money and position management, risk controls and volatility-based adjustments are at the core of the tactical nature of systematic macro strategies, which historically has proved quite successful in achieving strong returns for investors.

EVOLUTION OF SYSTEMATIC MACRO

Systematic strategies in the global macro space have been around for decades, dating back to when the list of markets that lent themselves to such trading was very limited, centered mostly on agricultural commodities. In the early days, the trigger to participate in market opportunities was typically based on a fairly simple set of mathematical formulas and some basic money management rules to identify price trends and momentum. Such trading strategies were commonly used by commodity trading advisors (CTAs), and their participation was limited to the futures markets, where they sought to establish a position on either the long or the short side of each market. Initially, they attracted the interest of high-net-worth individuals and funds of hedge funds that specialised in this field. Despite their ability to achieve high returns, the volatile nature of their return streams and the non-traditional approach to investing were responsible for a lack of interest on the part of traditional institutional investors. As is often the case, it was easier for investors to ignore something they found difficult to understand, especially if it was based on concepts that were foreign to their traditional 60/40 equity–bond world.

Systematic macro has evolved significantly since the early days of CTAs to become a legitimate and widely respected investment style, with many institutions, including public and private pension plans and sovereign wealth funds, feeling compelled to participate in what has proved to be a great diversifier to traditional portfolios. Many factors have contributed to its transformation from an underutilised investment vehicle to a valid and popular investment choice. In particular, its ability to provide historically strong and consistent returns, especially when other investment strategies failed to do so and most traditional portfolios suffered, as well as its increasing level of sophistication and tactical nature, have made this investment style more acceptable to once sceptical investors.

As is the case in many evolving fields, systematic macro firms continuously search for new frontiers to provide them with a competitive edge in the investment world. In doing so, they have expanded their horizons to all areas of science (mathematics, physics, biology, computer science, etc) to find more innovative ways to understand and navigate global macro markets. Equipped with constantly improving computing power and cutting-edge technologies, and supported by the proliferation of electronic trading, they are now able to screen vast market data for opportunities on which they can capitalise. Modern day systematic managers are participating in more markets and are utilising a wider range of models and algorithms than ever before. One of the main advantages of such strategies is their capacity to screen many markets across diverse sectors, utilising the same disciplined process, algorithms and models to consistently evaluate their relative and absolute appeal, something that discretionary macro managers may have difficulty doing on the same scale. This situation has been further improved by the proliferation of electronic trading, which increased the number of markets available for liquid trading as well as the ability to efficiently execute such trades. Electronic data collection and trading also opened new frontiers for analysis and enhanced oversight of quantitative programmes.

Systematic macro firms have become quite diverse in their philosophy, approach and the tools they use to achieve their objectives. Unlike most traditional CTAs, which focused on trend and

THE DISCIPLINE BEHIND SYSTEMATIC MACRO

Systematic macro strategies typically start with an idea or concept about how to trade in the markets based on the manager's experience and observations. These ideas are then researched and tested extensively to develop the core strategy. Some strategies are based primarily on complex formulas that define relationships between prices and other market data over time and across markets, often taking into consideration the correlation between markets and market sectors, while attempting to optimise returns. Other strategies focus on the behavioural aspect of markets and trading, which guides their participation based on disciplined trading rules, relying on price behaviour as the most important input. The key for all such strategies is model robustness, which is achieved by avoiding over-fitting and over-optimising the data.

In order to thrive and maintain their competitive edge, systematic managers need to invest heavily in research and development. They constantly look for new concepts, algorithms and behavioural approaches to enhance their trading and to provide them with more dynamic tools to identify and adjust to changes in the market, while leaving their core strategy unchanged. By constantly analysing changes in the patterns and dynamics of price behaviour, including its volatility and other data, and by employing new concepts to put such developments in the right context, systematic macro managers proved over time they could adjust well to changes in the economic and market environments both in periods of high and low volatility.

Modern systematic managers are different from the CTA strategies of the early days, not only in their use of more advanced concepts and algorithms, but also in the more active and tactical nature of their participation in the markets. While still benefiting from the ability to participate on both sides of the market (long or short) in a wide range of very liquid and transparent instruments (mostly futures), the evolution of systematic strategies has made them more adaptable in their screening of opportunities and participation in them. Thus, some strategies are moving to the side-lines when the picture becomes less clear, either due to elevated market volatility or some other indicators of a highly uncertain environment.

These active management and tactical characteristics, together with the trading programmes' explicit design to "listen to the

momentum, many systematic macro managers are now often able to identify and analyse a range of other market characteristics. While they are all based on disciplined quantitative analysis of price behaviour and other market-related data, the timeframes, tools and algorithms used to guide their participation span a variety of models and often lead to different positions in the markets. Most guide their participation in a "bottom-up" fashion by independently analysing the price behaviour of the many markets that are included in their universe. Others tend to add a "top-down" approach or an overall risk budget allocation to their screening and portfolio construction. Given their different objectives, models and algorithms, each systematic macro manager can process market data differently and thus draw different conclusions leading to different participation patterns. The differences in the structure, process, methodology, models and algorithms, together with other dynamic factors, often lead to divergent performance between quantitative managers.

Quantitative models and algorithms are the proprietary assets of systematic managers and are responsible, together with disciplined and dynamic behavioural rules, for their competitive edge and success in the markets. While systematic managers share with their existing and potential investors the philosophy and concepts behind their strategies, and often describe the dynamic processes that guide their trading activity, the specific formulas and detailed algorithms represent their trade secrets and, as such, cannot always alleviate the "black box" concern. Paradoxically, however, investors often regard that other "black box" – the mind of a discretionary manager – as somehow being more transparent and accessible to them than a rule-based computer programme, something they think they are able to understand and in which they can have a higher degree of confidence.

Many different technical terms are routinely used in discussions about systematic strategies: factor analysis, neural networks, machine learning, price patterns, rule-based, artificial intelligence, etc. They often describe the theme that underlies a model or algorithm that can employ concepts and tools from different fields of science. Yet, the wide range of objectives, concepts, tools, algorithms, timeframes and other factors make it very difficult to classify such diverse strategies into specific descriptive groups, thus adding to the confusion and misunderstanding that surround the field.

markets," position them to adjust participation in response to changes in the economic environment, policy shifts or other developments, which are reflected in price behaviour. Thus, historically they proved to benefit from turning points in the economic environment or periods of rising uncertainty in the global economy – periods when many other investments tend to do poorly. Consequently, since the last economic crisis portfolios seeking to benefit from global tactical asset allocation (GTAA) have been increasingly incorporating systematic macro trading models and algorithms. The more dynamic nature and wider scope of systematic macro strategies can often supercharge a GTAA process and add significant diversification benefits for traditional portfolios.

Modern systematic macro funds and CTAs still have certain things in common: both are disciplined in their use of quantitative algorithms, trading rules and formulas. However, they often differ in the specific methods and analyses used and the way they guide their participation. In particular, systematic macro managers often utilise more diverse and advanced algorithms and tend to be more tactical and dynamic with their positions. Their investment process is typically structured along these lines:

- quantitative analysis, with varying timeframes and algorithms, of historical price behaviour, its pattern and volatility;
- determining whether such analysis triggers position taking, either long or short, in a market or a group of markets, or whether it leads to sitting on the sidelines;
- sizing of positions based on market volatility and other risk parameters for the market, the portfolio and the overall environment;
- setting stop-loss levels to serve as a safety net in case the markets do not behave as expected; and
- dynamic rules to trigger profit taking or adjust positions in response to price behaviour, as well as other characteristics of the markets and the portfolio.

Stop-loss levels, which are typically associated with each individual trade, ensure that the system "cuts its losses" when it is wrong. Dynamic position management rules, which are typically based on risk, money management and price dynamics, on the other hand, are designed to ensure that the system will "let its profits run" when it is right. Thus, more successful strategies tend to achieve a higher average return on their winning trades as compared to a lower average loss on their losing trades. The combination of these characteristics enables systematic macro strategies to perform well even if less than 50% of their trades are successful.

SYSTEMATIC MACRO VERSUS CTA: AN ILLUSTRATION

The following figures illustrate some of the different characteristics of modern systematic macro strategies as compared to a more traditional trend-following CTA approach. Figure 3.1 shows a more tactical participation pattern of systematic macro strategies, which tend to avoid environments of elevated volatility and which have profit-taking rules in response to a rise in volatility, trailing stop-loss mechanisms and other automated decisions built into the system. This tactical participation approach implies the system moving to the sidelines whenever the market or the overall environment is not clear or too volatile. Thus, with quantitative macro strategies one can see extended periods in which a programme would intentionally move to the sidelines with regards to a specific market and in which it could have low levels of exposure for the overall portfolio.

In any given market, systematic macro strategies can choose to either enter a long position, a short position or to stand aside. In Figure 3.1, the dotted grey line indicates when the programme has taken a long position in the instrument, looking for prices to rise. The solid grey line indicates when the programme has taken a short position in anticipation of prices falling. In both cases, the plus sign indicates a partial reduction of the position to realise some profits while maintaining a reduced long or short position. This may be triggered by a number of factors, including – but not limited to – reaching a profit objective or due to extreme increase in volatility. Also, it is common for a systematic macro strategy to adjust, or "trail," its stop-loss to lock in profits after a market has moved in the anticipated direction. This is done so as not to give back too much profit, or lead to a loss, after a favourable market movement. The black line depicts a period when the programme has exited its existing position in entirety and is waiting for a clearer picture to develop before entering into a new long or short position.

On the top panel in Figure 3.1, focusing on the price action in the Swiss franc, the systematic macro programme stayed out of the

Figure 3.1 Systematic macro: tactical participation

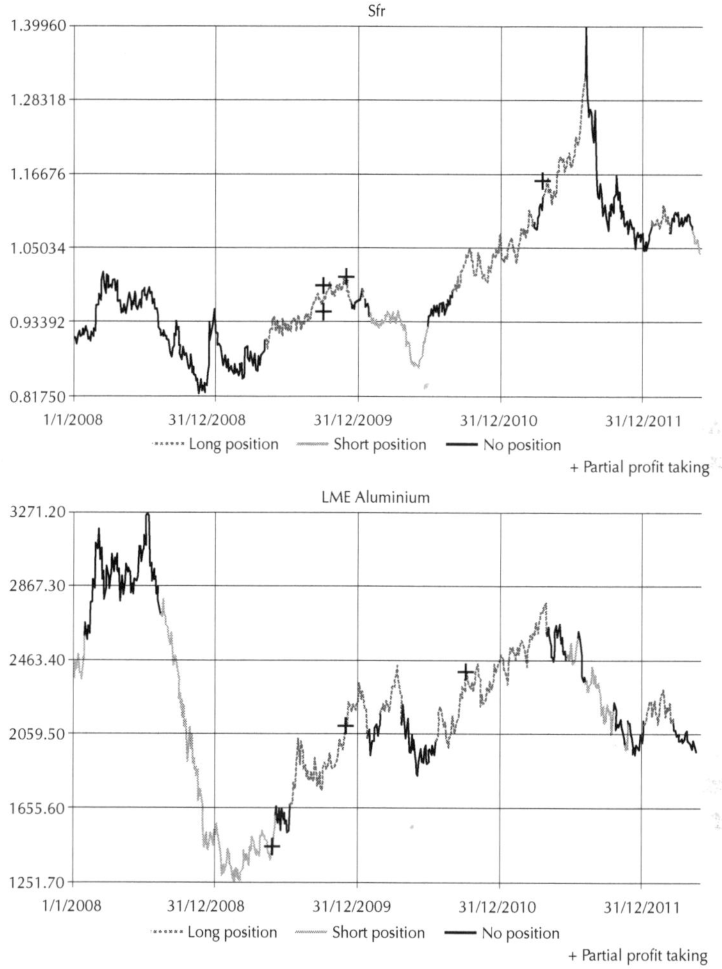

market for quite some time until a clearer price picture developed. Then, it entered into a long position. The system rode the price appreciation, taking profits several times while trailing its stop-loss to lock in profits, until a price correction resulted in exiting the position. A subsequent attempt to go short proved to be minimally profitable, even after prices corrected sharply higher. After a successful long position was exited, and after a few months of waiting for a clearer picture to develop, the programme entered into another long position. When the market moved in its anticipated direction quickly and decisively, partial profit was realised while letting the rest of the position ride the trend and trail its stop-loss. This ensured the trade would be profitable, and after the market spiked higher, the position was liquidated due to extreme market volatility.

On the bottom panel in Figure 3.1, focusing on the price action in the LME aluminium contract, a short position was exited and the programme waited for a clearer picture to develop before entering into another short position. The price then dropped extensively and, after the programme determined that prices lost their downside momentum, partial profits were realised. A subsequent rally in prices triggered the liquidation of the position, realising significant profits. The programme then made several successful trades going long, locking in profits along the way, before a minor failed attempt at going short. After waiting for confirmation of ensuing weaker prices, another short was attempted with greater success. Subsequent attempts at short and then long positions, with waiting periods in between, proved unsuccessful. Despite several failed attempts at positions that resulted in losses, it should be noted that the profits from the successful trades far outweighed the smaller losses on the losing trades, which is an important feature that differentiates systematic macro strategies from traditional CTAs.

Figure 3.2 illustrates a traditional trend-following CTA approach, which looks to always participate on the long or short side of every market it follows on the basis of some crossing of price-moving averages. While both approaches can benefit from extended moves in trending markets, especially if they develop within a well-behaved volatility pattern, the CTA approach can often give back a significant part (or even all) of its unrealised profits.

In Figure 3.2, the dotted grey line represents a long position in the market and the solid grey line represents a short position. At no time is the strategy ever sitting on the sidelines with no position, unlike systematic macro strategies. Rather, the CTA programme will always have either a long or a short position. When the CTA exits a long position, it will sell not only to close the long position, but it will also sell to immediately initiate a short position (position size may vary). The same holds true for exiting a short position: it is bought back and simultaneously a long position is initiated (in varying size).

On the top panel in Figure 3.2, continuing with the Swiss franc

Figure 3.2 CTA moving average-based constant positions in market

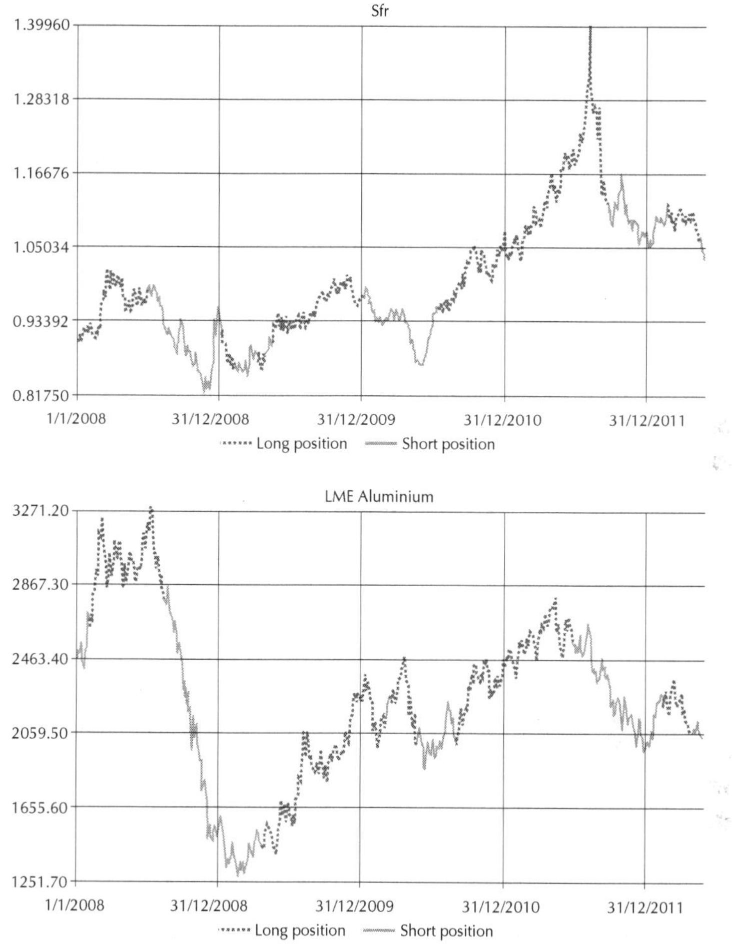

example, the CTA programme exits a long position and immediately enters a short position. The market quickly rewards the short position, but in a sharp rally it gives back over half of the profit before exiting the position. There are then several attempts at longs and shorts, all resulting in losses. This highlights one of the biggest drawbacks of a classic CTA: since it always has either a long or a short position, if the market price does not trend and becomes choppy, the system will suffer from "false" signals and can realise many losing trades until a trend develops. While the losses may seem small, they can add up quickly and become significant.

The CTA programme then had moderate success with a long position, but an attempt at a short position gave back all its profits after a sharp market rally. The subsequent long position benefited from the extended market rally, but gave back a significant portion of its profit after the sharp market sell-off before exiting and reversing into a short position. The resulting short and long position that followed both generated small losses.

On the bottom panel in Figure 3.2, continuing with the LME aluminium contract example, a short position was exited and the resulting long position achieved a minor gain before flipping back short again. The short achieved significant gains before reversing its position to a successful long. The next three trades resulted in losses of varying degrees, before enjoying subsequent successful long and short positions. The long position that followed suffered a loss.

Both systematic macro and CTA strategies can achieve significant gains, but the tactical participation of the systematic macro strategy enhances its return characteristics by its more opportunistic approach. This selective approach helps to filter out the market "noise" that results in fewer trades and a higher winning trade percentage. The profit taking and trailing stop-loss features also contribute to the higher winning percentage of the systematic macro system and, along with a volatility filter, help to smooth the return stream with less downside deviation.

OTHER ADVANTAGES OF SYSTEMATIC MACRO

Historically, both traditional CTAs and systematic macro strategies have always benefited from some additional characteristics that have made them attractive to investors. As they primarily trade in the futures markets, they are regulated by the Commodity Futures Trading Commission (CFTC) and the National Futures Association (NFA), which provide oversight as well as perform periodic audits. Such oversight is further enhanced as many systematic macro managers submit themselves to the registration and regulations of the Securities and Exchange Commission (SEC).

In addition, as futures markets are traded on organised and regulated exchanges, they benefit from exchange protection and transparency, as well as independent daily valuations. Trading in futures is performed via standardised contracts, which are defined by the various exchanges and involve a deposit with the exchange of a "margin" that is determined by the exchange and represents only a small percentage of the notional value of the contract. Thus, by executing and clearing their trades through the regulated exchanges, most systematic macro managers employ only a portion of their cash to support their positions and do not need to borrow to be able to execute and support their strategies.

Also, participation through futures contracts avoids the use of securities and derivatives and the counterparty exposure and risks that they entail. As futures markets attract participation by traders, investors and hedgers, they tend to have good diversity and liquidity with an orderly price discovery mechanism on which systematic managers can rely in their analysis and trading. Most futures markets are characterised by significant liquidity, which enables most small- and medium-sized systematic macro managers to fully participate in them in a balanced, diversified way without affecting price behaviour.

These qualities attracted considerable investor interest in quantitative macro strategies, as they stood in stark contrast to the experiences of other strategies in 2008, when liquidity suffered and many gates were imposed. Moreover, as many managers in the space have been around for a long time and have performed well in diverse environments, this "survival test" increased the level of confidence in their ability to continue doing well in the challenging environment that investors are facing.

While the bursting of the Internet bubble in 2000 triggered an increase in investor interest in systematic macro, the experience of 2008 was decisive in moving it into the mainstream. By performing well when most equity-based investments and hedge fund strategies failed to perform, and by avoiding the liquidity trap and providing investors with cash that they needed to survive, systematic macro has become the portfolio diversifier of choice. Furthermore, as distribution platforms and investment consultants embraced the space and provided transparent vehicles with high liquidity for institutional investment, the level of comfort and understanding of systematic macro increased even more. The universe of potential investors also keeps growing due to the rising use of UCITS (Undertakings for Collective Investment in Transferable Securities) funds in Europe and the inclusion of systematic macro mutual fund structures.

DIVERSIFICATION BENEFITS

The rising institutional interest and participation in systematic macro is the result of its well-documented ability to provide genuine diversification to typical institutional portfolios in periods of uncertainty, rising volatility and adversity. While the experience of 2008 is still fresh in investors' minds and is largely responsible for the latest surge in interest, such diversification characteristics have been observed on many past occasions of market stress and dislocation, not least in 1998 and 2001. Institutional investors with equity-heavy portfolios realised the need for other engines for return and alpha in their portfolios, and found systematic macro to fit the bill.

The ability of systematic quantitative macro strategies to perform well in periods of rising uncertainty and market dislocation reflects the fact that such periods often require many markets, across all sectors, to adjust to changing circumstances with extended price moves. As systematic macro strategies are designed to screen for and identify such opportunities, it often leads to their beneficial participation in market moves at times when most other traditional positions in investors' portfolios tend to suffer. Furthermore, many such extended price moves develop at a time when the global economy and the market environment have little shock-absorbing capacity, which tends to amplify the adjustment process even further. This is typically the kind of environment in which pressures in various markets and sectors start to build, reflecting a rising level of discomfort, which can often facilitate early identification and participation in new opportunities by systematic macro strategies.

The diversified participation of these strategies in many sectors and markets (fixed income, currencies, stock indexes and commodities) gives them the opportunity to benefit from such shocks across many positions, most of which move in the opposite direction from traditional equity or fixed income investments. Consequently, while we often observe positive correlation between systematic macro strategies and traditional portfolios during periods of rising equities, they have a significant negative correlation during periods of declining equities, which helps offset and smooth some of the bad performance of traditional portfolios during such periods. Most long-only or even delta-neutral equity strategies, as well as other hedge fund categories, fail to provide similar highly desirable diversification benefits.

In addition to their unique diversification properties in crises, systematic macro strategies can provide traditional institutional portfolios with exposure to markets that the latter may not normally cover (eg, currencies, commodities, volatility). The tactical nature of their participation in all markets and sectors and their ability to actively take either long or short positions enables systematic macro managers to perform well not only during periods of rising and declining equity and fixed income markets, but also during periods of rising and declining US dollar and commodity prices. These qualities can be clearly observed in Table 3.1, which shows the divergent returns of systematic macro as compared to other investment strategies, as well as their attractive correlation characteristics. In particular, the negative correlation that more tactical systematic macro strategies have to the more traditional asset classes during periods of adversity is responsible for their ability to provide beneficial diversified returns in periods when traditional portfolio or equity based investing need it the most (such as 2000, 2001, 2002 and 2008). Together with positive correlation in "good periods," systematic quantitative macro usually enhances returns with minimal, if any, adverse effect on volatility. Tactical systematic macro strategies can also have positive returns during rising and falling volatility environments.

The interest in systematic strategies as diversifiers and producers of alpha for institutional portfolios is further enhanced by their other favourable characteristics. The trading by systematic strategies on organised, regulated exchanges which facilitate liquidity, transparency and timely objective valuation, as well as mitigating the need for borrowing and minimising counterparty risk, were all welcomed by investors which suffered adverse liquidity, valuation, counterparty problems and the imposition of liquidity gates during 2008.

SYSTEMATIC VERSUS DISCRETIONARY MACRO STRATEGIES

While systematic and discretionary macro strategies have similar objectives, their philosophies, methodologies and the paths they take to generate returns can be quite diverse. The reliance of quantitative macro on vast data and computer models and algorithms allows them to analyse and participate in a much wider range of markets across all sectors and geographical areas. Furthermore, as they

Table 3.1 Performance of various investment strategies

	2000	2001	2002	2003	2004	2005	2006	2007	2008	2009	2010	2011	2012 thru April	Annualised ROR	Std Dev	Drawdown
NewEdge Macro Trading Quantitative Index	22.59%	14.91%	21.14%	26.73%	2.11%	6.14%	7.83%	5.05%	11.74%	-2.24%	10.08%	-4.24%	-1.17%	9.38%	6.94%	-6.61%
HFRI Systematic Macro	11.79%	4.09%	-3.25%	15.36%	6.42%	14.40%	16.84%	10.34%	18.06%	-1.68%	9.76%	-3.53%	-1.33%	7.61%	7.86%	-7.28%
NewEdge CTA Index	9.56%	2.49%	13.78%	16.05%	1.46%	3.20%	5.75%	8.05%	13.07%	-4.30%	9.26%	-4.51%	-0.47%	5.75%	8.95%	-10.30%
S&P 500 Index	-10.14%	-13.04%	-23.37%	26.38%	8.99%	3.00%	13.62%	3.53%	-38.49%	23.45%	12.78%	0.00%	11.16%	-0.40%	16.14%	-52.56%
MSCI World Index	-14.05%	-17.83%	-21.06%	30.81%	12.84%	7.56%	17.95%	7.09%	-42.08%	26.98%	9.55%	-7.62%	9.42%	-0.76%	16.70%	-55.37%
HFRI Fully Wgt Composite	4.98%	4.62%	-1.45%	19.55%	9.03%	9.30%	12.89%	9.96%	-19.03%	19.98%	10.25%	-5.24%	4.36%	5.90%	6.81%	-21.42%
Median Public Pension	2.65%	-5.28%	-8.06%	17.63%	10.29%	10.08%	11.42%	7.87%	-22.11%	15.93%	11.06%	2.05%	6.25%	4.24%	8.56%	-31.00%

Description of investments

HFR Indexes, note that HFRI Indexes data used herein is generally on a one-month lag as it is not updated until later in the month. The HFRI Monthly Indexes (HFRI) are equally weighted performance indexes which are designed to represent a larger universe of hedge fund strategies. Funds included in the HFRI Monthly Indexes must: Report monthly returns, report returns net of all fees, report assets in US$ and have at least US$50 million under management or have been actively trading for at least 12 months. (Source: Bloomberg)

NewEdge CTA Index is equal-weighted and reconstituted annually. The index calculates the net daily rate of return for a pool of CTAs selected from the largest managers open to investment. (Source: Bloomberg)

Newedge Macro Trading Index (Quantitative) is a sub-index of the Newedge Macro Trading Index covering the quantitative and GTAA strategies. (Source: Bloomberg)

S&P 500 Index consists of 500 stocks weighted by market capitalisation and is one of the most widely used benchmarks of US equity performance. (Source: Bloomberg)

MSCI World Index is a free-float equity weighted stock market index of over 1,600 world stocks and is often used as a common benchmark for global stock funds. The index includes a collection of stocks of all the developed markets in the world. The index includes stocks from 24 countries but excludes stocks from emerging and frontier economies. (Source: Bloomberg)

Median Public Pension Plan is derived from data published by BNY Mellon and represents the weight-adjusted median sector allocations for the referenced plan. Allocations to the alternative investments asset class are allocated equally to private equity, commodities and absolute return (hedge funds). Further, allocations to the private equity asset class are equally allocated between private equity and venture capital. Once the allocations are derived, an Index-replication process is used to create a hypothetical historic return stream for the plan by applying the sector asset allocation percentages to the monthly index returns by sector.

"listen to the markets" and lack emotions in their participation, they can quickly adjust to changes in the economic, policy or market environments, which contributes to their tactical nature.

The design and implementation of quantitative strategies involves an in-depth consideration and scientific support for all aspects of processing market data, discerning its meaning and drawing meaningful guidance for participation. In addition, their disciplined process supports consistent and clear risk control measures. In contrast, discretionary strategies tend to rely much more on the human factor, often coloured by emotional perceptions, when analysing sectors and assessing opportunities. Thus, their participation tends to be much more concentrated and, at times, they risk "falling in love" with their positions, which can make them slow to respond to fast-changing circumstances. While quantitative strategies always stay true and disciplined in their analysis and participation, discretionary strategies run by human traders always have the risk of an undesirable "style drift." Furthermore, in extreme market environments or when fundamentals are ignored for extended periods of time, such differences in style and method can be amplified.

Systematic strategies are often ambivalent with respect to price levels: typically they are not driven by relative value considerations or a notion of how far markets can move. In contrast, those discretionary or other strategies that have a value or fundamental component will tend to shy away from participating in market opportunities when prices reach extreme levels, which is likely to limit their returns. Prices often move to extreme levels in times of global dislocations and imbalances: in the year following the global financial crisis, investors have lived through interest rates in major developed economies hitting the zero lower bound; crude oil prices dropped below US$20 per barrel in late 2001, then rose inexorably above US$130 in 2008, only to collapse precipitously to US$35 per barrel in the same year. Investors had witnessed persistent moves towards an extremely high value of the Swiss franc. All of these developments represented unique profit opportunities for systematic macro managers.

Systematic strategies are mostly designed to "listen to the market" and actively adjust to changing circumstances, so they may be quicker to respond to new developments. This characteristic can be enhanced by their "bottom-up" analysis and building of exposures. Thus, they often build positions before there is much participation from other strategies, which are still coping with the change and need to unwind their previous state of mind before they can build enough conviction in the new reality. Furthermore, by the time such other strategies decide to participate, they will often face a less-favourable volatility environment. Consequently, investors observed much better performance by systematic strategies at times of turning points in the environment and market turbulence during the Asian financial crisis of 1997, the Long-Term Capital Management (LTCM) crisis of 1998, the Enron collapse of 2001 and the global financial crisis of 2007–09.

The difficult market environment of 2010–11 being another example. Those quantitative macro managers who had built into their systems sophisticated learning mechanisms to allow for more tactical trading managed to navigate it quite successfully. Specifically, the yield curve in the US was not in a normal trading mode at the time: it was openly and persistently manipulated by policymakers through various interventions, such as quantitative easing and Operation Twist. As such, the yield curve was not necessarily reflecting fundamentals such as the underlying economic activity or the level and dynamics of outstanding debt. When the government is that involved, it basically creates artificial levels of rates, making the markets much more vulnerable.

As a result, it was a particularly difficult environment for many discretionary managers who tried to relate the behaviour of fixed income markets to economic fundamentals. Yet, from a technical price-based point of view, between the spring and autumn of 2011 the markets were in a clearly pronounced move toward lower rates globally, which provided systematic macro managers with profit opportunities. During the latter part of 2011, global fixed income markets experienced elevated volatility that justified lower levels of exposure. This experience highlights the importance of "listening to the markets" and making tactical adjustments in response to changing circumstances.

The reliance of quantitative macro strategies on a vast body of data, and their ability with the advances in computing power and technology to constantly evaluate the robustness of existing models and algorithms (as well as developing new ones), better position them to adjust to changes in the economic and market environment. Discretionary strategies arguably have less technical capacity and scope to constantly monitor and rigorously evaluate such changes on a timely basis. However, discretionary traders can (and often do) take outsized positions based on their fundamental analysis of major evolving developments. While such concentrated bets can lead to highly profitable trading if the discretionary managers are right, it can also result in significant volatility and sizable losses if either their analysis or timing are wrong.

The focus of systematic managers on continuous research to assure the robustness of their concepts, models and algorithms, as well as their constant drive to develop new tools and approaches, allow them to stay current in ever-changing market environments. Thus, additional layers can be added to successful programmes to further enhance and improve their ability to deal with diverse environments. Their quantitative process also lends itself well to evaluating "what-if" scenarios on a wide range of parameters.

The more tactical nature of systematic strategies and their ability to generate good performance in diverse market conditions has led to a rebalancing in the global macro space: from historical concentration of assets in discretionary funds, the industry has moved toward a better balance between discretionary and systematic styles.

CONCLUSION

The constant evolution and increasing sophistication of the systematic global macro and CTA industry have made this space a more popular and valid investment alternative, not only for purposes of portfolio diversification, but also for pure alpha generation. The ability of systematic macro to transform itself from simple "one-dimensional" trend-following CTA programmes into a powerful and successful engine for screening, processing, analysing and dynamically participating in a vast and diverse range of global macro markets and environments earned it the respect of institutional investors. Rapid progress in technology and science, and the ability of quantitative macro managers to harness them to their advantage, has made quantitative macro strategies some of the most dynamic, adaptive, tactical and innovative strategies in the global macro space. But the most important shift in investor sentiment that tipped the balance decisively in favour of systematic macro was its spectacular performance during the financial crises and dislocations of 2000–02 and 2008. The transparency and liquidity of systematic macro strategies, the reliable regulatory framework in which they operate and the rising number of consultants and investors who have embraced them have given systematic macro managers their final seal of approval.

4

The Different Shades of Macro

Igor Yelnik

This chapter will concentrate on similarities and distinctions between various global macro styles of investing, with a particular focus on an institutional investment approach, typically referred to as global tactical asset allocation (GTAA). The author believes that a clear delineation between different macro styles, including GTAA, is sometimes difficult to achieve. While distinctions between the approaches are rooted in the underlying technologies, they also stem from historical reasons and different philosophical and structural frameworks. Reflecting the author's professional background, the chapter will look in some detail at the development of systematic macro as a style, with a particular emphasis on issues related to risk management and the role of "big picture" vision. It will also elaborate on risk management as a cornerstone of successful alpha generation in systematic macro.

THE PRIMARY COLOURS OF GLOBAL MACRO

As a child, the author, like many Jewish boys growing up in the old Soviet Union, liked to play chess. His coach used to say: "Chess is a combination of art, science and sport. Mix them in different proportions, and you will see different styles. Focus more on science, and you will get the great Botvinnik. Focus more on art, and you will get the inimitable Tal."[1] What he did not say, but certainly seemed to imply, was that no matter what proportion of each ingredient one chose to include, there were still no substitutes for the innate gift and the hard work one had to put in to reach the summit.

We can extend this analogy to global macro investing, which can also be viewed as a mix of art, science and sport. If you focus more on art, you will see the enviable ability of successful discretionary managers to call big market moves. On the other hand, if you focus more on science, in an extreme case you may end up wondering how some successful systematic managers can consistently make money in the market without having any views about its direction. As for the sport component, the parallel is obvious: managing money is a highly competitive game, in which the score is always available for everyone to see, expressed in terms of risk-adjusted returns and hard cash earned for investors. Metaphorically, art, science and sport, mixed in different proportions, form the full spectrum of global macro strategies, encompassing managers of all styles in the same way that the primary colours – red, green and blue – form the full spectrum of perceivable colours.

The similarities between discretionary and systematic macro styles are fairly easy to spot.[2] In essence, both are based on global risk taking and top-down analysis on market and asset class level. To express their views, macro managers take positions in equity, fixed income, commodities, currencies and other markets, while predominantly using derivative instruments or exchange-traded funds (ETFs). Use of individual securities, such as stocks of specific companies, is very limited. Both discretionary and systematic macro managers have the goal of delivering positive returns in all market environments, regardless of general market direction, while producing low correlations with traditional asset classes and other hedge fund strategies.

In both styles, risk tends to be allocated dynamically, with higher conviction bets consuming a bigger share of the risk budget. Similarly, capacity in both styles is generally large, but admittedly not unlimited. At a certain point, which varies depending on the specifics of a particular strategy, most managers will start thinking seriously about possible limitations that market liquidity may introduce. Another similarity is the ultimate reliance on human capital and employee skills as a cornerstone of any alpha generation process. No macro business, discretionary or systematic, can survive without serious investment in the human talent behind the investment process.

Distinctions are rooted in the technology of decision-making.

While in the purest case of discretionary macro both the analysis and the final decision are made by a human trader, in the purest case of systematic macro they are performed by a computer, which generates trading positions based on a programmed algorithm. It is difficult to come across a discretionary manager who would base their investment decisions on intuition alone and would not rely, at least to some extent, on quantitative tools. It is equally difficult to come across a systematic manager who would not apply their intuition, judgement and knowledge of markets to shape and guide their trading system. Since the two extremes of the spectrum – pure art (discretionary) and pure science (systematic) – are so rare, what does one see in actual reality as one shifts the fader from the former to the latter?

First, one will see how the day-to-day investment process becomes increasingly independent from key individuals. With systematic macro, whatever was incorporated in the model at the time it was built will remain there unchanged until someone makes an explicit decision to alter the set of rules guiding the trading system. However, there is an important caveat, which will be addressed later in the chapter, as we touch upon the role of individuals in the systematic space.

Second, one will see how the day-to-day investment process becomes far less emotional. The model does not "fall in love" with its trading positions and is able to take losses without hesitation. It is not concerned with job security or bonuses; it never has a headache; it never worries about sick children; and it never longs for a vacation. Profit or loss, earthquake or war, the model will do whatever it is designed to do. This is not meant to imply that a systematic approach is always better than a discretionary one or, in this particular case, that a totally cold and unemotional state of mind always trumps empathy. Models do have certain disadvantages, which will be discussed later in the chapter.

Third, computers have the indisputable advantage over humans in terms of their sheer computational power; thus, one will see a dramatic increase in the number of independent trading ideas exploited by the systematic macro process in contrast with discretionary managers. As one shifts the fader, one moves from a set of highly concentrated high-conviction bets towards a much more broadly diversified portfolio, where both the sign and the size of each individual trading position are outcomes of a computerised decision-making process. In a world where many seemingly unrelated phenomena may all of a sudden prove to be related, the ability to get exposure to as many truly independent risk factors as possible is valuable.

Fourth, as one shifts from discretionary to systematic, risk management systems and techniques tend to become more elaborate, simply because systematic approaches lend themselves more readily to quantitative risk modelling and sophisticated risk analytics; we see how the various economic and financial phenomena become much more strictly defined. In the process we might lose the unique ability of the human mind to adjust to an entirely new environment and to handle entirely new types of information. On the other hand, we gain the ability to analyse vast arrays of data, quantify risks in an objective fashion and avoid cognitive inefficiencies of the human brain.

Fifth, in contrast to discretionary macro, systematic managers tend to have more flexibility in customising and calibrating their products to meet investors' needs to a much higher degree of precision. For example, running portfolios with different levels of target risk or with different trading universes becomes easy. It requires no more than simply setting up separate portfolios with different parameters in respective portfolio management systems. It is often possible for systematic managers to turn certain parts of their strategy on and off with the click of a mouse. While this ability may be less important for those investors who are moving towards unconstrained mandates, it may still be relevant when investors' guidelines prevent them from getting exposure to certain asset classes, for example, commodities or emerging markets.

Finally, as one shifts from discretionary to systematic, one often sees the universe of traded instruments become simpler and more liquid. The reason for this is that non-linear relationships are much more difficult to model while keeping the right balance between complexity and robustness. In contrast, a skilled and experienced discretionary manager may have a very good understanding of prevailing market conditions and the peculiarities of specific instruments, and can therefore make productive use of fairly complex and opaque over-the-counter (OTC) derivatives.

While it is perfectly acceptable to mix and match different macro styles in one's portfolio, investors need to make sure that they get exactly what they pay for. For example, with systematic managers there is always a risk of key principals overriding their own trading systems and using discretionary judgement. While there may be situations that justify such actions, if it becomes a common occurrence, at some point one must question the nature of the strategy and the implications for the portfolio (eg, an increase in key man risk or dissipation of diversification benefits). In keeping with our earlier chess analogy, one must beware the infamous chess-playing automaton: not only did it turn the art and science of chess on its head, it was also decidedly unsportsmanlike![3]

THE TWO CONVERGING STREAMS OF SYSTEMATIC MACRO

Systematic macro strategies have come a long way since the early days. A steady influx of mathematics and natural science PhDs into the industry, persistently high spending on research and development, and spectacular improvements in information technology have all contributed to rapid progress in the field. But if one were to take a bird's eye view of the industry, one could characterise its long-term progression as a history of two separate and distinct streams which have developed in parallel but started to converge:

- GTAA; and
- commodity trading advisors (CTAs), also known as managed futures.

GTAA has its roots in a relatively naïve and simple strategy of tactical reallocation between three core domestic asset classes – cash, bonds and equities – as practiced in the late 1970s and 1980s (Muysken, 2006). Over time, the concept evolved to become global in scope and to include more asset classes and strategies. One feature that made the GTAA approach distinctly different from CTAs is that it was contrarian in nature and focused on mean reversion: it only took relative value positions. If the strategy was long one market or asset class, it was necessarily short an equal dollar amount in other markets or asset classes. While it was originally implemented in the underlying cash and securities markets, the flexibility and cost savings associated with futures and forward contracts quickly became apparent, so most GTAA strategies started to be executed as derivatives overlays. Typically, a GTAA process would include the following four modules (see Potjer and Gould, 2007; Yelnik, 2007).

- *Asset class selection:* the output of this model would recommend long and short positions in global equity and global bond markets, usually implemented via index futures or ETFs.
- *Stock country selection:* this model compares the relative attractiveness of individual country stock markets and results in a long/short portfolio of such markets.
- *Bond country selection:* this model compares the relative attractiveness of individual country bond markets and results in a long/short portfolio of such markets.
- *Currency selection:* this model's recommendations are long and short positions in different currency pairs, typically implemented via FX forward contracts.

These modules, or variations thereof, are largely mutually independent and in many cases can be run on a stand-alone basis, and represent an important part of most GTAA processes. Many modern GTAA products add dimensionality by including commodities, yield curve plays, emerging markets, investment style rotation (eg, value versus growth, small cap versus large cap) and even real estate, although some of these components may entail higher trading costs and capacity issues. Up to fifteen developed equity markets, eight bond markets and a dozen currency pairs can be traded without limiting the capacity too much. This is why most large GTAA managers allocate the bulk of their risk budget to models that trade these liquid markets.

GTAA processes are typically implemented via futures and forward contracts and ETFs. They may also use other derivatives, like swaps or options. The latter are used mostly when a volatility module is included in the roster or when a tail protection component is employed.

As a product developed primarily for institutional investors, GTAA was typically executed in the form of overlays, implemented via managed accounts with a low targeted volatility of returns. Such mandates were constrained by the parameters of the client's underlying portfolio, which effectively determined the opportunity set available to the GTAA manager. The realisation that limiting a manager's ability to freely express their views hampers risk-adjusted returns was the main driver behind the evolution towards unconstrained GTAA mandates. Specifically, GTAA is now increasingly viewed as an independent source of alpha, and as such is often allocated a separate risk budget in institutional portfolios. When this happens, the question of whether to invest in GTAA using managed accounts or funds becomes a matter of preference largely unrelated to the investment features of the product.

Historically, GTAA products started with valuation-based models. However, over time other ideas and concepts gradually entered a GTAA manager's lexicon and toolkit. Among these, one deserves particular attention for purposes of this chapter: momentum. It is a well-documented risk factor that is typically associated with trend-following models. As the latter are generally uncorrelated with valuation-based strategies, their combination within one product should, and usually does, improve risk-adjusted returns. Therefore, it is only logical that valuation-driven GTAA managers have started to diversify their investment processes by adding momentum-based components.

This brings us to the second stream of systematic global macro: CTAs, or managed futures, which have their roots in trend-following models. The concept of trend following based on technical rules is older than GTAA. Moving averages, the simplest method for signal filtration, were easy to calculate – even with the primitive computers of yesteryear. However, the explosion of institutional interest in CTAs began in earnest in the 1990s, and managed futures have gone from strength to strength ever since.

CTAs tend to have a much broader eligible universe compared to their GTAA peers: it is not unusual for a managed futures programme to trade up to 100 markets globally. Like GTAA managers, they primarily use futures, forwards and, to a lesser extent, other derivatives to express their views (Kaminski, 2011). In addition, although CTAs typically model each traded instrument separately, the resulting portfolio is global in scope, which also makes them look and feel similar to GTAA. These similarities have two consequences.

First, some CTA managers started rebranding their products as GTAA, which allowed them to move from the hedge fund risk bucket to the GTAA risk bucket in institutional portfolios, resulting in less competition and larger-sized allocations. Since the universe of traditional GTAA managers was relatively narrow at the time, this shift made perfect sense from a business development perspective. Although CTA strategies are mostly directional and GTAA strategies are mostly relative value based, not too many investors concerned themselves with such subtleties. From a theoretical standpoint, this minor complication was easily resolved by reinterpreting outright directional positions as functionally equivalent to relative value positions *vis à vis* cash.

Second, GTAA and CTA specialists started to borrow pages from each other's playbooks: while the former increasingly looked at momentum and adopted methods of technical analysis, the latter paid more attention to relative value models and started incorporating some traditional GTAA approaches. The once clear-cut distinction between the two methodologies began to blur, which can be clearly seen in increased correlations of returns among most – although certainly not all – GTAA and CTA managers.

This cross-pollination (or, depending on one's views, cross-contamination) could progress at an even faster pace, but is tempered somewhat by managers' fear of being accused of "style drift." However, as the diffusion continues, we are clearly witnessing a slow but sure convergence of the two streams into a more generalised concept of systematic macro.

Conceptually, the two styles complement each other. Trend-following strategies often produce attractive returns during periods when elevated volatility triggers pronounced trends. However, when volatile markets are range-bound, they are doomed to lose money. On the contrary, many GTAA processes are susceptible to "value traps" and may underperform during strong trends, whereas rational and mean-reverting markets are good for them. The synergies are obvious, and the goal of producing the best risk-adjusted returns will continue to drive progress in this area.

This point is illustrated in Figure 4.1. It shows the price action in A$/¥ over a time span of eight years, from 2002 to 2009. There is a long upward sloping trend, followed by a period of elevated volatility in 2007, then a sharp reversal in 2008 and another rising trend in 2009. A very simple purchasing power parity (PPP) based model, which was practically neutral early on, steadily accumulated a sizeable short position, relentlessly increasing its bet against the trend. While the model continued to incur losses during the better part of the period in question, it approached the time of the market collapse in 2008 very well prepared. As the Australian dollar plummeted, the model returned to an almost flat position and started building a new short position in 2009, countering the new trend. In contrast, a trivial momentum-based model, which would take a long position whenever the 20-day moving average was above the 60-day moving average and a short position otherwise, changed its signal much more frequently, adapting to the prevailing market direction. Even without running a correlation analysis, just from examining the figure, one can expect the two models to produce low correlated returns (indeed, in this particular sample, the correlation was a mere 0.2).

On a separate note, as one looks beyond systematic macro, one can see how the logic of risk diversification and risk allocation inevitably points towards the development of a super-quant product, which would include not only the top-down macro strategies discussed above, but also various other quantitative strategies.

Any trading position in the market entails exposure to some risk factors, both known and unknown. One can say that a market

Figure 4.1 A$/¥ and positions suggested by two simple models, momentum and PPP

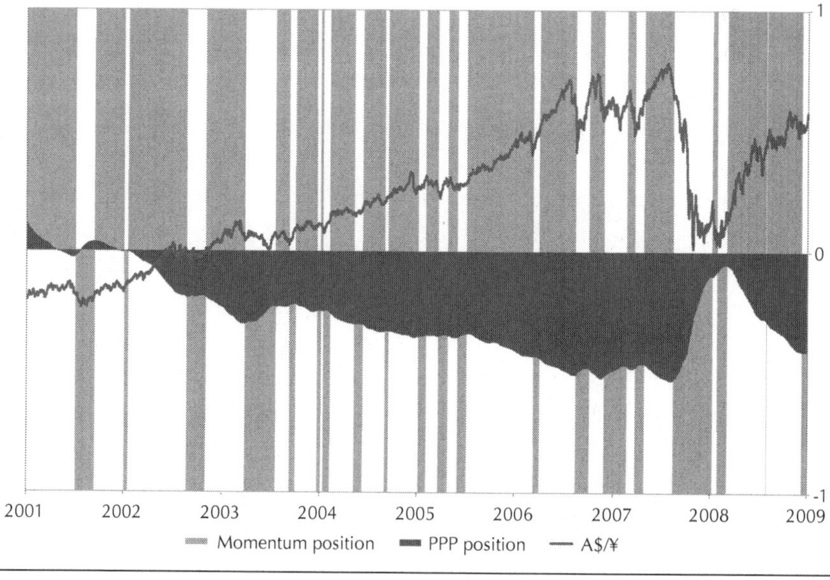

position is a way of expressing a view of which risks one wants to bear, and not only an expression of what assets one believes will outperform going forward. By extension, the difference between investment strategies can be identified by what risk premia they exploit, how explicitly these risk premia are specified and what mechanisms are used to size exposures to these risk factors over time.

When viewed from this angle, some positions that might be traditionally considered different will actually offer very similar risk exposures. For example, if someone wants to earn an equity risk premium, they can do so by taking a long position in S&P 500, but they can also achieve practically the same result if they go long FTSE 100 instead. (Obviously, the outcomes will not be identical because of the presence of idiosyncratic risk factors.) Similarly, a carry risk premium in currencies may be expressed via different currency pairs: for instance, long A$/Sfr and long NZ$/¥ positions, while not perfectly correlated, will expose the investor to carry as a well-defined risk factor.[4]

This change of perspective, from asset classes to risk factors, has conceptual implications that may help determine which strategies represent a good mutual fit. It is not only traditional long- and medium-term momentum-based strategies that can help diversify classic GTAA models – it is also true for shorter-term CTA strategies, which take risks that are different from those assumed by their longer-term peers. Arguably, the same can be said of high-frequency trading models, although, admittedly, capacity issues may represent too high a barrier for this approach to take up a decent share of institutional risk budgets. At the time of writing, certain event-driven, pattern recognition and fixed income relative value strategies have found their way into systematic macro portfolios.

WANTED: PRAGMATIC SCIENTISTS WITH "BIG PICTURE" VISION

Achieving success in systematic macro requires a unique combination of skills. On the one hand, you need to be a well-trained and highly competent scientist, with an appreciation of both the scientific method and its practical limitations in real life. On the other hand, you need to have a "big picture" vision to understand how the world at large works. When building a systematic process, one obviously needs technical knowledge and skills to research, construct and rigorously back-test a quantitative model. However, these skills are no substitute for a clear and logical *qualitative* view of why it would be reasonable to expect the model to make money in the market, what risks will be taken and whether and how these risks will be compensated.

One needs to focus on the distribution of returns and their characteristics, all the while being alert to multiple hidden risks that often come with uncertainty and complexity. Often ideas that look independent in theory end up exploiting very similar effects in practice. Sometimes these dependencies may be captured by a statistical analysis, but other times they may not. Sometimes tests show that the effect is significant, but in other cases they do not. Sometimes something as innocuous as changing the starting date of a back-test by a year or two may completely change your opinion of whether the idea will work at all. For example, Figure 4.2a shows an investment process with an information ratio of 0.31, while Figure 4.2b shows exactly the same process, except the figure starts 15 months later. Even at a glance, the second picture looks far less attractive, which is confirmed statistically by the fact that the information ratio is only about half of that shown in the longer sample.

Suppose an idea seems to have worked in the past and back-test results are promising. Should it become part of the model? How do you decide? What about a previously successful model that suddenly starts underperforming? Has there been a structural change in market dynamics, or is it just a temporary outlier within acceptable tolerance limits? How long do you wait before you get concerned? Should you replace the model with an updated version, or do you drop it altogether? These are just some of the challenges a systematic macro manager will inevitably confront from time to time.

In many cases, the length of available historical data will not be sufficient to allow statistically significant proof that the idea should work. That leaves a lot of room for judgement by the individual manager based on their investment beliefs and convictions, which in turn are based on their profound understanding of the market, the model and the risks taken. This is where "big picture" vision is critical.

This brings us back to the discussion of similarities and differences

Figure 4.2 Same back-test of a risk factor in a model that trades developed market bond futures on a relative basis (different starting dates)

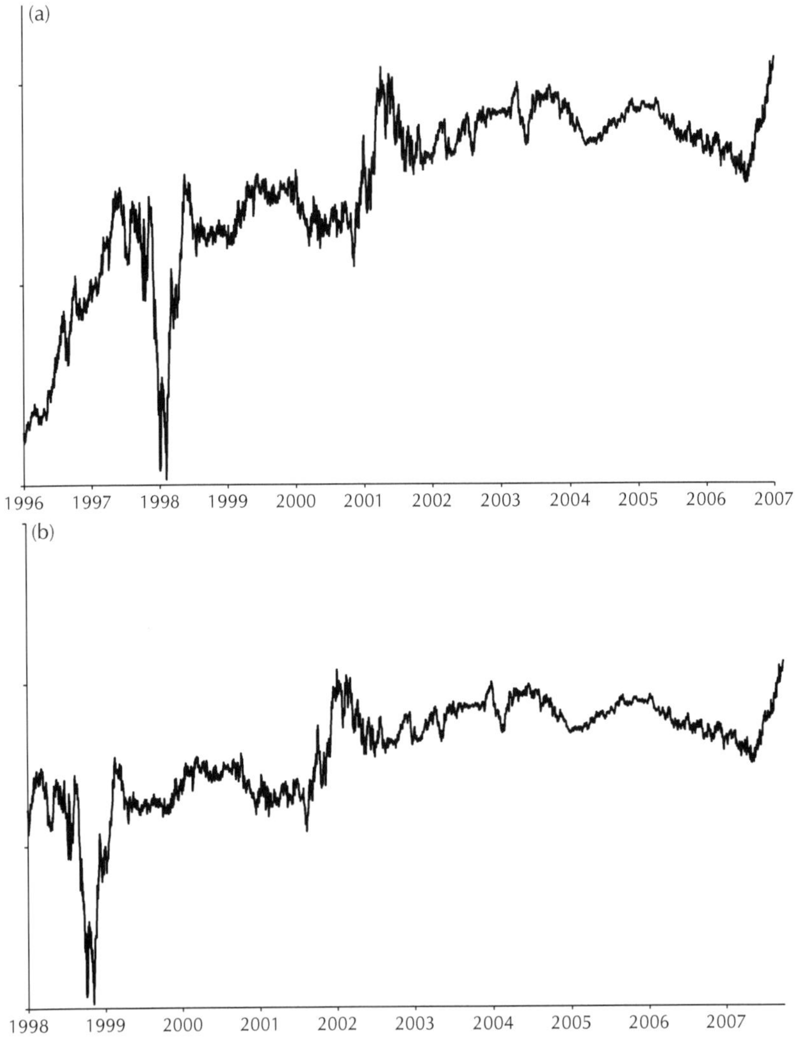

between discretionary and systematic strategies. Both need to have a visionary behind the product. However, while in the case of discretionary macro this vision is applied in day-to-day decision-making about actual investment positions, in the case of systematic macro such vision is applied at the stage of model construction. In the former case, a manager's decision will have its impact during the lifetime of the trade. In the latter case, it will persist during the lifetime of the model.

It is incredibly easy to construct a model that will successfully trade the markets of the past. It is considerably more difficult to achieve the same result with the markets of the future. Since, apart from one's beliefs and convictions, back-tests are the only indication of what can reasonably be expected in the future, a lot of effort is typically spent on optimising the model such that its back-tested returns would look compelling. However, if one is not careful, such impressive results may be due to a "creative" choice of parameters and as such will be totally meaningless and unhelpful going forward. While models that have been over-optimised in terms of parameter choice are relatively easy to spot, over-optimisation in terms of investment ideas or risk premia may prove to be somewhat more difficult to identify.

When a researcher works on a model, they are susceptible to selection bias: if they test two ideas which are so similar that only one of them can be included in the model, they are most likely to select the one with the better back-test. This bias is very hard to resist. Extraordinarily strong belief is needed to insist that an idea that has not proven itself in the past will work in the future. Even more extraordinary persuasion skills are needed to convince one's colleagues on the investment committee. In real life, such things practically do not happen.

Another temptation is to model as much as possible, especially the most significant events of the recent past. Modelling a financial crisis that started with unsustainable leverage in the economy, drawing conclusions from one-off central bank interventions or liquidity squeezes produces superb results in sample. Unfortunately, one-off events by definition do not recur out of sample. In general, the relationship between model complexity and stability must be well understood. Attempts to model everything lead to too much complexity and unreliable results. In contrast, simple models will not capture everything, but will tend to be much more robust.

In other words, it is naïve to think that a systematic strategy can be safely left alone to operate entirely on its own. To use an aeroplane analogy, it takes skill to design a good autopilot system, but no matter how good it is, one should never underestimate the role of a talented and experienced pilot manning the cockpit.

RISK MANAGEMENT: IS THERE LIFE BEYOND STOP-LOSSES?

There are not many areas of human activity in which financial results become so abundantly clear as quickly as they do in asset management, especially when liquid instruments are involved. Prices get published in real time, and P&L becomes known immediately. One of the more fascinating aspects of comparing and contrasting discretionary and systematic managers has to do with their approach to loss management.

How do people normally react to losing money? A host of studies shows that human behaviour is asymmetric with respect to losses and gains. The tendency to "run" the losers and "cut" the winners is well documented and explained as clearly sub-optimal behaviour even in the most basic investment literature. One of the key tenets that all discretionary managers learn in their apprentice days is: "to cut your losses quickly and let your winners ride." Furthermore, they learn to trade less whenever losses have been incurred. Some managers even stop trading altogether for a certain period of time once their losses exceed a predefined limit. This is perfectly reasonable behaviour. The human mind is distracted by the pressure of mounting losses in a very competitive environment with extremely high performance expectations. Getting out of the market and taking time off may help the trader regain self-confidence, think of new trading ideas and return to the game with a refreshed mind. Such is human nature.

In contrast, a systematic trading strategy, whether based on technical analysis or fundamental drivers of asset returns, does not suffer from this problem. It is entirely unemotional and its nature is decidedly not human. Along with its ability to process huge quantities of data, the absence of human weaknesses and fallibilities is widely considered to be a major reason for such strategies to exist. And yet, most trading systems still have stop-loss rules and mechanisms coded inside them, leading them to manage losses in ways very similar to human traders. But what would be the reason for a computerised strategy to reduce or entirely cut its positions while incurring losses? Will it be under psychological pressure thinking about its bonus and potential client redemptions?

There may be various reasons for introducing stop-loss rules in trading systems. Some of them are perfectly justified, while others have to do with human imperfection. Implicitly, the use of stop-losses is based upon the assumption that returns of a strategy are positively auto-correlated (Kaminski and Lo, 2007). If this assumption is correct, instituting stop-losses can be expected to add value. If not, it may lead to deteriorating returns in the long run. In many systematic macro and particularly GTAA strategies, returns are not positively auto-correlated. Simply put, their realised returns do not predict next period returns. Use of stop-losses in these systems would thus tend to subtract value. However, model builders are human and have limitations, just like the rest of us. As for the psychological pressure usually accompanying drawdowns, some of them consider it prudent to have an "anthropomorphic" stop-loss mechanism built in.

Many religions and philosophic theories of ancient times were anthropomorphic, in that they attributed human characteristics to non-human phenomena. Natural to human beings and making intuitive sense, anthropomorphism allowed our ancestors to comprehend and explain on a certain level events and phenomena they would not be able to comprehend and explain otherwise. Despite all the technological innovations of the recent centuries, how different are we really from our progenitors?

A strategy endowed with such anthropomorphic elements may also be more appealing to the end-investors in the fund. Their expectations are not always managed well: all too often they have preconceived notions and misconceptions about how the investment process works and what they should expect from it. For example, an investor in a programme targeting 20% annualised volatility would sometimes profess grave concerns over a 5% monthly loss. Yet, with any reasonable assumption about the Sharpe ratio, such monthly loss is not that far beyond one standard deviation from the mean! While a loss of this magnitude is not particularly worrying in itself, a stretch of such losses occurring more frequently than the live track record and out-of-sample back-tests show may hint at a break in some assumptions and relationships upon which the model is based. A sensible stop-loss rule built into the system would appear to help mitigate such eventuality, while also reassuring end-investors. However, while its ability to actually improve the return pattern is indisputable in some cases, in others it may prove illusory.

In a complex strategy like systematic macro, multiple reasons may cause underperformance. It is paramount that the manager does their homework and monitors carefully the workings of all individual moving parts in the machine. In most cases, when a complex strategy has experienced a drawdown exceeding its previous maximum level, it is likely that at least one (and perhaps even several) part has underperformed versus their previous worst results. That is the point when the manager should be seriously concerned and ask themselves whether an underperforming factor or risk management methodology needs to be replaced.

Any stop-loss methodology is by definition backward looking: the manager cuts their position not because they expect it to underperform going forward, but because it has underperformed in the past. One aspect that is often forgotten is that, after some time has passed following a position cut, one must take risks again. While a discretionary manager may use the pause to explore other trading ideas or to simply lick their mental wounds, a systematic strategy should have a systematic way of getting back into the market. If a strategy changes its signals frequently, timely return to risk taking is not an issue. However, in the case of a slow-moving strategy with a longer time horizon, this might present a challenge. For example, if a currency is considered undervalued today, it will likely be considered undervalued in a few months' time as well. What would be the trigger for the strategy to switch such a position on again?

Stop-losses can help safeguard against human fallibility, but introducing them in a trading system requires as serious and objective consideration as introducing any other element of the system. The full gamut of risk management approaches and tools available to professional systematic macro managers stretches far beyond stop-losses. As such, they should not be viewed in isolation from the underlying strategy: the best managers think of return generation and risk management as two inseparable parts of one whole.

KNOW YOUR COLOURS

Global macro is a universe of strategies that may be broadly categorised as discretionary or systematic. A clear delineation between these styles is not always possible, as the distinction is sometimes blurred. However, conceptually the two approaches are sufficiently different to allow a meaningful comparison.

In the systematic part of the spectrum, GTAA and CTA are the two dominant styles that have been in existence for decades and, being complementary to each other, have exhibited a tendency towards convergence. The advantages of these styles, based on a computer's ability to process vast arrays of data in a consistent and unemotional fashion, do not negate the role of a skilled human manager who must remain firmly in charge. This person must have a unique combination of skills, which can be broadly described as those of a well-trained scientist with a pragmatic approach and a "big picture" vision.

Risk management is an integral part of any systematic macro process. While risk management tools utilised in a systematic strategy may include those available to a discretionary manager, such as stop-losses, they may also involve other approaches and methodologies that fit well and work in harmony with other elements of the strategy.

Successful allocators to global macro are able to easily navigate between discretionary and systematic styles of management, and between GTAA programmes and CTAs. For them, it is not a question of which approach is better; it is a question of what combination of different approaches makes the most sense for their portfolios. In other words, it is a question of arriving at the optimal mix of art, science and sport.

1 Mikhail Botvinnik, 1911–95: three-time world chess champion. Apart from playing competitive chess, he pursued the career of an electrical engineer and a computer scientist. He developed and implemented one of the first chess-playing computer programmes based on so-called "selective searches." Mikhail Tal, 1936–92: world chess champion. Widely regarded as a creative genius, he played with a daring, combinatorial style. His play was known mostly for improvisation and unpredictability. Every game, he once said, was as inimitable and invaluable as a poem.

2 In the context of this chapter, the term "systematic" is used as the antonym of the term "discretionary." Thus, systematic macro combines all styles where risk taking is global and the analysis is done chiefly on a market or asset class level, while decisions are driven by computer programs. It is important to note that for different market practitioners this term may have different connotations: for some it alludes mostly to GTAA strategies, while others may use it to refer primarily to CTA programmes.

3 The chess-playing automaton (also known as the "Mechanical Turk") was a fake machine constructed in the late 18th century. From 1770 until its destruction by fire in 1854, it was exhibited by various owners as an automaton, although it was exposed in the early 1820s as an elaborate hoax. Constructed and unveiled in 1770 by Wolfgang von Kempelen (1734–1804) to impress the Empress Maria Theresa, the mechanism appeared to be able to play a strong game of chess against a human opponent. The Turk was in fact a mechanical illusion that allowed a human chess master hiding inside to operate the machine. With a skilled operator, the Turk won most of the games played during its demonstrations around Europe

and the Americas for nearly 84 years, playing and defeating many challengers, including statesmen such as Napoleon Bonaparte and Benjamin Franklin.

4 We assume that interest rates in Australia and New Zealand are higher than in Switzerland and Japan, respectively.

REFERENCES

Kaminski, Kathryn, 2011, "In Search of Crisis Alpha: A Short Guide to Investing in Managed Futures," CME Education Group, April.

Kaminski, Kathryn and Andrew W. Lo, 2007, "When Do Stop-Loss Rules Stop Losses?" working paper, MIT Sloan.

Muysken, Bill, 2006, "Tactical Asset Allocation: Back in Favour," *Investments & Pensions Europe*, May.

Potjer, Daan and Chris Gould, 2007, *Global Tactical Asset Allocation* (London: Risk Books).

Yelnik, Igor, 2007, "Is Global Tactical Allocation A Hedge Fund Strategy," *Hedge Fund Journal*, February.

5

The Role of a Global Macro Strategist

Grant Wilson

Civic Capital

This chapter will evaluate the role of a global macro strategist. It is a timely focus, as strategists are playing an increasingly important function within the discretionary macro arena, and yet it can be difficult to describe what they do, and how they do it.

Three main arguments will be advanced here. First, that the role of a global macro strategist is distinct from that of a financial markets economist, even if the divide is not always observed in practice. This is a fairly straightforward distinction, and one that will be highlighted in the first section.

Second, that a global macro strategist has two main functions: analysis and prediction. The analytical function involves the strategist deploying a range of research techniques to further their understanding of a particular macro topic, with a view to providing their clients with a meaningful transfer of intellectual capital. The predictive function relies upon this analysis, and involves the strategist making forecasts as to the future direction and volatility of financial markets. Both these functions are important, and will be examined in the second section.

Third, that it is possible to distinguish between macro strategy that is predominantly fundamental in its method, and that which is behavioural. The fundamental school draws heavily upon macroeconomic influences, and has a rich and storied tradition. The behavioural school, of which Civic Capital is a part, is novel by comparison, and is focused more upon understanding how financial market participants may respond to incoming stimuli. These approaches are introduced and compared in the third section.

In order to provide some real world context, a case study is also provided, with an emphasis on the speculative surge of the Swiss franc in the period 2008–11. Some of the tools that were used to analyse and predict the move are illustrated, and a contrast is drawn between how fundamentally oriented strategists tended to evaluate the situation compared to behaviouralists.

Global macro strategy will be evaluated from a critical perspective in the final section, both in terms of its analytical and predictive contributions. An attempt is made to distinguish between the good, and the not so good. In a world where content is increasingly abundant, this is a useful note on which to conclude.

ECONOMICS AND MACRO STRATEGY: A FUNCTIONAL DISTINCTION

Macro investing has long been regarded as closely related to, if not synonymous with, the field of macroeconomics. From this perspective, the great skill of a macro investor is to be able to project economic developments with some degree of prescience, and to monetise these forecasts by investing in a range of financial instruments.

This approach, were it accurate, would leave very little room for the macro strategist. Economists would dominate the agenda, crowding out all other forms of analysis. However, since around the turn of the century, strategists have proliferated, both on the sell-side within global investment banks, and on the buy-side within hedge funds, sovereign wealth funds and other asset managers. That most strategists have some form of formal training in macroeconomics makes the situation even more confusing.

What has emerged is a basic division of labour. The primary role of a financial markets economist is to analyse and predict the economy, whether defined at a global, regional or national level. In contrast, the macro strategist focuses on financial markets, and on any economic, political or social development that may have relevance.

For the economist, a typical focus is the set of economic variables that are deemed by clients or policymakers to have importance. So it is not uncommon to find an economist devoting a lot of time to understanding the composition and interrelationships of benchmark statistics on economic activity, inflation and unemployment, or on more esoteric areas such as trade and capital flows. An economist will often bring their technical expertise to bear in interpreting how and why such data may have deviated from consensus expectations.

The role of an economist is, however, much broader than this. A typical preoccupation is to abstract away from the incremental data flow in order to create a narrative as to how the economy is structured, and how it is expected to evolve. A critical focus is the use of macroeconomic policy tools, such as interest rates and fiscal policy. Following the global financial crisis of 2007–09, this emphasis has become increasingly important, particularly with respect to the use of non-standard policy measures, such as quantitative easing and intervention in foreign exchange (FX) markets. An essential part of the role is to explain the new toolkit of the global central banking community, along with the initiatives of key multilateral institutions, to an ever-expanding and increasingly informed audience.

Having said that, it would be unusual to find an economist who is quarantined entirely from commenting upon financial markets. Economists are expected to "have a view," at least informally, and in many cases it is the economics team at a global investment bank that takes responsibility for forecasting the benchmark interest rates set by global central banks. This is where lines start to blur, and where turf is sometimes fought over. However, at a conceptual level, the distinction is evident enough and, in practice, it is clear that macro strategists have carved out an important role.

MACRO STRATEGY: ANALYSIS AND PREDICTION

Every macro strategist is a little bit different. The differences stem from a variety of factors: academic background, cultural heritage, methodological bias, professional environment, etc. However, every macro strategist is faced with an analytical and predictive imperative. Some may weight their role more toward one than the other – but these two functions are never far apart, and excellence in both is the hallmark of an effective macro strategist.

The analytical function

The analytical function of a strategist consists of a methodical examination of issues with macro relevance, without any requirement of an associated prediction. At first glance, this function may seem trivial, but this is not the case at all. The complexity of modern financial markets, and the rapidity of developments, ensures that strong, independent analysis will always find a committed audience.

The typical form of macro analysis consists of client-facing reports, which are produced either on a regular schedule, or intermittently. The content may be authored by a team or by an individual, with attribution typically provided. Macro strategy tends to be data-rich, in the sense of being accompanied by charts and tables, which often provide much of the perspective on offer. However, many strategists favour a narrative approach in order to convey the subtleties of their thinking.

When it comes to content, the focus of a macro strategist is any economic, political or social dynamic that has the capacity to move markets. Part of this perspective is to analyse the structure of financial markets, including the identities and interests of different participants, with a view to predicting their behaviour. The first-order objective, however, is to offer informed, distinctive and timely analysis of macro developments.

Like economists, macro strategists have faced new challenges since the 2008 crisis erupted, as traditional drivers of financial markets have broken down and the involvement of policymakers has deepened. This has played to the strengths of many strategists, especially those who operate within a relatively unconstrained remit. The flexibility to operate across product silos, and to avoid being compartmentalised by country or region, has facilitated new lines of inquiry. The interconnectedness of global vulnerabilities, as well as the interdependence of policy responses, have become key focal points.

The core characteristics of macro strategy have not, however, changed. It remains a holistic, all-encompassing discipline, one that is open minded regarding the analytical methods that may be deployed, and one that is continually striving for new insights.

The predictive function

As important as rigorous analysis is, the predictive function of a macro strategist is crucial. Clients expect strategists to make forecasts, and to be accountable for those forecasts in a timely fashion. Arguably, the predictive function is more onerous for a strategist than an economist. The shortcomings of economic forecasting are widely accepted, and it is common practice for economists to revise their numbers with very little fanfare. Macro strategists, for the most part, are not afforded the same sort of lenience.

Having said that, there is a great degree of variability when it comes to the formality of the forecasting process. Some strategists are content to describe their views in narrative form, allowing their readers to make an assessment of their expectations, and to track their view as it evolves. At the other end of the spectrum, there are strategists who issue precise forecasts, which may be further conditioned by profit targets and review triggers, and there are some who go as far as maintaining model portfolios. There is no right or wrong approach here, but there is a requirement for the strategist to maintain continuity with how the view has been expressed.

A critical focus of the strategist is to develop an understanding of the reaction functions of other market participants. In the context of the division of labour outlined above, consider a single data point, such as a non-farm payrolls report. The strategist has very little business in forecasting the extent to which this report may deviate from consensus expectations; however, comprehending how other market participants may respond to the deviation is entirely relevant.

The broader challenge for a macro strategist is to anticipate the decisions of policymakers. Increasingly, this involves a thorough understanding of the political contexts within which such decisions are made. In this sense, the strategist takes on a wider role than an economist, a role that is not dissimilar to a political economist, whose primary focus is the interaction between states and markets. The macro strategist and the political economist share a common interest in analysing and then predicting the exercise of discretion by powerful market participants.

A final point is that a strategist focuses not merely upon predicting the direction of financial markets, but on the associated volatility. Arguably, this observation holds for an economist as well, yet in the case of the strategist, the distinction is critical as forecasting direction without forecasting volatility is not nearly as useful. The importance of an accurate volatility forecast is that it enables the associated positions to be scaled in an appropriate size. A volatility forecast that is too high may encourage position sizes that are too small, an outcome that may be sub-optimal, but quite benign. A volatility forecast that is too low may encourage position sizes that are too large, an outcome that may be quite dangerous. A strategist needs to have a keen sense of both direction and volatility when engaging their clients.

FUNDAMENTALISM AND BEHAVIOURALISM

While the macro strategist cannot escape the analytical and predictive imperatives, there is considerable scope within the role to improvise and innovate. The market is always looking for novel ways of examining situations, particularly if the methods deployed are credible and replicable. In broad terms, however, there are two main schools of macro strategy: fundamental and behavioural.

Macro: Fundamental

The fundamental school of macro strategy holds that economic variables are the main drivers of financial prices and that, over the long run, the intrinsic logic of the relationship will assert itself. The qualifier is important in this formulation. The fundamentalist acknowledges that economic variables are not the only driver, and that deviations from a concept of fair value may persist for prolonged periods. Equally though, there is a sense that fundamentals are inescapable, and will inevitably win through.

Keynes's famous statement, that: "the market can stay irrational longer than you can stay solvent," typifies the mindset of the fundamentalist. There is an assumption that underlying all the noise there is still a rational basis for price action, one that might be discovered by those with the requisite economic insight. It is this mindset that explains the enormous efforts that go into economic forecasting and modelling.

As outlined in the first section, however, the remit of a macro strategist is much wider than economic statistics. It involves locating economic developments within their broader social and political contexts. A logical relationship between economic variables and financial markets is seen, but there is also an acknowledgement of the feedback loops between how the economy is tracking and how policymakers are responding. This removes the macro strategist from the domain of "true science," where financial markets might have been viewed as a form of dependent variable. Instead, there is recognition of a complex mode of interdependence, where the economy and financial markets are in a constant state of iteration.

Importantly, the fundamentalist retains a commitment to basic economic logic. In addition, considerable support for the perspective is derived from the many instances where fundamentals are seen to have overwhelmed the responses of policymakers. So, on this view, the succession of financial crises which have been witnessed over the past 30 years have less to do with the deregulation of financial markets, and more to do with economic fundamentals ultimately asserting themselves.

The perspective is encapsulated well by the so-called "impossible trinity" of international economics, popularised by the Mundell–Fleming model. From this perspective, a fixed exchange rate cannot persist with an open capital account without the central bank foregoing control over monetary policy. A country in breach of this basic condition would quickly be identified by a macro strategist as vulnerable. The same sort of logic underpinned criticism of the role of the US dollar in the latter phase of the Bretton Woods system. The Triffin dilemma, as it came to be known, implied that the expansion of the US current account deficit, which was required to satisfy the increasing global demand for a reserve currency, would eventually threaten the fixed system of exchange rates by oversupplying the US dollar relative to its backing in gold. This perspective was validated in 1971 when Nixon closed the gold window, and may also be viewed as a prototype for fundamentally oriented macro strategy.

A more formalised example is the canonical currency crisis model, a phrase popularised by Paul Krugman.[1] Here, the currency of the country in question is pegged and backed by a central bank with finite reserves. However, in the presence of open capital markets, and a budget deficit that is persistently funded by money creation, a logical inconsistency arises. This encourages a speculative attack, which is repelled initially by higher interest rates. As the political constraints to higher interest rates come into view, and reserves are run down, the peg is abandoned, enabling speculators to exit with substantial profits. The central bank, meanwhile, is left to rebuild its policy platform, its reserves and its credibility.

There have been many famous instances of this type of situation over the years, and there are many variations on the theme. The departure of the UK pound from the ERM mechanism in 1992 is arguably the most famous macro trade of all time. Also, the role that speculators played in the Asian currency crisis of the late 1990s has been extensively documented and debated. These are classic examples of macro strategy in action.

There is also a more mundane side to fundamental macro strategy, in which the strategist may simply present a range of economic data and argue that a particular set of financial markets outcomes is more likely than not. Advances in computer science have greatly assisted this endeavour, both in improving the quality of data that is used, and in facilitating increasingly sophisticated modelling techniques. While the conclusions yielded by garden variety forms of macro strategy are not as strong, there is a commitment to the same philosophy. Namely, that observable economic data matter, and that economic fundamentals are best situated within an appropriate social and political context.

Macro: Behavioural

The behavioural school of macro strategy focuses less upon a logical relationship that may be perceived between economic fundamentals and financial markets, and more upon understanding the perspective of market participants with the power to influence future outcomes. A behaviouralist is prepared to displace their own predispositions and value system, and to relax any assumptions regarding actor rationality. The aim is to thoroughly understand what others mean, with a view toward predicting what they might do. If this can be achieved, then it may be possible to predict the direction and volatility of financial markets with reasonable regularity.

Behaviouralism, in this sense, is distinct from the microeconomic theorising of Daniel Kahneman and Amos Tversky. There is a shared acknowledgement of the inadequacy of the rational actor model, as well as a specific emphasis on the individual level of decision-making. But this is where the substantive similarities end. The behavioural macro strategist is not particularly interested in cognitive biases of others. The focus instead is upon achieving a form of empathy with powerful market participants, and for this to be the basis of informed predictions.

The academic heritage for this approach can be traced all the way back to Max Weber, the pioneering German social theorist. Although he referred to financial markets only in passing, the core of his writings on sociology provide a platform for the behavioural school of macro strategy. Weber advanced the concept of *verstehen*, which translates to "interpretative understanding." This involves rejecting the possibility of objectively studying social phenomena. Instead, the aim is to develop a sense of empathy with others, whether intellectual or emotional, almost as a form of thought experiment. Weber's approach is entirely subjectivist, where it is "a great help to be able to put one's self imaginatively in the place of the actor and thus sympathetically to participate in his experiences."[2]

This is an apt description of how a behavioural macro strategist approaches the day-to-day. There is a continual relevance to understanding the ideas and interests of powerful market participants, such as central banks, governments and private sector entities. Economic fundamentals are still significant, but not because of a logical connection to financial markets. Rather, economic fundamentals derive their relevance from how powerful market participants may react to changes in their trajectory, and the study of this reaction function becomes a central preoccupation. In this way, the fundamental/behavioural divide in macro strategy comes to mirror the objectivist/subjectivist divide in broader social theory.

In keeping with Weber, an important aim of the macro strategist is to intellectually empathise with those in positions of influence. This does not mean the strategist has to agree with the intellectual framework in question, but understanding is key. To take a simple example, when Ben Bernanke became Chairman of the Federal Reserve in 2006, there was a lively debate among the economic fraternity concerning the merits of his various intellectual positions. To a behaviouralist, however, the principal aim was not to critique but to study these same positions with a view to predicting how his leadership may evolve under different scenarios.

Another example involves the transition in leadership at the European Central Bank. The role of the strategist in this instance was to recognise that Mario Draghi was prepared to engage in more aggressive and creative policy responses than his predecessor, Jean-Claude Trichet, particularly in respect of collateralised lending. Draghi's academic background was suggestive of this, and his early press conferences were studied carefully by the macro community. A related challenge was to interpret how his policy initiatives would be received by market participants in the private sector, and over what time horizon.

It follows that the most straightforward instances of behavioural strategy involve a thorough and ongoing engagement with the foundations of public policy. When policy is well calibrated and transparently applied, this mode of analysis becomes quite conventional.

All that is left to speculate upon is how policy may evolve, which will be an incremental process, one which operates within orthodox boundaries, and which has any number of prior examples from which expected volatility may be quantified.

Where macro strategy becomes more interesting is where the constructs of the market participant in question begin to break down. A strategist who has pursued the aim of intellectual empathy will be quick to recognise when this occurs. It may be that economic developments have diverged sufficiently from expectations that the framework has been brought into question. Alternatively, or additionally, it may be that financial markets have moved far enough to invalidate the perspective. In either case, the strategist will be highly attuned to the situation, and to the attendant impact on the credibility and resources of the institution in question.

These are the sorts of situations where financial markets can become wild and unruly, whether to the upside or the downside. There is, for example, an extensive literature on bubbles and manias, such as the "irrational exuberance" of technology stocks in the late 1990s. Conversely, there are many examples of currency markets undershooting valuation parameters, particularly following the break of a peg. In these instances, the concept of intellectual empathy has limited use.

In its place, Weber encourages the study of the reaction function not of the individual, but of the herd. He refers to this as emotional empathy, where there is explicit recognition of the propensity of the collective to behave in an irrational fashion. In these instances, the role of the macro strategist morphs from intellectual engagement with the accepted wisdom of the day into a dispassionate analysis of euphorias and panics. There is still an attempt to empathise with market participants, but there is a recognition that rationalist bounds no longer apply.

The broader challenge for the behaviouralist is to stay true to process. The fundamental school of macro strategy is clearly ascendant, and its reductionist qualities appeal to many. The behaviouralist, by contrast, is required to focus upon a broad range of actors in highly personalised terms, where different viewpoints, even if well understood, need to be weighed, balanced and ultimately resolved. This is a demanding task, and one that often leads to unremarkable conclusions. However, as the case study in the fourth section shows, there are instances where a macro strategist operating in the behavioural tradition is able to provide an entirely differentiated form of analysis, which yields a more accurate set of predictions.

FROM THEORY TO PRACTICE: THE SNB, 2008–11

The role of a global macro strategist has been defined in terms of its analytical and predictive functions, and it has been contrasted to that of a financial markets economist. The experience of the Swiss National Bank (SNB) between 2008–11 is helpful in illustrating these points, and in further distinguishing between the fundamental and behavioural schools.

Some background

In the wake of the global financial crisis, the SNB commenced an aggressive programme of outright intervention in Eur/Sfr. The Governing Council argued at the time that the rapid appreciation of the Swiss franc posed a risk to the nascent recovery of the Swiss economy, and that FX intervention was an appropriate policy response. In the decade prior to the intervention, the SNB had maintained FX reserves in the range of Sfr 43–64 billion, or some 8–13% of GDP at current prices. By the time the programme ceased in May 2010, FX reserves had swelled dramatically to Sfr238 billion, or 42% of GDP.

Through this period, the Swiss franc resumed its appreciation, in part driven by negative developments in the eurozone. Early in August 2011, with Eur/Sfr approaching parity, the SNB announced that it was reducing interest rates and expanding its balance sheet via an increase in sight deposits, a development illustrated in Figure 5.1. The dramatic increase in money market liquidity helped to stabilise Eur/Sfr. Then, on September 6, 2011, the SNB went a step further, by making an unconditional commitment to uphold 1.20 as a lower bound in Eur/Sfr. The announcement effect was significant, with Eur/Sfr relocating above the limit without the SNB having even intervened.

The economist, the fundamentalist and the behaviouralist

In keeping with the distinction outlined in the first section, the main focus of the financial markets economist through this period was the

Figure 5.1 SNB balance sheet: Liabilities

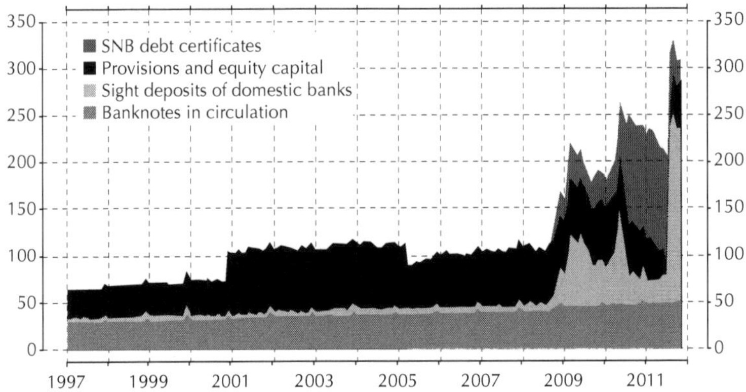

Source: SNB
Note: The SNB commenced unsterilised intervention late in Q3 2011, as shown by the surge in sight deposits.

Swiss economy. It was, of course, impossible to ignore the pronounced strength in the Swiss franc, but the priority was to evaluate the impact currency strength would have on the economy, and especially on the trade balance, rather than to analyse whether the state of the economy justified the move.

The economics fraternity did, however, engage in a very active debate regarding the SNB's policy stance, and specifically regarding the effectiveness of FX intervention. This debate centred on the scale of the intervention, and theoretical differences between sterilised and unsterilised intervention. A useful example of the debate is the IMF's Article IV review of Switzerland, published in May 2011.[3] Here, the IMF challenged the SNB on the degree to which the Swiss franc was overvalued, and also highlighted some of the macro-prudential risks that the scale of the intervention programme entailed.

In contrast to the financial markets economists, the focus of the macro strategist was the Swiss franc itself, along with Swiss interest rates, equities and property. The reaction of the SNB to Swiss franc strength was keenly studied, but less as a form of policy prescription, and more in terms of assessing its effectiveness. Different strategists, of course, held different views on this point. But the main divide was between how strategists of a fundamental and behavioural orientation approached the move.

The typical starting point for the fundamentalist was a measure of Swiss franc valuation. While a variety of methods are available in calculating fair value, all of these measures suggested that Swiss franc overvaluation was already extreme. Figure 5.2, for example, shows the real exchange rate for the Swiss franc against its 15-year moving average. The high point reached in 2010, at roughly 10% overvalued, matched the highs seen in 1995 and 2003, which proved to be opportunities to sell Swiss francs on a multi-year basis.

This starting point coloured the analysis of most fundamental strategists, who found it very difficult to justify an even stronger Swiss franc. The slowing economy, the expected deterioration in the trade balance and the radical interventions of the SNB were all posited as fundamental reasons for the move to reverse. This can be seen in consensus currency forecasts for the period, which tend to be dominated by the contributions of fundamentally orientated strategists. Figure 5.3 highlights the dramatic extent to which forecasts of Eur/Sfr for Q3/Q4 of 2011 lagged the move in spot.

The approach of the behavioural macro strategist was quite distinct. The starting point was to disavow any logical connection between the state of the Swiss economy and the possible level of Eur/Sfr. The next step was to identify and then evaluate the ideas

Figure 5.2 Sfr REER versus long-term average

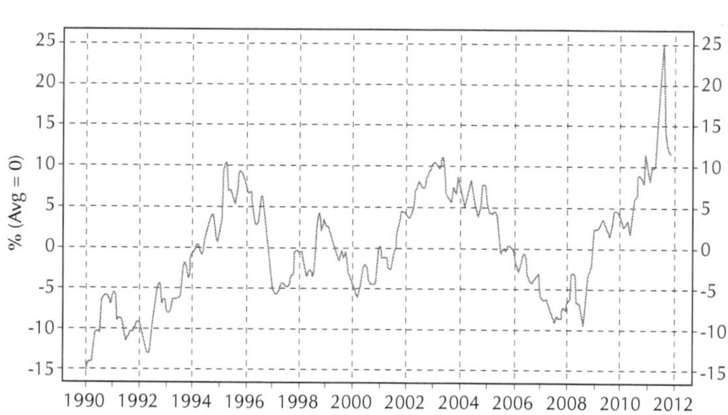

Source: Haver
Note: Sfr REER shown against its 15-year average; a positive number represents the percentage by which Swiss francs were said to be overvalued; the surge through Q3 2011 is notable.

and interests of the most influential market participants. In this instance, the SNB became the predominant focus given their monopoly over Swiss money market rates, and their capacity to intervene in Swiss francs.

The focus was then on attaining a level of intellectual empathy with the SNB. At a minimum, this involved a thorough inspection of the public essays and speeches of the members of the Governing Council. A deeper dive involved a comprehensive examination of their website, including a compilation of the main data series which are published. An even closer inspection delved into the SNB's mandate, including its constitutional underpinnings and its relationship to the cantons. A further overlay involved understanding the relationship of the SNB with other influential parties, such as the Swiss parliament, the IMF and the private banking network.

For the strategist who pursued these lines of inquiry, it became increasingly apparent that the intellectual framework that the SNB was using to think about the Swiss franc was breaking down. Not only was the market ignoring the surge in valuation, it was ignoring the SNB's verbal interventions. This dynamic became particularly acute in the context of the SNB's balance sheet, where the rally in Swiss francs had the impact of eroding the SNB's equity and provi-

Figure 5.3 Eur/Sfr: Consensus forecasts versus spot

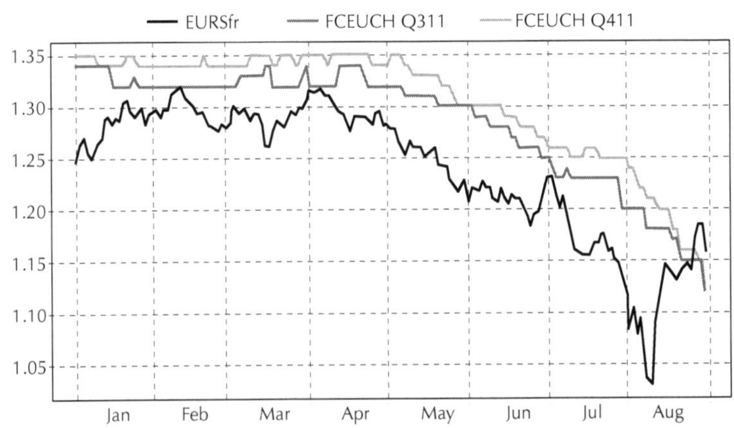

Source: Bloomberg
Note: Consensus currency forecasts are dominated by fundamentally orientated strategists; the forecasts for Eur/Sfr, which reflected 39 contributors, lagged the move through Q2/Q3 2011.

sions. The depletion of equity was in turn generating unwanted headline attention, particularly as the annual profits of the SNB had been a mainstay for the budgets of the cantons in previous years.

Fundamentally oriented strategists were, of course, aware of these issues. However, few engaged with any coherence. In addition to the perceived valuation constraint, many pointed out that the SNB had an unlimited ability to sell Swiss francs, which distinguished this situation from the canonical crises mentioned earlier. This insistence on a logical basis for the move was the main reason it was missed by fundamental strategists.

Behaviouralists, in contrast, were able to ignore the categorical distinction, and focus quite precisely on the SNB's predicament. In Weberian terms, the failure of the SNB's intellectual framework left open the possibility of an emotional market response, one that ignored typical rationalist boundaries. There was explicit recognition of the crisis of credibility that the SNB faced, seemingly unwilling to intervene even as Eur/Sfr plunged toward parity.

A very useful tool through this period was to measure the SNB's equity base in real time. Figure 5.4 shows one such measure, and highlights how official data lagged by one month. The main advantage of a real-time measure was that it highlighted when the SNB exhausted its equity base. Given the political sensitivity of this development, it was possible for a behavioural macro strategist to predict that a bold reaction might occur before the end of month mark printed in negative territory. In the event, the SNB commenced the re-expansion of its balance sheet within two days of its equity moving into negative territory, and within a month the lower bound had been established. In doing so, the SNB reasserted its authority and created a new intellectual framework for interested parties to evaluate.

While this case study is supportive of a behavioural approach to macro strategy, its main purpose is to highlight the difference of methods. There will be many instances where the two schools converge, and where strategists reach opposing conclusions even when of the same persuasion. As will be highlighted in the last section, what ultimately matters is the quality of the analysis and the accuracy of the predictions.

Figure 5.4 SNB equity and provisions

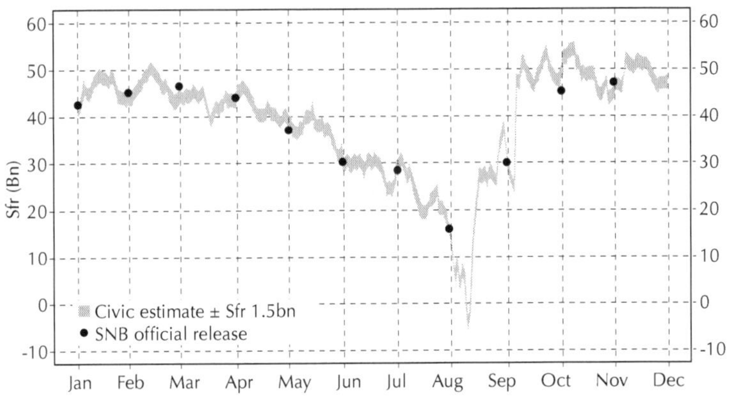

Source: SNB, Civic Capital
Note: A real-time estimate of the SNB's equity position was a very useful tool in predicting the SNB's behaviour, and thereby predicting Eur/Sfr; the black dots represent official SNB marks for equity and provisions, whereas the grey line represents a real-time estimate constructed by Civic Capital.

WHAT GOOD MACRO STRATEGY LOOKS LIKE

To conclude, it is helpful to examine some of the characteristics that are typically associated with successful macro strategy. This task is best addressed in terms of the core functions of the strategist: analysis and prediction.

Good analysis

The hallmark of good analysis is that it involves a genuine transfer of intellectual capital. It furthers the understanding of a complex topic, its presentation is coherent and consistent, and it is entirely independent. It is also timely, in that it focuses upon topics of contemporary relevance. Good analysis is an end in itself: it need not be accompanied by a prediction.

The most useful touchstone in assessing the quality of macro analysis is client feedback. If the clients of a strategist consistently learn something new and interesting by engaging with the work in question, the job is largely done. If not, the strategist has either failed to meet the qualitative standards expected, or may be failing the test of relevance.

A typical client complaint is that the analysis in question is too orthodox. The sheer volume of content available implies a premium is commanded by analysis that is informed, yet distinctive. This poses a challenge to the strategist, who is required to continually push the boundaries. For those strategists who are required to publish on schedule, it can be particularly difficult to find something new to say.

The attribute of distinctiveness is closely related to the topic of independence. Many of the most sought-after strategists operate from boutiques, to avoid any form of editorial interference. It is not uncommon for these strategists to pursue the most innovative forms of analysis, and to be of a generally creative mindset. Independence of thought is a key attribute, and eccentricity can often be a virtue.

For many strategists, the concept of independence conveys a right to criticise policymakers, or at least to advocate various forms of policy action. Others disagree with this, preferring to draw a hard line between positive forms of analysis (that which is), and normative (that which ought to be). There is no single right answer here, but good analysis does not allow for *ad hominem* attacks, nor does it permit unqualified advocacy.

Good analysis may be qualitative or quantitative in its composition, and is frequently a blend of both. However, in striving for quantitative rigour, data are often misused. Data mining is a common fault, as is the misapplication, or misinterpretation, of statistical techniques, which often occurs even with good intentions. The best practice is to comprehensively acknowledge data sources, and to be meticulous in the use of statistical methods.

An important step for the macro strategist is to seek client feedback on their analysis, whether formal or informal. The feedback mechanism not only ensures that strategists understand the attributes and shortcomings of their approach, it often leads to a mutually beneficial dialogue. Even the most talented strategist has room for improvement, and a good part of this is accepting and engaging with the constructive feedback of clients.

Good prediction

Good prediction is typically preceded by good analysis, and has two main attributes: accuracy and accountability. It is also important that predictions are timely and are constructed in a way that is helpful to clients. But a macro strategist who is able to deliver accurate and accountable trade recommendations will already be ahead of most.

While it is not commonly recognised, accuracy and accountability are closely interrelated concepts. A strategist who boasts a track record of accuracy will often fail the most basic tests of accountability. This is a hot-button issue. As distinct from risk takers, who are able to measure their contribution in terms of profit and loss, it is sometimes very difficult to pin a strategist down. There are few things more frustrating for a risk taker who has followed the lead of a strategist and lost money, only to observe the strategist spin the view around in such a way as to avoid association.

This is a difficult problem. And in many ways it is just as frustrating for a strategist who may believe, justifiably or not, that their contribution warrants greater recognition. It is the curse of the strategist to feel underappreciated when things are working out well, and overexposed when things are not.

Many strategists attempt to address this imbalance by tracking the performance of their recommendations on a line-by-line basis. This is a helpful step for those strategists who view precise trade construction as one of their deliverables. But while the approach may lend some credibility, it is still very difficult for a strategist to replicate a holistic portfolio environment, where volatility needs to be accounted for on an intraday basis, and where the management of drawdowns often compromises the ability of a risk taker to hold to a view. It is possible to construct an authentic synthetic portfolio to replicate profit and loss, but this is a very demanding task.

An alternative approach is to discard quantitative rigour, and instead pursue a narrative approach, where discipline is imposed via the written word. Many of the best strategists pride themselves on acknowledging when they are wrong, even if they are not keeping an accurate score. These strategists are very precise with their use of language, so that it will be clear to a client when a particular view has been ceded. The avoidance of ambiguity becomes an important pursuit.

A related point is that a strategist needs to be clear regarding the time horizon that they are working toward. A forecast without a temporal element may be useful, but to a risk taker it is not nearly as useful, or accountable, as one which is time-specific. This point is particularly important given the increased market segmentation that has developed between low-frequency and high-frequency traders. A strategist may also be short-term or long-term, but the two horizons should not be conflated and, where possible, key risk events should be analysed in isolation.

In the final determination, it is the responsibility of the macro strategist, whether of a fundamental or behavioural orientation, to deliver good analysis and good prediction. Clients are the final arbiter of excellence, and actively discriminate on the basis of merit. Even in a world which is content-rich, or perhaps especially in such a world, it is not difficult to identify the best macro strategists. They will teach you something new, and help you make some money along the way.

1 At http://web.mit.edu/krugman/www/crises.html.
2 At http://ssr1.uchicago.edu/PRELIMS/Theory/weber.html.
3 At http://www.imf.org/external/pubs/ft/scr/2011/cr11115.pdf.

6

Emerging Markets in Global Macro Investing

Gene Frieda

Moore Capital

Brazil has some of the savviest global macro investors in the world. While financial engineers from Ivy League schools were busy turning trash into triple A-rated securities in the early part of the 21st century, Brazil's traders were applying their own sophisticated engineering to global markets.

In the 1980s and 1990s, Brazilian fixed income traders were on the cutting edge of financial innovation, as they sought to "hedge" against hyperinflation and to circumnavigate a web of capital controls. It was no coincidence that, when Brazil was faced with its own exchange rate crisis in 1999, the government called on a talented 42-year old Brazilian economist and hedge fund manager, Arminio Fraga, who happened to be managing a dedicated pool of emerging market investments for George Soros's Quantum Fund, to save the day. Upon becoming the governor of the central bank, Fraga instituted inflation targeting and helped steer the economy through a harrowing 2002 election campaign won by leftist candidate Lula da Silva.

With relative stability restored, Fraga resigned at the end of 2002 and promptly founded his own hedge fund the following year, focusing initially on global macro investing. After inflation stabilised and capital controls were eased in tandem, a number of other hedge funds were soon launched, initially focusing on Brazil. However, realising the advantages of their own past experiences of booms and busts, the Brazilians turned their sights on the global markets, quickly becoming leaders of the macro investing pack.[1] Like a player turned coach, the Brazilian wave of hedge funds highlighted just how flat the global macro world had become in the wake of the global financial crisis.

This chapter will posit several timeless characteristics of emerging market investing, focusing in particular on underlying market liquidity and institutional maturity. We will first set the stage with a brief overview of emerging market investing since the early 1990s. We approach the evolving story of emerging markets from the perspective of a macro hedge fund strategist tasked with spotting investment themes that are both tactical and strategic in nature. The chapter will conclude by looking at how the framework of analysis for emerging market investing has become increasingly relevant for macro investing in mature markets.

Emerging markets tend to be characterised by higher volatility and often non-normally distributed returns with fat tails. These characteristics, by definition, require tighter risk management and dedicated credit analysis skills. These are markets where sleuths prosper, because data are more opaque, policymaking more volatile and the rule of law far less secure. Risk of adverse price movement is often swamped by more unique hazards – such as expropriation of assets, suspended exchange rate convertibility or outright sovereign default. Emerging market investors are more likely to find themselves reading the last three versions of the country's constitution than dissecting the reasons for a 0.1 percentage point surprise to the latest monthly inflation data – as might be the case in a developed market.

The need to differentiate between an emerging market "situation" and an emerging market country reflects an inconvenient truth: that in the wake of the 2007–09 global financial crisis, many economies previously deemed developed look far more like traditional emerging markets than the emerging markets themselves. And this highlights why the old emerging market hands of the 1990s global macro world have shifted their sights to the European periphery: it is a region that largely resembles the crisis-prone emerging markets of that prior era.

There are a number of issues that this chapter will explicitly seek to avoid. It does not address the question of whether emerging markets as an asset class offer higher risk-adjusted returns than developed markets, or indeed what the optimal portfolio allocation to emerging markets within a traditional fixed income or equity portfolio should be. The focus, instead, is on how a macro fund identifies opportunities in sovereign fixed income and currency markets that are inherently less liquid and more opaque than those of developed markets.

A short history of emerging market investing since the early 1990s shows how two strains of emerging market trading have developed. One is more traditional and inherently appealing to global macro traders, while the global financial crisis of 2007–09 spawned a more faddish strain.

THE RISE OF GLOBAL MACRO INVESTING IN EMERGING MARKETS

Born from the rubble of the Latin American financial crisis, the rise of the Asian export machine and the fall of the Berlin Wall, emerging market (EM) investing was still a niche story as the dot com bubble was coming to a head (see Figure 6.1).

EM fixed income and currency trading was primarily the domain of commercial banks with residual experience in securitising the defaulted loans of the 1980s debt crisis into Brady bonds. Macro hedge funds were drawn into the sphere amid declining US treasury yields, strong economic growth in the early 1990s and relatively high EM sovereign yields, both on dollar-denominated debt and in local currency fixed income. Low correlations to advanced markets and high potential returns, albeit with higher volatility to boot, led to the development of performance tracking indexes such as those of MSCI

Figure 6.1 Net private capital flows to emerging markets

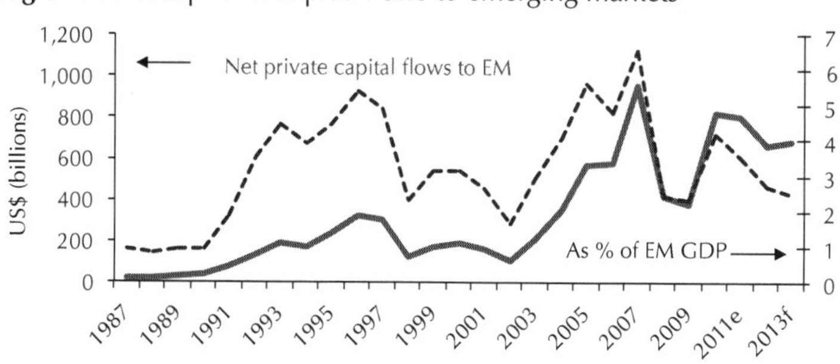

Source: Institute for International Finance

for equities and JP Morgan for fixed income, and a new asset class was launched (see Figure 6.2).

Markets were inherently illiquid, and material advantage in the pre-Internet world could be gained from frequent travel to the country or even by reading faxed copies of local newspapers. Jim Rogers, co-founder of the Quantum Fund with George Soros, popularised the appeal of EMs in a 1995 book, *Investment Biker*, where he described travelling 100,000 miles across six continents, analysing and investing as he went.[2] The advantages of time spent on the ground were material.

The example of Mexico between 1990 and 1994 is a microcosm for the broader story of macroeconomic imbalances, financial dislocations and political disruptions that set that stage for global macro investing in emerging markets during that tumultuous decade. Having emerged from a sovereign debt default in 1982 and subsequent hyperinflation, Mexico agreed to negotiate a free trade agreement with the US and Canada at the end of 1992. Mexican inflation had receded from a peak of 180% in 1988 to less than 20% at the start of 1992. The exchange rate was a "crawling peg," allowing slight depreciation each year, but effectively fixed in order to anchor inflation expectations.

The exchange rate anchor worked to bring down inflation, but the corresponding decline in interest rates, helped in part by strong foreign interest in Mexican peso-denominated paper, led to a boom in domestic demand. Three-month interest rates fell from 24% at the start of 1991 to as low as 11% in early 1992. The current account responded in kind, worsening from a deficit of 2% of GDP in early

Figure 6.2 Correlation between emerging market and world equity indexes

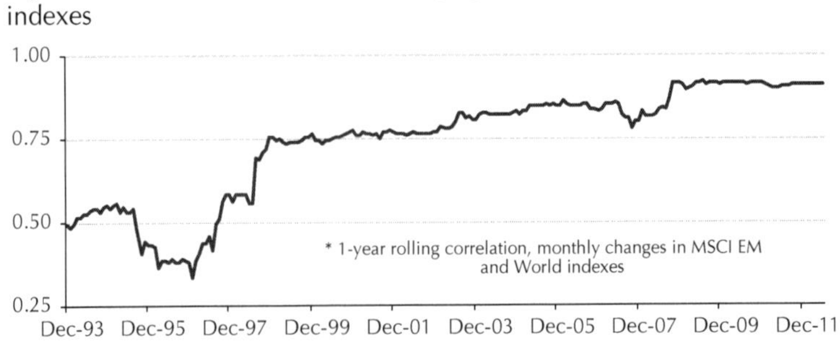

Source: Ecowin

1991 to 5.5% of GDP by the end of 1992. The party continued unimpeded for another year until a random confluence of events – typical of emerging markets – ensued. On January 1, 1994, the Zapatista Army of National Liberation, a group of previously unknown guerrillas, seized a number of towns and cities in the southernmost state of Chiapas. Armed clashes ensued over the following year.

Then followed on March 23 the assassination of the ruling PRI party's presidential candidate, Luis Donaldo Colosio. The PRI party had ruled Mexico for the previous seven decades. Faced with an uncertain transition, foreign confidence in Mexico evaporated. Forced to defend the *de facto* fixed exchange rate, the Banco de Mexico quickly spent most of the country's foreign reserves.

With reserves nearly exhausted and faced with the prospect of another sovereign debt default, the Mexicans finally gave in and floated the peso on December 20, 1994. Only with a last-minute intervention by US President Bill Clinton, in the form of an unprecedented bilateral loan made from the US Treasury's Exchange Stabilization Fund (together with support from the International Monetary Fund and the Bank for International Settlements), was another default averted.

Global macro investing in emerging markets came to prominence during the 1997 Asian financial crisis. The industry was still relatively young, but a number of global macro funds spotted growing macroeconomic imbalances and financial risks among several Asian tiger nations not that dissimilar to what had happened in Mexico only a few years earlier. Using the old metrics of external debt sustainability, they speculated that foreign reserves were no longer sufficient to defend two competing macroeconomic objectives: defending exchange rate pegs to the dollar, while keeping monetary policy loose enough to support strong and increasingly credit-led economic growth.

The low volatility typically associated with fixed exchange rate regimes allowed global macro funds to employ substantial leverage to challenge Asian currency pegs. The end result – the exit of several Asian fixed exchange rate regimes from their dollar pegs – was not that dissimilar to that of several developed European economies that were forced out of the ill-fated European exchange rate mechanism (ERM) back in 1992.

Just as Mexico's so-called Tequila Crisis of 1994 was a magnet for macro hedge fund interest in the wake of the large gains wrought from the collapse of the ERM in 1992, Argentina's crisis in late 2001 served as a tombstone on a decade of destabilising currency crises that swept across emerging Europe, Asia and Latin America.

An overlapping phase between 1998 and 2005 forms the core of what can be deemed traditional EM investing. This phase focused on deep structural reforms, both fiscal and monetary, which led to a period of strong GDP growth (see Figure 6.3).

During this period, emerging market investing gradually shifted from "special situations" to that of levered bets on the global economic cycle (see Figure 6.4). The advent of the BRICs (composed of Brazil, Russia, India and China) symbolised the nexus between emerging markets as a driver of global demand growth and the seminal role these countries played in supplying key inputs – namely commodities and labour – to the world economy.

In the early years, there was little question as to what an EM was: by comparison to high-income Organisation for Economic Co-operation and Development (OECD) countries, these were low- to middle-income countries that, more often than not, had been beset by some sort of macroeconomic crisis within the past decade. Emerging markets tended to have sub-investment grade ratings, reflective of a past tendency to default, hyper-inflate, or both.

Mexico joined the OECD in 1994, while Korea and three central European countries joined within the next two years. All five experienced crises within two years of joining this previously elite group of "developed" nations – but, nonetheless, the definition of an emerging market was gradually being muddied.

Figure 6.3 Emerging market GDP growth* rates

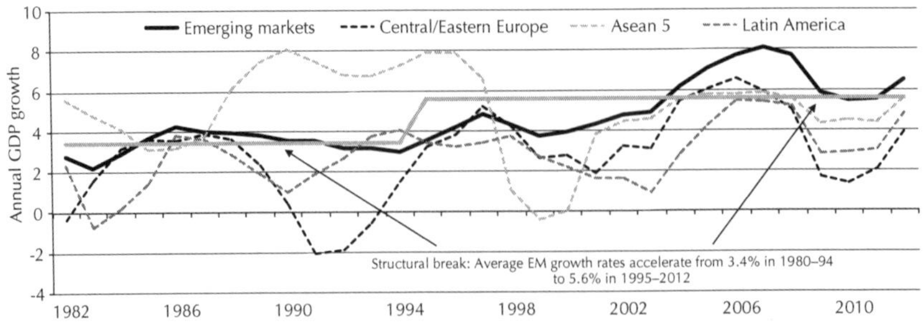

Source: IMF WEO Database, * three-year average GDP growth

Figure 6.4 Emerging market bonds spreads and sovereign ratings trends

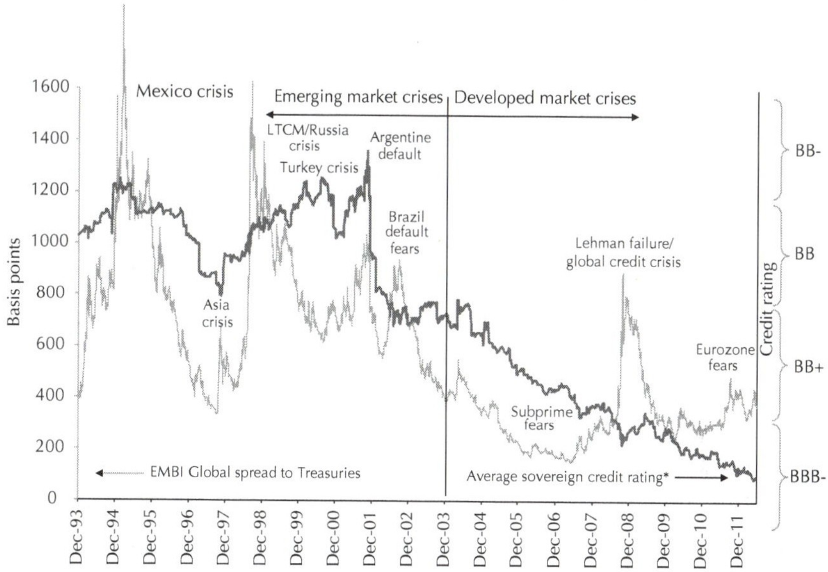

Source: JP Morgan Securities
* Average of S&P and Moody's

Fast-forward to the post-2008 global financial landscape, and there almost seems to have been a role reversal. The majority of tradable emerging markets have investment grade ratings, external and public sector debt levels below 60% of GDP, single digit inflation and annual per capita incomes of more than US$10,000.

The fundamental improvements and strong growth seen by less-developed economies underscore a crucial point: the emerging markets are not a static club. Several countries, like Singapore, Korea and the Czech Republic, have graduated. At the same time, some countries, like Argentina and Venezuela, have regressed deeper into dysfunctionality, while some advanced economies, such as those on the periphery of the euro area, are looking ever more similar to the emerging markets of old.

REGIME CHANGE: THE NEW EMERGING MARKET THESIS

While having a resemblance in genesis and exodus to the speculative attacks on the European Exchange Rate Mechanism (ERM) of the early 1990s, the economic consequences of the Asian crisis were far more severe, and arguably generational in the way they changed the behaviour of emerging market policymakers (see Figure 6.5). This behavioural change, in turn, led to a shift in emerging market investing, away from uncorrelated special situations, either going into or coming out of a crisis, and towards high beta plays on global growth.

Chastened by the economic collapse following the successful attacks on various exchange rate pegs, Asian policymakers – foreshadowing later episodes in Russia and Latin America – decided to re-orient their macroeconomic policies toward the primary goal of avoiding external debt crises at all costs. This included the adoption of somewhat more flexible exchange rate regimes, which allowed for greater day-to-day volatility, and the build-up of massive war chests of foreign exchange reserves.

Whereas leveraged macro funds had been the kings of the market mountain in the 1990s, the new and increasingly powerful kids on the block in the first decade of the 21st century were emerging market central banks. They intervened in foreign exchange markets to hold down the value of their currencies, and then reinvested their burgeoning foreign exchange reserves in developed markets. Five macro trends developed as a result.

First, exchange rate intervention reflated emerging market economies. Currencies did not adjust as rapidly as their strong balance of payments would have suggested. Undervalued currencies became self-reinforcing as manufacturing shifted away from devel-

Figure 6.5 Growth impact of financial crises in Europe and emerging markets

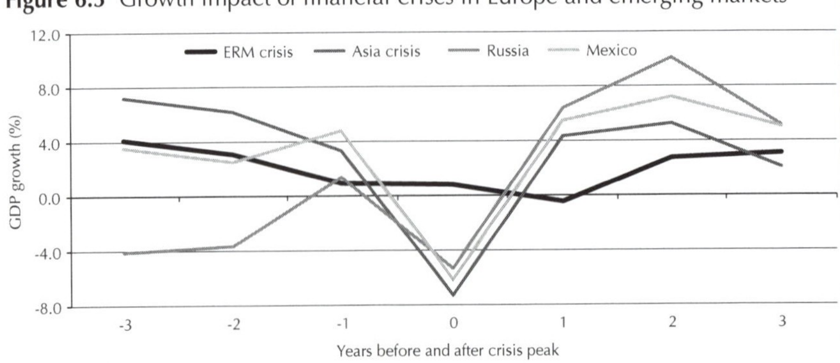

Source: IMF

oped economies at a faster pace. Sovereign spreads narrowed as a result of strong growth and reduced external indebtedness, thereby reinforcing a cycle of credit rating upgrades, strong equity performance and rising foreign investment appetite.

Second, loose monetary conditions were then re-exported back to the developed economies as growing foreign exchange reserves were invested in US treasuries and other developed economy sovereign bonds. As the 2000s wore on and foreign reserves reached mammoth proportions, the exchange rate intervention became contagious and self-propagating. This was inherently bullish for emerging equity and local currency fixed income markets, via rising commodity prices and strong developed country growth.

Third, larger foreign reserve cushions became a fast ticket to investment-grade status, which in turn allowed emerging markets to move past the "original sin" of being unable to issue much debt in their own currencies. Again, this trend fed on itself, with a shrinking supply of hard currency-denominated emerging market sovereign debt leading a growing posse of emerging market fund managers to shift their mandates toward local currency fixed income instruments.

Fourth, central bank intervention also served to suppress financial market volatility more broadly. In a mirror image of the 1990s speculation against emerging market exchange rate pegs, falling volatility led to ever-larger leveraged bets – this time on currency appreciation.

Figure 6.6 Emerging market foreign reserves and implied S&P 500 volatility

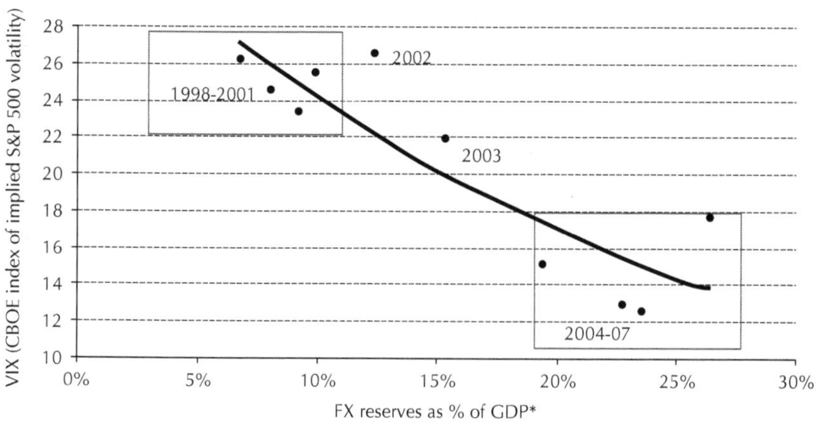

*Brazil, China, India, Japan, Korea, Russia, Taiwan

The trend was so pronounced that in spite of an average sovereign credit rating below investment grade levels,[3] the benchmark JP Morgan EMBI global debt spread over US treasuries collapsed, reaching as little as 151 basis points in mid-2007. Equity market volatility also declined significantly between 1998 and 2007 (see Figure 6.6).

Finally, the flip side to the pressure on emerging market exchange rates was a steadily depreciating US dollar, which followed efforts to revive the American economy after the bursting of the technology bubble. The collapse of Asia's tiger economies in the late 1990s was followed by a historic slump in the price of those commodities, most notably oil, which had fed Asia's boom. But, from 2002, steady dollar depreciation exacerbated a rise in commodity prices that was already developing as a function of Asia's recovery. (In contrast to the 1990s, China went from follower to leader of this trend after joining the World Trade Organization in 2001.)

THE ROLE OF EMERGING MARKETS IN GLOBAL MACRO TRADING

In many respects, the above narrative is a gross simplification. Economists have sought to explain the flood of money to emerging markets in terms of "push" and "pull" factors.[4] For market participants, it should be clear from the five trends cited above that the relationship between emerging and developed markets is inherently symbiotic.

In a world where risk-free rates in advanced economies have converged toward zero, emerging markets have become a more central component to global macro portfolios. The conservative "home bias" of developed market investors has waned amid a global wave of financial market liberalisation. And, perhaps most crucially, America's response to the global financial crisis has set in train an inexorable decline in the dollar's dominance as a reserve currency. For all the caution that follows in this chapter on the danger of underestimating risks within emerging markets, it is the US dollar's declining reserve currency status that looks set to ensure a permanent role for emerging markets within the global macro investing suite.[5]

The dichotomy between the two types of emerging market trading styles noted above again underscores a key point: almost by definition, the "who", the "what" and the "how" of emerging market investing is constantly changing.

From a global macro perspective, emerging markets are conceptual more than definitional. They constitute country-driven situations where financial markets are, or become, deeper over time, or disintegrate rapidly, and where distributional tails are prone to extremes. As a result of such experience, emerging market investors have been quicker to understand the consequences of the eurozone crisis than many developed market investors. The old emerging market hands were among the first to bet strongly that European policymakers' promises to socialise debt problems were not credible.

Global macro funds bet on the credibility of macro regimes. Is an exchange rate peg credible given a country's macroeconomic fundamentals? Can the central bank credibly raise interest rates to defend the exchange rate peg without undermining growth? Are real interest rates unnecessarily high given a country's shift from current account deficit to surplus following an earlier crisis? Can a country afford to restructure its banking system after a burst credit bubble without bankrupting itself? Global macro funds question the credibility of governments' promises. In an emerging markets context, these promises tend to be backed up by higher-than-normal yields.

However, there is a limit on the extent to which emerging markets can replace developed market assets. This limit is largely a function of liquidity. Also, the rise in correlations between developed and emerging financial markets over time has mirrored the growing integration of emerging and advanced economies.

Emerging markets are inherently less liquid and, accordingly, more volatile in periods of strong risk-seeking behaviour and of risk aversion. The best and most careful analysis of individual emerging market economies can go awry as a result of broader macro trends emanating from the larger developed economies.

TRENDSPOTTING IN EMERGING MARKETS: A CASE STUDY

Recognising that developments in the largest economies tend to set the cyclical stage for emerging market asset behaviour, global macro traders tend to approach emerging markets from a top-down perspective. They devise macro scenarios for the US, Japan, China and Europe, with a heavy emphasis on the monetary policy stances of their respective central banks. Macro trading themes are then translated to emerging markets and used to identify specific absolute or relative value investment ideas.

Separately, there is a bottom-up process conditioned on the credibility of the macro regime and expectations about global growth and financial conditions. This process seeks to monetise country-specific idiosyncrasies – both positive and negative – that stem from structural economic or political developments.

The intersection of these two processes is the dynamic relationship between global financial conditions and a country's macro policy settings. Whereas a country's macro policy settings and resulting imbalances may be unsustainable in one state of the world, they may persist well beyond the macro trader's imagination in another state of the world.

A good example has been the conventional wisdom, partially backed by empirical research in the 1980s and 1990s, that current account deficits beyond 3% of gross domestic product were generally not sustainable over time. This maxim fit the experience of most emerging market economies that suffered attacks on pegged exchange rates during the 1990s, but it has failed miserably since the early 2000s.

After the current account deficit reached "unsustainable" levels of 3.7% of GDP in 2000, Turkey's crawling exchange rate peg to the dollar blew up in early 2001. The currency depreciated 60% in nominal terms and 35% in real trade-weighted terms over the space of nine months. The depreciation and ensuing growth recession led to a swing in the current account to a surplus of 1.9% of GDP in 2001. But thereafter, the current account quickly deteriorated, reaching a new record deficit of 4.6% of GDP in 2005 and worsening to nearly 10% of GDP in 2011.

It was not until late 2010 that the currency started to weaken materially and, even then, the paucity of yield available in developed markets enabled the central bank of Turkey to successfully arrest the decline in the Turkish lira with only modest interest rate increases. Whereas real interest rates (nominal interest rates minus annual consumer price inflation) had turned negative during 2011, the currency was stabilised at interest rate levels that would have been record lows only two years previously.

Turkey's heterodox policy regime had proven unsustainable in spite of record low interest rates in advanced economies, but at the same time, the looseness of global financial conditions allowed the Turkish monetary authorities to restore currency stability without much remedial action. Moreover, the eventual rapid adjustment in the exchange rate did not destabilise the economy, or indeed political institutions, as it had on numerous occasions in the past. In this respect, Turkey looked more like a developed than an emerging market.

A strategist tasked with identifying opportunities in emerging markets is challenged on a number of fronts – opaque information, lack of liquidity,[6] and dependence on macroeconomic and financial conditions in the largest developed economies. A starting point for identifying trends is reflected in Table 6.1, where basic scenarios for the US, Europe and China are considered in the context of what might be deemed as a good, neutral or negative scenario for risk appetite. Probabilities are attached to each of the individual country scenarios, and joint probabilities are then calculated, together with some basic market implications.

There are obviously many more combinations of scenarios than those highlighted in the table, but the framework serves for making adjustments to strategy as these different combinations materialise. The exercise amounts to being pre-emptive in thinking about different scenarios that are unpredictable *ex ante.*

With thought having been given to the global backdrop for emerging markets, there is an interim stage to trade identification from a top-down perspective before considering trade ideas at the country-specific level.

Using Table 6.1, which referred to the outlook for the second half of 2011 as an example, the conclusion of the scenario analysis was that the global recovery was moving into a state of "thin air," with modest upward progress achievable only with great effort and with substantial downside risk in the event of new shocks. Fiscal policy retrenchment was assumed to be the defining feature of advanced economy policy orientation, deepening the divide between emerging and advanced economies.

The US was assumed likely to outperform in this scenario, but without a major dose of additional monetary policy easing following the end of QE2[7] in June 2011, the backdrop was biased more toward risk aversion than risk-seeking behaviour.

The conclusions derived from these premises – a macro environ-

Table 6.1 Indicative strategic scenario analysis

	Good	Market implications	Probability
US	Labour market improves; Fed dovish on softening core CPI	US$ negative; bond negative + steepening; equity positive	15%
Europe	German growth anchor remains; Spain clearly decouples; No Greek programme trouble until 2012	ECB tightens to 3% by year-end and 3.5% by mid-2012	20%
China	CPI falls below 5% year-end; growth stays 9–10%	Chinese monetary policy neutral from September	15%
Other	Commodity price decline boosts real incomes in advanced economies and eases headline CPI pressures in EM	Faster monetary tightening; US$ positive; equity positive	25%
Joint probability			**18%**
	Neutral		
US	Growth between 2–2.5%; Fed neutral	Most US$ negative and modest equity positive	60%
Europe	Greece contained; Spain stays sub-250bps versus bunds; Euro area stress tests "successful"	ECB hikes in July and November and then on hold; EUR range-bound 1.35–1.50	45%
China	CPI slows toward 5% year-end; Growth stays 9–10%	Chinese monetary policy neutral from October–November	50%
Other	*Status quo* on commodity prices (easing); geopolitics (stable Middle East/Pakistan); capital controls (none)	US$ neutral/negative; equity neutral/positive	50%
Joint probability			**52%**
	Bad		
US	Growth sub-2%; weaker labour market; Fed neutral or small QE3	US$ neutral/positive; equity negative; bond positive; better for low yielding safe havens than high yielders	25%
Europe	Greece defaults without intl. support; Spain and Italy infected; Euro area bank funding stressed	ECB cuts before year-end; deeper fiscal tightening across eurozone; negative EUR, bank equity and Spanish, French and Italian sovereign spreads	35%
China	CPI stays high (above 5.5%); growth slows to sub-8%.	Chinese monetary policy tightens through year-end	35%
Other	Natural disasters; geopolitical conflict; capital controls	Looser monetary and fiscal policy; negative for highly indebted advanced economies and US$	25%
Joint probability			**30%**

Weights: US 35%; Europe 35%; China 20%; Other 10%. Joint probability = sum of country weights × scenario probabilities

ment characterised by less loose monetary and fiscal policy, deficient growth in advanced economies and a disconnect between policies in emerging and developed markets – were as follows.

- Expect a continued search for "alternative" safe havens given sovereign debt uncertainty, likely to be exacerbated by fiscal tightening – and corresponding growth drag – that aims to address the problem where currencies cannot offset the tightening. This favours safe "alternative" currencies as well as gold and EM local currency fixed income.
- Diversify funding away from US dollars and toward UK pounds, and especially euros. Eurozone periphery tail risk and greater potential for growth disappointment in the eurozone are judged to carry high probabilities.
- The backdrop is not particularly conducive to equity market gains. The second half of 2011 is likely to see either modest gains or significant declines.
- EM equities behaved predictably in the wake of Lehman Brothers' collapse, during QE1 and in the lull between QE1 and QE2. However, EMs underperformed in QE2 despite strong inflows – a genuine surprise. EM equity underperformance during QE2 is potentially a "canary in the coal mine."
- Japan, the US and the UK are more disadvantaged than most by having little monetary scope to counter fiscal tightening. Recourse to QE is only a second best.
- Sticky core inflation and positive output gaps in EM suggest no major monetary easing, but there is scope for hikes to be priced out of some markets.

Based on these conclusions, a number of trade ideas were recommended based on a bottom-up analysis of various countries' starting positions (imbalances, valuations, etc) and likely policy reactions (based on the scope for, and historical bias of, policy response to external shocks).

- The continued search for "alternative" safe havens in the face of sovereign debt uncertainty favours the Swiss franc, the Singapore dollar, the Canadian dollar and the Swedish krona, as well as EM local currency exposure in the likes of Brazil, Mexico, Korea and South Africa.

- Go short EM currencies that are more sensitive to EM equity performance. The Indian rupee stands out.
- Go short central European currencies. Central Europe was the regional currency outperformer against the US dollar during QE2. This reflected the cyclical strength of Germany, engendered in European Central Bank (ECB) rate hikes, and the benefits of easy funding for a traditionally mid-yielding, high current account-deficit bloc. The risk backdrop was likely to be much less favourable in the second half of 2011, with embedded tail risk stemming from the European periphery. Our relative value expression would be to short the Polish zloty versus the Czech koruna.
- Remain core long Asian currencies, but with a bias toward low rather than high yielders. Low yielders tend to be those with stronger current account positions and offer better protection during periods of risk aversion.
- Short the Turkish lira and payer[8] positions in five-year cross-currency swaps are core thematic positions given the Turkish economy's overheating problems, as reflected in the burgeoning current account deficit and an ideological central bank unwilling to react to these pressures. A weaker currency will put upward pressure on inflation. And since the Central Bank of Turkey continues to resist an orthodox tightening in monetary policy, the impact of higher inflation should come on the long end of the yield curve.
- Asymmetric trades for a neutral scenario that becomes bad include the euro as a funding currency, short Spanish and Italian sovereign debt.
- We would focus receivers on two-year South Africa, Malaysia and Mexico as the market prices out expectations of central bank rate hikes.
- Go short oil proxy currencies, including the Russian rouble and the Norwegian krone, and long China-sensitive commodity proxies like the Canadian dollar, the Indonesian rupiah and the South African rand (see Figure 6.7). We expect more growth relief than policy easing relief from China. Chinese growth should hold up at 9–10%, leading to outperformance by raw materials commodity prices relative to oil prices. But the cost will be persistently high inflation and continued money leakage to the non-traditional financial sector.

- If China's credit problems come to the fore earlier than expected, they will manifest themselves where stresses have already emerged: Chinese bank equity and credit default swaps (CDS). But Hong Kong should also be vulnerable, having experienced an even bigger lending boom than China (eg, bank credit-to-GDP went from 178% at end-2007 to 264% in May 2011). We buy a one-year 7.85 US$/HK$ one-touch binary call option for 4% of payout.[9]

The above recommendations were meant to give a group of global macro portfolio managers a sense of likely market direction, relative performance of various assets and specific trade ideas. Implicit in the analysis is recognition that all portfolio managers have their own biases (in terms of products and countries), focus and trading style.

There is a clear bias in our recommendations toward EM local fixed income exposure and against EM high-yield currency exposure, against the euro and European periphery fixed income and in favour of "new" safe haven assets, and against central Europe and in favour of some Asian currencies.

With the above outlook for the second half of 2011 as a guide, a quick check of what actually transpired reveals several key lessons about the challenges of investing in emerging markets.

Figure 6.7 Ratio of raw materials to oil prices as a currency trade proxy

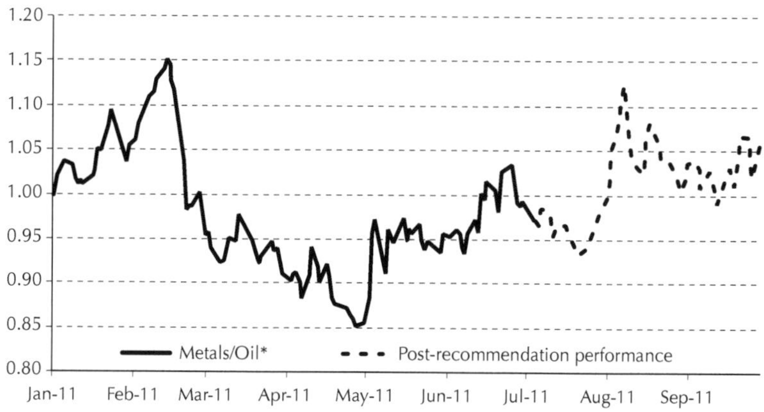

Source: Bloomberg, Jan 1, 2011 = 100
*Raw materials = CRB RIND Index; Oil = WTI crude

- The assumed global macroeconomic and policy backdrop proved generally correct. Nonetheless, the translation of this backdrop into specific trades was far from perfect.
- The list of trade ideas was designed as exactly that: ideas. They did not constitute a portfolio and there was no consideration given to scale. This is where trading style comes in. On this score, there should be little difference between emerging and developed markets in how a portfolio manager scales position size up or down. The main difference is in recognition of the higher volatility and potentially lower liquidity often inherent in emerging market assets.
- In the specific case outlined above, the outlook was over a relatively long period – the second half of 2011. The outlook was strategic in nature and did not address the question of tactical positioning.
- It is rare that one can identify unexpected shocks before they materialise. Often too much time is spent trying to predict triggers rather than vulnerability and consequences. Strategic outlooks should always seek to identify asymmetric opportunities that can lead to trades that work under a variety of scenarios. The Chinese bank equity and CDS recommendations were such examples.

TACTICAL CONSIDERATIONS

Beyond the challenge of identifying trends and serving as a compass for those trends, a strategist must pay heed to a macro hedge fund's greater aversion to daily profit and loss (P&L) volatility compared to, say, a long-term institutional investor. Shorter-term factors, including market positioning and news flow, are material considerations.

Surveys of market positioning, sentiment and asset class flows, public data on non-commercial exposures in currency and interest rate futures markets, and options market behaviour (namely, the "skew" in risk reversals) are all useful quantitative measures of positioning. Price action is another: are particular markets failing to react to good news or overreacting to bad news? Both quantitative and subjective measures of positioning feed into considerations of how and when to implement the type of recommendations outlined above.

The use of derivatives deserves special mention as a further complication for gauging the underlying market positioning. The explosive

Figure 6.8 Global OTC derivatives market volumes

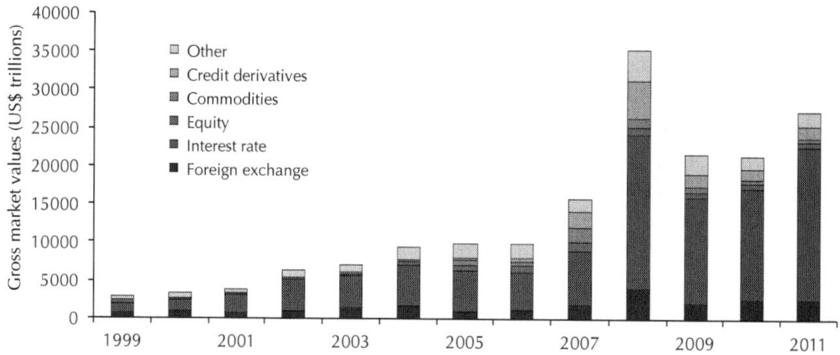

Source: BIS

growth of currency and fixed income derivative products, as much in emerging as in developed markets, has served to deepen market liquidity (see Figure 6.8). But this also leads to potentially higher basis risk (ie, the risk of a mismatch between a derivative and its underlying instrument) and contributes to non-linear price movements in the underlying instruments in response to exogenous shocks.

For example, as the global financial crisis began to unfold in earnest in 2008, several emerging market currencies, such as the Brazilian real, the Mexican peso, the Polish zloty and the Korean won, suddenly became extremely volatile. None of these economies were experiencing significant macro imbalances, such as burgeoning current account deficits or sharply accelerating inflation, yet all four currencies suffered disproportionately dramatic depreciations after the collapse of Lehman Brothers in September 2008. The declines belied perceptions of speculative positioning in these markets.

The culprit was soon unveiled to be a form of exotic currency option known as a knock-in, knock-out (KIKO),[10] or a target accrual redemption note (TARN), that had been sold by investment banks to less-sophisticated corporate clients. Used to enhance yield, the options created a long position in the local currency, with gains capped or limited by barriers or termination provisions once a certain gain was accrued.

Because they were mostly sold during a multi-year period in which the dollar constantly depreciated and emerging market currencies correspondingly appreciated, the corporate buyers of these options tended to ignore downside risks. These products were especially attractive because they were sold to buyers at "zero cost" (ie, buyers did not have to post any initial premium). Downside was normally unlimited, and the pace at which losses accrued was normally at twice the rate of any gain for a given change in the underlying exchange rate.

Just as the excessive sale of credit default protection by AIG Financial Products on subprime mortgage products contributed to the US housing bubble, so did these toxic exchange rate options contribute to mistaken perceptions that emerging market currencies were highly liquid. The IMF estimated the direct cost to financial firms (mostly within the emerging markets) from such options at US$530 billion. But the indirect cost to others that had invested in the affected local currencies was also substantial, as they discovered that liquidity in these normally liquid markets had evaporated.

Despite sophisticated analysis of market positioning by macro hedge funds, most failed to recognise the destabilising power of such exotic currency options until the underlying currencies had already blown up. Indeed, few hedge funds were aware of how widespread the use of KIKOs had become, given that they were mostly transacted between banks and corporate clients.

An important lesson derived from this experience is that even the most sophisticated attempts to measure market positioning are partial and static. They will not fully capture the underlying market liquidity, which can amplify or shrink value-at-risk (VaR) for a given net position size, nor will they reflect how derivative exposures can magnify or lower position exposures based on directional price movements.

CONCLUSION

It should be clear at this stage that the definition of an emerging market, at least in traditional terms, has become muddied. Per capita incomes in the several Asian tigers of yore now exceed those of many, if not most, advanced economies in North America and Europe. Public debt levels are generally low, and sovereign ratings are well above investment grade. "Reforming basket cases," the informal descriptive of emerging markets used in the early 2000s, now seems to define either serial defaulters or advanced economies, most notably those in the European periphery.

Three main factors have driven the shift in the nature of emerging market investing: the rise in global imbalances and the corresponding rise of emerging market central bank reserve management and trading activity; the collapse in developed economy interest rates and the post-crisis shortage of "safe" assets; and the structural improvements in emerging markets themselves.

EM investing is inherently more challenging than trading advanced economies, not only in terms of liquidity but also because many of the traditional macro "rules of thumb" do not apply. This failure underscores the tendency of macroeconomic theory to be based on observations in more advanced economies.

Blindly superimposing advanced economy macro thinking onto EM portfolio management can inevitably be hazardous to one's investment health. Some have gone so far as to devise a list of certain macroeconomic "rules of thumb" that tend not to hold in emerging markets.[11] A short list of stylised facts on the relationship between emerging market macro performance and asset price behaviour underscores the need for caution.

- Higher GDP growth rates do not necessarily translate into stronger asset returns. This applies to both currencies and equities.
- Asset price booms have a greater tendency to occur and tend to be mistaken for structural breaks. Once they burst, the consequences tend to be more destabilising.
- Nominal interest rates tend to be divorced from nominal growth rates and are more sensitive to exchange rates (because most emerging markets are open economies, inflation tends to be more sensitive to exchange rate movements).
- Because most emerging markets are small relative to the size of global capital flows, their ability to respond to positive and negative shocks with traditional policy mechanisms is limited. Macro-prudential tools, including financial transaction taxes and capital controls, are much more likely.

The decade following the early 2010s is set to be a challenging one for emerging markets, and it is likely that the faddish attraction of thematic investing in these countries will be tested. Liquidity risks notwithstanding, the period should be a fruitful one for global macro investors that are willing to test the credibility of individual emerging market policy frameworks as much in good times as in bad.

The greatest threat to the emerging markets investment story stems from challenges faced by countries with immature institutions and inherently less developed markets. Emerging markets' performance in the wake of the global financial crisis underscored both their vulnerability to financial shocks as well as a resilience borne of a decade of reforms. The "who", the "what" and the "how" of emerging markets will inevitably continue to evolve, but one guiding principle for EM investing will persist: think the unthinkable and do not expect normal rules to apply.

1 For a more detailed discussion of Brazil's hedge fund industry, see Alexander Ragir, 2011, "Brazilian hedge funds trounce competition," *Washington Post*, June 11.

2 Jim Rogers, 1995, *Investment Biker: Around the World with Jim Rogers* (Holbrook, Mass: Adams Publishing).

3 The minimum credit rating for investment grade is BBB–. In June 2007, when JP Morgan EMBI global spreads troughed at 151 basis points, the weighted-average credit rating for sovereign bonds in the JP Morgan index was BB+, one notch below investment grade.

4 See, for example, Atish R. Ghosh, Jun Kim, Mahvash S. Qureshi and Juan Zalduendo , 2012, "Surges," IMF Working Paper 12/22, January.

5 See Barry Eichengreen, 2011, *Exorbitant Privilege: The Rise and Fall of the Dollar and the Future of the International Monetary System* (Oxford, England: Oxford University Press).

6 Investment banks are especially notorious for recommending emerging market trade ideas in highly illiquid markets and instruments. It may well be the case that a smaller emerging market currency or bond market is poised to move 20% in one direction or the other, but it is arguable whether the diversification benefit outweighs the inability to achieve scale in a market with minimal liquidity. Moreover, as should be clear from the earlier discussion (where central banks lean against capital inflows), it is quite possible that the market's inherent illiquidity only manifests itself when the investor is trying to exit the position.

7 QE1 and QE2 refer to the first and second rounds of quantitative easing carried out by the US Federal Reserve after the global financial crisis of 2007–09.

8 Payer positions imply a bet on higher interest rates. In a payer interest rate swap transaction, the investor borrows at a fixed rate and lends at the floating rate (normally three- or six-month Libor). If interest rates rise by more than is priced into the yield curve, the investor profits. Receiver positions are the opposite: a bet on lower interest rates.

9 A one-touch barrier option is a deep out-of-the-money bet that pays out if the spot exchange rate touches the strike price at some point during the life of the option contract. For a US$1 million payout, the buyer would be required to pay US$40,000.

10 Randall Dodd, 2009, "Exotic Derivatives Losses in Emerging Markets: Questions of Suitability, Concerns for Stability," IMF Working Paper, July.

11 Jonathan Anderson, 2010, "The "Bad Rules" Compendium," *Emerging Markets Perspectives*, UBS, Hong Kong, August 23.

7

Risk Management in Global Macro Funds

Barry Schachter

The purpose of this chapter is threefold. First, to provide an overview of some key principles of risk management as they apply to global macro investing. Second, to consider how risk controls are applied in the day-to-day management of global macro funds, while emphasising that the risk management function is much broader than just its quantitative elements. Third, to explore some open challenges, both conceptual and practical, to risk management in global macro and the investment industry more generally.

There are two broad categories of global macro strategy: the systematic approach, with computer-driven algorithms at its core, and the classic discretionary approach, which is built around qualitative analysis and risk taking by individual portfolio managers. Within these categories the strategies may be further sub-divided based on types of trades (eg, directional versus relative value), geographic focus (eg, developed versus emerging markets) and asset class specialisation (eg, currencies, commodities, volatility). There is also a broad range of possible investment horizons.

Within funds that pursue global macro strategies there are different approaches to risk management. Some of that variation is adaptation to the specific risks of the strategy, some is adaptation to the investment and corporate cultures of the firms running the strategies, and some of it is random adaptations arising from the idiosyncrasies of the individuals performing the risk management function. This variation across funds is healthy and is an important source of innovation. By contrast, prescriptive regulation has driven much of the evolution of risk management in banking, thus significantly limiting the variation in how risk management is practiced across the regulated sector. That approach has placed a very strong emphasis on the concept of independent risk management, with heavy reliance on specific quantitative risk measurement tools.

Prior to the global financial crisis of 2007–09, hedge funds had been largely free from prescriptive regulation of their risk management function. This engendered some significant differences between the sell-side and the buy-side. In the hedge fund industry, it is not as straightforward a task to discuss risk management as a function separate from risk taking. It is viewed more as a value-added function, effectively being conducted in partnership with risk taking to advance the goal of improved risk-adjusted performance. While the same quantitative tools are found in hedge funds as in banks, they are not as heavily relied upon in the conduct of risk management. In global macro especially, qualitative aspects of risk management are more in the forefront.

It is generally considered that greater independence means better risk management. However, this notion arises from a simplistic view of risk management as purely a control function. If its purpose were simply to prevent violations of risk controls, then keeping it free from external influence does enhance risk management. But this kind of independence has a price: an adversarial relationship between risk taking and risk management. In such a relationship, risk takers often view risk managers as preventing profitable trades. As a result, the two-way flow of information – which is essential, not only to effectively managing risk, but also improving risk-adjusted returns – is reduced. Thus, a careful balance must be struck between independence and service orientation, a balance that can be characterised as a partnership, where risk management has significant enforcement authority, but is also committed to working with the risk takers to improve their risk-adjusted performance.

PRINCIPLES OF GLOBAL MACRO RISK MANAGEMENT

While the 10 principles of global macro risk management discussed below are certainly not exhaustive or all encompassing, they do highlight many critical elements of risk management as they apply to global macro trading. Together they also demonstrate that, in order to be effective, risk managers need to be "in the trenches" and getting their hands dirty.

Only take those risks that are central to the view being expressed

Any expression of a global macro view, unless it is riskless arbitrage in the purest sense, entails uncertainty of the outcome. Given that even a star alpha generator may be correct only 55% of the time, taking on unintended risks as part of a trading position can adversely affect results. Unfortunately, the instruments chosen to express a view often bring along with them exposure to factors unrelated to the view.

Consider the following example. Assume a manager has a view on future increased divergence between the short-term "risk-free" rates in the US and Europe. They choose to express this view by trading a three-month US dollar OIS swap versus a three-month Euribor future. Unfortunately, by doing so, the manager takes on other risks as well. In particular, the Euribor rate will fluctuate not only with the level of the European Central Bank's administered policy rate, but also with liquidity and credit conditions in Europe's interbank market. As a result, it is entirely possible for the original view on the divergence of short-term rates to be correct, only to be offset by events that affect liquidity and credit conditions in the eurozone, thus preventing the trade from profiting from the original insight. In this particular example, the manager can avoid such an outcome by substituting the Euribor leg of the trade with an EONIA swap.

Do not expose a position to "unknown unknowns" that are affecting price

Many factors taken together determine the realised price dynamics in a market. Sometimes price changes cannot be explained by the flow of public information. If poorly understood forces are in play, then the level of confidence in one's ability to capture alpha from a macro idea is eroded. For instance, price behaviour may be temporarily affected by a large commercial firm implementing a hedging strategy on a massive scale, or by a large speculator closing out a big position, or a dealer updating its hedge position against a large exposure to Wall Street. Even when a position has been in place, price behaviour that is inconsistent with the flow of market news is a signal to hedge, reduce or eliminate the exposure.

Whatever can go wrong probably will go wrong

There are many ways for a trade to go wrong. Some risks can be addressed at the trade construction phase. But it may be deemed too costly, in the sense of reducing expected return, to take precautions against every possible contingency. Markets have an unlimited capacity to surprise the risk taker (and the risk manager). Historical studies of worst-case scenarios can provide help only to the extent that history is relevant and representative of future potential market moves. Because all possible adverse states cannot be known in advance, a desirable approach to risk management is one that is robust under such limits to foresight. One approach is to structure positions such that they have a known limited downside. Long option positions can sometimes be used to achieve this goal at a tolerable cost to expected return on the position.

The ultimate risk management strategy against this uncertainty is to assume that the market *will* turn against the position at some point and to set an explicit exit strategy before putting on the trade. The exit strategy should take into account, among other things, the proposed position size, risk tolerance, level of conviction in the view, market volatility and possibly technical charting factors (to the extent they can provide information about the likely behaviour of other market participants).

Trading liquidity is a fickle friend

Trading liquidity affects the cost of entering and exiting a trade, through the market impact of size traded at a point in time and the volatility impact over the time it takes to enter and exit. While this can be factored into a trading decision, liquidity risk estimation is complicated by the fact that trading liquidity fluctuates unpredictably. Markets characterised as "roach motels" – easy to enter, impossible to exit – should generally be avoided, but if a trading view is to be expressed using such a market, the risks are best viewed in terms of a hold-to-maturity investment horizon.

Crowded trades, where significant speculative interest is concentrated in the same position, can give rise to episodic illiquidity, if a situation arises in which large speculative traders are simultaneously exiting – also known as a "liquidity black hole." This is a significant risk in global macro, where the number of unique big picture views is relatively small, while the number of risk takers is large. A risk manager looks for indications of "crowdedness" as part of an early warning system. An indicator commonly used for this purpose is the weekly reports of large speculative positions in the US futures markets by the Commodity Futures Trading Commission (CFTC).

In other circumstances that often develop during financial crises, illiquidity in one market may arise as a spill-over effect from the price action in another market. It has been argued for some time that the use of risk limits based on value-at-risk (VaR) can induce this effect: a spike in volatility in one market pushes up portfolio risk as measured by VaR, which in turn forces the trading unit to reduce positions elsewhere in order to bring overall risk back below the limit. This behaviour would be replicated simultaneously across the Street, as many trading desks respond similarly to a rise in measured portfolio risk.

The best hedge is to exit the position

While this is an age-old maxim, it is still valid, although it is not always possible to follow in practice. If a position needs to be hedged, where a hedge was not initially contemplated in the trade construction process, it is probably the result of a sudden discontinuous market move against the position. Exiting is the best protection against further losses; however, an exit may be difficult because trading liquidity is likely limited (eg, selling into a falling market). Putting on a hedge may reduce exposure, but if the hedging instrument is not perfectly correlated with the position being hedged, it will introduce basis risk. This is more often the case than not, as executing a hedge requires liquidity and, in the face of a violent market move, liquidity may only be available in a different, but related market. If this is the case, the hedge should be lifted as soon as it is possible either to exit the underlying position or initiate a direct hedge.

Beware of changes in risk regimes

Experience suggests that global markets often go through sudden shifts in the risk environment. These shifts are driven by positive feedback effects in the behaviour of individual market participants. Different regimes result in very different cross-asset (and cross-asset class) correlations and individual asset volatilities. Portfolio construction and overall risk are significantly affected by the possibility of regime shifts, so risk managers should seek to identify and monitor factors that are effective precursors to these shifts.

Unfortunately, conventional financial theory does not pay much attention to the interplay of investors in determining price dynamics. Models that focus on feedback loops and adaptive behaviour (eg, models of investor "herding") have seen only limited application. They frequently do not lend themselves to analytic solutions, requiring a simulation approach. The global financial crisis of 2007–09 has sparked interest in modelling feedback effects in macroeconomic models (eg, in dynamic stochastic general equilibrium models). Interest in early warning indicators of systemic fragility has given rise to a large number of empirically driven systemic risk indicators. In 2012, the US Office of Financial Research published a taxonomy of systemic risk measures.[1]

Diversification is about the number of risk factors, not individual positions

The real sources of risk in a portfolio are individual risk drivers, not individual positions. This is especially important in global macro, where the potential number of instruments in a portfolio is vast, but the risk factors operating on those positions may be quite small. Keeping track of this has important implications for managing portfolio diversification/concentration and hedging.

The Mexican peso/US dollar exchange rate exhibits an extremely high correlation to the S&P 500 index, and the S&P 500 index exhibits a very high correlation to emerging market equity indexes. These very high correlations suggest that a single risk factor explains the predominant part of their returns. In this author's experience, even very large global macro portfolios, when subjected to principal component analysis, have more than half of their volatility explained by significantly fewer than 10 risk factors. Risk must be understood in terms of the common risk factors driving value changes within the trading book.

Good fences make good risk takers

Discipline is key to successful risk taking. The best global macro traders understand this and embed strict discipline in the manner in which they trade their ideas. This author has rarely encountered a risk taker who would object to their trading being subjected to a set of mutually agreed risk guidelines. Such guidelines are not just risk control mechanisms, they help risk takers by alerting them whenever their trading takes them outside their typical trading parameters. They also provide an independent means to enforce their trading discipline. Analyses of risks taken in relation to trading guidelines also provide useful feedback to risk takers on trends and tendencies.

Do not be dogmatic

Risk management decisions are made amid a fog of uncertainty about the future. In the face of this, risk managers must be both sceptical and pragmatic in pursuit of their purpose. Practically speaking, this means not putting too much faith in any model or any set of historical observations. It means being willing to entertain non-scientific approaches to risk management. It also means learning to live with a sense of fatalism, because risk management will never be 100% proof against all adverse outcomes. By the same reasoning, however, risk managers should incorporate this understanding of their inherent limitations by building a risk management framework that will increase the likelihood of surviving the inevitable errors.

Everyone is a risk manager

Risk management must be part of the very fabric of the trading organisation: it cannot serve its purpose if it is a function that is simply bolted onto the risk-taking process. The culture of the organisation must be one of prudent risk taking guided by sound risk management principles. Senior management determines that culture, in which the front line of risk management is the risk taker. In such an environment, the risk manager can provide significant added value, with further assistance from execution traders, analysts, operations and treasury staff.

RISK CONTROL "NUTS AND BOLTS"

Risk controls (position limits, stop-losses, drawdown controls, etc) are quantitative constraints on the risk-taking ability of portfolio managers, who tend to view them as part of their own trading discipline. In a multi-manager macro fund, risk controls serve a further purpose by acting as a way to control aggregate risk taking. While *risk control* and *risk management* are not synonymous, the former is an important element of the latter. If risk controls are to be effective, they must be set based on a good understanding of the risks being taken, the manner in which those risks are taken and the fund's tolerance for risk, also known as risk appetite.

Risk and return are not independent. The overall goal of risk management at the portfolio manager level is to help the risk taker make more money through better risk management. This goal is achieved by improving the clarity with which the risk taker evaluates risk and return and by supporting the portfolio manager's risk-taking discipline. It is nevertheless true that some aspects of risk control will lower expected return. This is the case, in particular, for risk controls that reflect the fund's risk tolerance.

To be effective, risk controls should be tailored to each individual portfolio manager: they should be defined by the markets and instruments the manager trades and by their trading style, which in turn is defined by the typical holding period, number of positions managed, approach to portfolio construction and risk mitigation strategy. No single quantitative measure of risk is sufficient for effective risk control. It is naive to think that any given set of risk controls will be a guarantee against something going wrong. Also, no positive relationship exists between the level of detail and the degree of effectiveness of risk controls. For these reasons, quantitative risk controls, while supporting good risk management, cannot be a substitute for proactive and collaborative risk management by the risk taker and the risk manager, which requires prudent and positive intervention and sound judgement of the appropriateness of the risks being taken at any given time.

Because the scope of global macro trading is so broad, risk controls are usually broad as well. A portfolio-level VaR-based control is common, with the maximum allowable risk for a 95th percentile one-day VaR being around 3% of allocated capital. Other risk measures may be employed in addition to the VaR control: for example, parts of a portfolio may be subject to controls based on notional exposures, especially in the case of credit instruments, where the principal is at risk. Credit instruments may also be subject to controls based on maximum exposures by ratings category or by specified ranges of market credit spread.

Controls may be stated in terms of price sensitivities as well, especially for interest rate instruments and option positions. For example, in the case of fixed income instruments, the control might be stated in terms of the maximum price impact per one basis point change in the underlying interest rate. Equity risks may be limited in terms of the maximum net or gross market value, beta or other equity factor exposures. Also, a global macro portfolio will often embody views on future volatility, which may be expressed in many ways. Controls on volatility risk will therefore be broad, perhaps referencing only the aggregate "vega" exposure by asset class. The level of detail will depend on the intensity and variety of volatility bets within the strategy.

A significant portion of a global macro book may be non-directional, with trades expressing views about the relative movements in two (or more) market prices: for example, the 2-year versus the 10-year US Treasuries or the 3-month versus the 15-month Brent crude futures contracts. When risk controls are employed for relative value trades, it is essential to take into account the fact that instruments with different tenors are exposed to different risks (or to recognise that multiple risk factors are influencing the dynamics of their prices).

Because risk controls are tailored to the risk taker's usual scope of trading, it is entirely appropriate that an individual risk control may be exceeded on rare occasions, given a particular set of circumstances in the markets. At such time, it is the risk taker's responsibility to initiate a discussion with the risk manager in order to request a temporary waiver of the guideline. When this conversation does not happen and a risk control level is exceeded, the risk manager has the authority to require portfolio adjustments.

Risk tolerance is enforced through controls on absolute loss and drawdown. Control on absolute loss takes the form of a maximum amount of portfolio loss, usually expressed as a percentage return on capital, measured over a given time interval. If a manager's losses reach the maximum loss level, then further risk taking is halted by closing out all positions. Global macro trading books can take time to unwind if market impact is to be kept low, as position sizes can be large in relation to immediate market liquidity. Therefore, in practice, the trading halt must be managed dynamically if the act of closing the book is not to generate further losses beyond the control threshold.

Following the trading halt, a management decision is made whether to allow risk taking to recommence. Because the maximum allowable loss is known to the risk taker at the outset of the period, like a buoy marking the safe channel for ships, the maximum loss should be treated as a limit that must never be crossed. For this reason, in the author's experience, a manager who exceeds the maximum loss threshold typically is not allowed to resume trading. Exceptions do occur, with the portfolio manager permitted to resume risk taking under a significantly reduced capital allocation and more stringent risk controls.

Control of drawdown is similar to control of absolute loss, but reflects a different management philosophy about trading profit. Drawdown is closely related to cumulative return. A portfolio manager's drawdown at the current time is equal to the difference between the maximum historical cumulative return and the cumulative return as of the current time. A drawdown control may state that if the current drawdown reaches a certain level, then further risk taking is halted. A drawdown control limits the amount of profits that are given back before risk taking is halted. Implicitly, a drawdown control, in contrast to an absolute loss control, reflects the view that profits earned by the risk taker are owned by the fund. Drawdown controls may have a greater adverse impact on expected return than loss controls. First, macro managers will typically increase their risk-taking levels as they accumulate profits, but a drawdown control can act as a disincentive, as higher risk increases the likelihood of a drawdown of any given amount. Second, because expected drawdown is positively related to the volatility of a strategy, higher risk strategies will be risk-managed more tightly to avoid hitting the drawdown threshold.

The approach to risk control by global macro funds varies enormously across funds and reflects not only differences in the risks being taken, but also in their risk-taking cultures. In all instances, however, effective risk control reflects the cooperative efforts of the risk taker and the risk manager.

RISK MEASUREMENT AND RISK MODELLING

Risk measurement is a significant component of risk management, with risk aggregation being one of the biggest challenges. Aggregation is a significant issue in global macro trading simply because interactions among the variety of risks (or risk factors) that fall within the global macro trading universe – including every asset class and every exchange-listed and OTC instrument – make portfolio-level risk assessment very difficult. Modelling portfolio risk helps improve a macro manager's understanding of complex risk interactions in their portfolios.

However, risk modelling itself has inherent limitations and presents pitfalls to risk managers looking to those models for insights about portfolio risk. This section will look at several risk measurement challenges that loom large, not only for global macro strategies, but for all hedge funds and the financial industry more broadly: the focus is on VaR models, the role of common sense, scenario-based stress testing and issues surrounding tail risks.

In defence of VaR and other models

VaR is the generic name for a family of methods used to measure aggregate uncertainty about the near-future risk of loss in a portfolio containing a number of different financial instruments. VaR has been widely used throughout the financial services industry for many years, and is also widely used by hedge funds.

VaR is an important element of risk measurement for global macro trading, where the book of trades may include highly disparate individual bets, and as a result the overall risk of the portfolio may be difficult to judge. VaR provides a way to meaningfully aggregate these individual risks. It can also be used to explore ways in which those risks interact to assess the effect of potential hedges or new positions, and to identify efficient approaches for adding to or reducing portfolio risk. In spite of multiple well-documented issues and challenges with implementing VaR in practice, and many actual cases of investors misusing or abusing it in the past, it is this author's firm belief that a risk manager's toolbox should continue to include VaR among other quantitative models and approaches.

Criticisms of VaR models can be reduced to an epistemological dispute about what a model represents when it is put forward to answer questions about financial risk. To call a VaR model flawed implies using a conceptual framework in which models are intended to be accurate descriptions of the world as it actually works (a "realist" perspective). An opposing view (an "instrumentalist" perspective) considers models as useful tools of convenience, even although they do not represent the world as it actually works. In this view, to call a VaR model flawed is a statement with no meaningful content. From an instrumentalist's perspective, the appropriate question to ask is whether VaR is a useful model in the context of an agreed scope for risk management.

The distinction between these two views is very important, because in the first case the onus of success is on the model, while in the second case the onus is on the risk manager, where this author believes it belongs. Two unfortunate consequences have flowed from the predominance of the mistaken realist view. First, energy has been diverted from identifying and addressing the truly relevant limitations of VaR models. Second, reliance on VaR models is viewed more sceptically than it should be.

Risk in trading usually means *risk of loss*. The scope of experience that VaR models are meant to explain depends on the operational definition of risk of loss. For VaR, this risk means a loss amount likely to be exceeded with some small chance, say, one in a 100. However, since the onset of the global financial crisis in 2007, risk of loss has been increasingly interpreted as losses from extreme market upheavals or tail events. These two definitions are not interchangeable: VaR does not explain the scope of experience represented by losses in tail events. Using the latter definition, a realist would conclude that VaR models must be an oversimplification of the true dynamics of market prices, because they fail to measure risk well when they are most needed, and that therefore they are flawed. As such, a realist believes that VaR is a model of market price dynamics as they really are, but this is an untenable belief. We are a long way from discovering universal laws of financial market price dynamics, if there are any. At best, VaR models show a correspondence to certain observed empirical regularities. Few risk management professionals would be prepared to claim more than this for VaR models.

Risk management can be carried out without claiming to have to hand a risk model that describes the world as it actually works. Without attaching a claim to VaR models that they explain experience truly, they can provide very reasonable risk forecasts in ordinary market environments. VaR models provide a view into portfolio risk that is helpful to risk management, even if they do not provide a comprehensive view into portfolio risk. The limitations of VaR models are not flaws; rather, they are indicators to be used by risk managers about when and in what ways the VaR model is useful. In this instrumentalist view, VaR models are tools of convenience. Their wide adoption is not the same as exclusive use: it signals no more than sufficient utility to warrant adoption. It is important to emphasise that risk management is *not* science. This is not an apology, nor an admission of defeat: it is a declaration that risk management works best when it does not purport to be what it is not.

Some pundits have concluded after the global financial crisis that reliance on all quantitative risk models should be put aside in favour of the risk manager's common sense thinking. This is mistaken for two reasons. First, common sense has its own limitations and is itself model-based. Second, this is evidence of confusion between the question of whether to use quantitative risk models and the question of what is the proper scope for use of such models.

Common sense models of financial market dynamics share the same potential problems associated with quantitative models. For example, both may suffer, albeit in different ways, from over-fitting to historical data. Common sense is limited by what our mind can directly perceive about the way the world works from the sense data it receives. Our senses can mislead us, especially in situations of great subtlety or complexity. The way we interpret sense data is conventional, reflecting social constructs through which we interpret the world. And our interpretation of sense data is subject to various well-documented cognitive biases. Financial market dynamics are both complex and subtle. If our risk management decision-making is completely governed by the prejudices of common sense, we will sometimes fail in situations where, had we employed quantitative models, we might not have failed. Therefore, it is not appropriate to mechanically disregard quantitative risk models any more than it is to rely on those models mechanically.

Risk managers must use their common sense judgements in deciding when and how to employ quantitative risk measurements as tools for decision-making. They must manage their quantitative risk models, actively assigning more or less weight to their respective outputs according to their assessment of which of the models are more or less relevant for a given set of circumstances. The need to eschew a mechanical approach to risk management decisions also argues against a prescriptive approach to risk regulation that mandates both the particulars of quantitative risk models to be used and how those models are to be used. In sum, it is difficult to credit the argument that quantitative risk models should be replaced by common sense. Both common sense models and quantitative risk models should be part of risk management.

Macroeconomic scenario-based stress testing

Portfolio stress testing is the name given to a variety of non-statistical, non-model-based (but still quantitative) risk assessment methods. Scenario-based stress tests, which examine a portfolio's potential for loss arising from a comprehensively specified alternative economic environment (eg, the outbreak of a war) are an important component of risk measurement for the global macro trading strategy. They are less reliant on projecting recent historical experience into the future than VaR models.

In response to criticisms of VaR, scenario-based stress tests have become increasingly prominent, used not just as a complement to VaR-based risk models, but carrying equal or even greater weight than those models. This partly reflects an increased focus on extreme tail risk, which will be discussed in the next section. Despite this increased emphasis, however, scenario-based stress tests have several potential problems of their own.

In general terms, the construction of a scenario-based stress test proceeds as follows.

1. Identify the economic scenario of interest. This part of stress-test construction is subjective. In global macro investing, any useful scenario needs to be global in its implications to allow for meaningful exploration of the complex and varied risks in a global macro book of positions.
2. If the scenario is to be purely hypothetical, operationalise it by selecting a core set of trading markets in which the scenario's impacts are likely to be the most immediate and from which they will be assumed to radiate to other markets. If the scenario is to correspond to market behaviour from an actual historical period, all markets with available prices from that historical period are used, once beginning and ending calendar dates of the historical scenario are determined.
3. For a hypothetical scenario, specify the magnitudes of the changes to be applied to core market prices, called *factor shocks*. These are set subjectively, usually with inputs from in-house

economists and strategists, after considering historical price behaviour and estimates from a macroeconomic model. For a historical scenario, some market prices may be missing and appropriate shocks for the relevant instruments will have to be assigned subjectively or perhaps using statistical data analysis.

4. In a hypothetical scenario, the core market shocks will be propagated to all remaining market factors affecting portfolio valuations – for example, through the betas of the non-core market positions to the core market positions. Before this can be done, however, restrictions may be placed on how these non-core market prices will move, for example, whether no-arbitrage relations will hold, or whether spreads will be allowed to change their sign.
5. The factor shocks are used to re-price each instrument in the portfolio, and scale the result by the size of the position.

A completely objective construction of a scenario-based stress test is impossible. Two risk managers creating a "euro break-up" stress scenario for the same portfolio will almost certainly end up with different portfolio impacts as a result of the subjectivity involved in the scenario construction. Even an "historical" stress scenario, ostensibly relying on objectively observed historical factor changes, requires subjective judgements about start and end dates, how missing data are handled, restrictions on how the core shocks propagate to the rest of the portfolio, differences in values among data sources, etc. This subjectivity necessarily implies some uncertainty in the message transmitted by the scenario to the risk manager about potential portfolio risks and particular points of vulnerability.

Historical stress scenarios lose their usefulness the further into the past they go: markets change in their structure; the way investors use instruments changes; and often the instruments themselves change. Attempts to faithfully replay the effects seen in the more distant past – for example, during the 1987 stock market crash – may be more misleading than meaningful.

A scenario-based stress test provides no information about a portfolio's behaviour other than for the specific values of the factor shocks in the scenario. Thus, in complex portfolios, unless there is further analysis, the user cannot know if the outcome of the stress scenario is robust to small changes in the core shocks, and therefore whether the result is anomalous or representative of the expected impact of a similar set of shocks. This is important because the exact values of the shocks in a future stress event cannot be anticipated precisely.

The only scenarios that can be modelled are those that can be imagined, both in terms of the underlying economic environments and in how they are translated into shocks to portfolio positions. This challenge is often framed as the infamous *Black Swan* problem, or that of "unknown unknowns." For example, in March 2011, a major earthquake triggered a powerful tsunami that in turn instigated a large nuclear accident in Japan, with significant consequent moves in market prices. To the best of the author's knowledge, there were no risk managers anywhere in the world who had simulated a stress scenario based on this particular confluence of events.

A variation on the standard stress scenario approach, called reverse stress testing, does not rely on identifying stress scenarios in advance. The idea originated in 1995 as *maximum loss optimisation.*[2] In this approach, a search mechanism is used to find the set of shocks that results in the greatest portfolio loss, subject to high-level constraints placed on what shocks are allowable.[3]

A reverse stress test is portfolio-centric in the sense that the worst-case scenario is determined by the positions in the portfolio. It provides insights about the portfolio from interpretation of the environment implied by the worst-case scenario. Also important is the information about the largest contributions to the loss (eg, by country and individual risk bet) along with the price moves corresponding to those significant contributions, especially when viewed in light of the level of conviction in the views which gave rise to those positions in the first place.

Unfortunately, global macro may be one of the least suitable strategies for this type of stress scenario analysis: the benefits of reverse stress tests are lessened if the trading book turns over quickly or if exposures are dynamic. In these situations, the utility of reverse stress tests for portfolio management decays rapidly unless they are conducted frequently. In contrast with conventional stress-test scenarios, it may be very difficult to draw inferences about the evolution of total portfolio risk over time from observed reverse stress-test results, as both portfolio exposures and the shocks that correspond to the worst-case outcome change constantly.

Another problem with implementing reverse stress tests is the computational challenge, which can be stated as searching through an m-dimensional space of factor changes efficiently. Complicating matters, a global macro portfolio's risk factor dimensionality may be high and individual position exposures may be non-linear or even discontinuous functions of the risk factors. Significant computational time may be required and the optimisation may not guarantee that the maximum loss will be found.

These computational problems have workarounds. For example, it may help to employ quasi-random Monte Carlo methods, or redefine the factor space to be of lower dimensionality after applying principal component analysis to the market factors. Whatever optimisation method is employed, a reverse stress test should be accompanied by a perturbation analysis to satisfy the user that the worst-case scenario is robust to small changes in the factor shocks that generated the scenario. To economise on computational time, this diagnostic process may be limited to those positions that are seen as contributing the greatest losses to the outcome, or representing the highest conviction trades in the portfolio, or exhibiting the greatest non-linearity (or "gamma") in their pricing functions.

Tail risks and global macro

At least partly due to well-documented cognitive biases, many investors seem to underestimate the probability of devastating rare events during normal times, only to dramatically and systematically overestimate the same probability immediately following such events. The latter is called the *availability bias* and it dominates investor behaviour after a rare dramatic event. The global financial crisis of 2007–09 was no exception, as it refocused people's minds on extreme left tail risks. Many investors rushed to buy prohibitively expensive insurance in the form of dedicated tail risk hedges.

A tail risk strategy is dependent for its success on identifying risk factors that will behave in a predictable manner in a crisis, the specifics of which cannot be known in advance, as tail risk events are, by their nature, not predictable in their details. Two approaches are possible. A tail risk strategy may be designed to hedge against extreme losses in the portfolio – for example, by purchasing equity index puts. A more general tail risk strategy is constructed without reference to existing positions, but rather with an eye toward market crises generally. While there is no such thing as a "typical" crisis, there are fairly typical market reactions to crises. Based on this, positions are established in markets that will react predictably to a wide range of events. For example, in a flight-to-safety scenario, a tail risk mitigation strategy would imply being short equity indexes and long credit protection. Other choices are long volatility exposures (using volatility derivatives or vanilla options like puts on equity indexes), long positions in "safe haven" currencies (traditionally, US$, ¥, Sfr) and long positions in risk-free sovereign debt (again, traditionally, US Treasuries, German bunds and Japanese government bonds). Positions in individual stocks or debt instruments would be unsuitable, because of their idiosyncratic risks and the high degree of uncertainty about how a particular instrument would behave in a systemic crisis.

It may seem counterintuitive, but the economic logic for a global macro fund to incorporate a dedicated tail risk strategy is not strong. By virtue of being nimble and flexible, and limiting their trading to the deepest and most liquid of markets, global macro funds have the ability to react quickly and decisively to crises, closing out losing positions and capitalising on various trends that develop as markets collapse and policymakers deploy anti-crisis measures. If anything, global macro strategies – and systematic trend-followers in particular – can serve as substitutes to dedicated tail risk hedges in investor portfolios, albeit with a lower degree of convexity compared to many volatility-based tail risk strategies.

Often, global macro funds may put on individual trades that resemble tail risk hedges, especially if they are consistent with the alpha component of their strategy. For example, one such trade in 2011 was very popular among macro funds that were bearish on the future prospects of the eurozone: long the Danish krone against the euro. Although Denmark is an EU member of good standing, in the 1990s it was granted an opt-out from joining the eurozone to help facilitate domestic approval of the Maastricht Treaty. However, the krone is effectively pegged to the euro by the Danish central bank. It was widely expected that, if the eurozone were to break up, this peg would be abandoned and the krone would be allowed to appreciate significantly. The asymmetric nature of the risk in the trade, combined with the low volatility of the Dkr/Eur exchange rate and the low carrying cost of this trade, made it an attractive component of a longer-horizon bearish euro trade.

CONCLUSION

Throughout this chapter, our focus has been on the key risk management principles, as well as some salient issues and challenges, as they broadly apply to all types of global macro strategies – ie, discretionary and systematic styles of trading. This is not meant to imply that, in practical terms, risk management functions will be identical in both types. Historically, there have always been noticeable differences between the two styles. For example, while at discretionary funds risk controls are often enforced by a separate and independent risk unit, at systematic funds they are typically hard-wired into the trading systems and algorithms. They are extensively researched, coded and back-tested during the model-building phase, but once the model has been rolled out, risk controls become part of the system.

Another interesting, albeit minor, point of difference that can sometimes be observed between risk managers at discretionary and systematic funds is in how they view leverage: while the former often describe it as a percentage of assets under management, the latter would typically refer to it in margin-to-equity terms. However, most of these differences have to do with style and implementation preferences, not with substance and core philosophy. This author firmly believes that most of the key points discussed in this chapter apply equally to discretionary and systematic funds.

This chapter has described a global macro risk management function whose focus is on risk of loss generally, and not just on loss given a tail event. Driven by the complexity of the global macro strategy and the dynamic properties of the macroeconomic environments generating the trading opportunities, risk management needs to be multi-layered, proactive, flexible, pragmatic, sceptical and instrumentalist. It matters less whether the risk function is embodied in a separate or independent risk manager, and more that the actual functioning of risk management in the organisation has these characteristics.

1 **Bisias, Dimitrios, Mark Flood, Andrew W. Lo and Stavros Valavanis,** 2012, "A Survey of Systemic Risk Analytics," US Department of Treasury, Office of Financial Research (WP 0001, January), see http://www.treasury.gov/initiatives/wsr/ofr/Documents/OFRwp0001_BisiasFloodLoValavanis_ASurveyOfSystemicRiskAnalytics.pdf.

2 See **Studer, Gerald,** 1995, "Value at Risk and Maximum Loss Optimization," RiskLab Technical Report, ETH Zurich (see http://www.gloriamundi.org/Library_Journal_View.asp?Journal_id=4941).

3 For example, a constraint may be necessary to prevent the search mechanism from using a set of factor shocks that are either improbable (eg, equities up 10,000%) or impossible (eg, negative volatilities).

8

Geopolitical Risk in Global Macro Investing

David Murrin

Emergent Asset Management

Global macro managers have to navigate a complex web of interconnected risks: market, credit, liquidity, financing, counterparty and operational, to name but a few. While all of these risks are different – and reasonable market practitioners can disagree about how best to deal with them – in at least one respect they are all similar: the nature of these risks has been well researched and documented, and as such they are relatively well understood. Dedicated risk management functions, with sophisticated infrastructures and high-calibre quantitative staff, have been built up over the years to measure, monitor and manage these risks.

In contrast, geopolitical risk, which can have a material and lasting impact on an investment portfolio, is neither well researched nor particularly well understood. While risk management systems and methodologies have evolved dramatically since the 1970s, there has been no visible progress in the way market practitioners analyse and manage geopolitical risks. There are no geopolitical analogues to commonly used market risk models such as value-at-risk (VaR), or analytical frameworks linking geopolitical "risk factors" to expected returns. Geopolitical experts and analysts working in boutique advisory firms still operate more as a cottage industry than as a well-defined and structured discipline within the broader risk management function.

Interestingly, this lack of analytical sophistication with respect to geopolitics is not at all the result of under-appreciation by market practitioners: early macro traders were highly attuned to geopolitical risk and the opportunities it presented.[1] Rather, the reason at least in part has to do with the fact that the "golden age" of global macro – the 12 years from 1987 to 1999 – coincided with one of those rare "unipolar" moments in world history: the Cold War was coming to an end; the US reigned supreme and unchallenged as the only remaining superpower; the US political establishment famously proclaimed the "end of history"; economic policymakers were congratulating themselves on taming the business cycle and achieving the state of "Great Moderation"; and Western-dominated international financial institutions were laying down the law across the developing world in the form of the so-called "Washington Consensus". Geopolitical risks all but faded into the background.

However, this all changed dramatically in the following decade. First, 9/11 shattered the myth of American invincibility. Multiple geopolitical challenges started emerging along with the rise of Islamic fundamentalism, China's growing economic and financial clout, and Russia's sooner-than-expected resurgence on the back of rising commodity prices. Then, the crisis of 2007–09 shattered the myth of Western economic and financial supremacy, leading to huge debt overhangs, high unemployment, anaemic growth and bleak prospects for most developed countries, bringing social tensions and political discord. Suddenly, it became painfully obvious that global economic and financial power was shifting decisively from the West to the East. As a result, concerns over geopolitical risks re-emerged with a vengeance.

This chapter will propose one possible approach to analysing geopolitical risk in the context of global macro investing – a model called "Five Stages of Empire." This is a proprietary concept developed by the author and explained in detail in his earlier book, *Breaking the Code of History*. It is not a model in the traditional *quantitative* sense: there are no well-defined data inputs processed by a computer and translated into actionable trading signals. Rather, it is best viewed as an internally consistent analytical construct based on three principles that have guided and shaped much of human activity throughout the millennia. We start with a brief review of these three principles, before describing the Five Stages of Empire model, the core of the chapter. The final section considers how to apply this model in practice, with a particular focus on global macro investors.

The philosopher George Santayana famously wrote: "Those who cannot remember the past are condemned to repeat it." We must not only remember the past, but understand it. Only by deciphering the code of history are we able to understand the markets around us and the trading opportunities ahead of us.

THE THREE PRINCIPLES

A market technician's approach to history and geopolitics

As a former geophysicist based in the jungles of Papua New Guinea and a former market technician situated on the trading floor of one of the largest global investment banks, the author has had the privilege of working in vastly different environments, with multiple opportunities to observe the peculiarities of human nature and the dynamics of collective behaviour. One of the striking early discoveries during his career in the City of London was the realisation that the same patterns of collective subconscious behaviour that he had observed among the primitive tribes were clearly discernible in financial markets. Primordial emotions of fear and greed, coupled with a strong tendency to herd, manifested themselves time and again in market price patterns and trends. But if a market technician can successfully identify and, to a certain extent, predict repeatable patterns of collective behaviour in one area of human activity, then surely it would be logical to extend the same technical approach to other areas.

This was the genesis of the first principle: all collective human activity – underlying not only financial markets, but also history and geopolitics – is driven by the same emotional and psychological forces and result in the same behavioural patterns. Therefore, in order to understand the dynamics of history and geopolitics, it would be logical to approach them from a market technician's perspective.

History and the collective behavioural patterns that determine its course are products of the human decision-making process, and therefore, by extension, the brain. The earliest part of the human brain to develop was the stem, which governed the majority of the body's basic functions. During the early stages of human existence, it was also instrumental in assessing the place of an individual within the tribe. The acceptability of every action, and the continued inclusion of a single member of the tribe, was gauged within the collective. Rejection by the tribe meant a severe reduction in an individual's ability to survive. Those who did survive would, by definition, have developed a keen sense of what was required to preserve their place. As a result, the tribe developed a collective consciousness to which all its members were connected to various degrees.

Only relatively late in human development have we acquired sophisticated functions in the middle part of the brain, where emotions are processed, and in the frontal lobes, where logic and reasoning are enabled, allowing for a more comprehensive thinking process. The recently evolved frontal lobes have not yet had time to assume complete control of human thought and action; the older sections of our brains still predominate, producing highly emotional behavioural patterns that can, at times, override the brain's higher centres. The inescapable conclusion is that logic has not governed human history, which has instead been influenced by collective emotional responses. Although individuality is valued in many societies, we are all to some extent deeply linked to each other via our lower-brain functions. Few people are able to maintain their independent-mindedness in the face of strong group response.

Human social constructs, such as a city-state, regional power, empire or religion, all manifest a collective consciousness that processes information and then responds on a predominantly emotional basis. It is this group engine that drives both short- and long-term patterns; individuals may not recognise their part in this dynamic, but, when observed from a distance, these responses can be perceived as existing within a cycle. Once the algorithm of a natural cycle is understood and recognised, its characteristics can be used to discern where a society or societies are situated within it and where they might be heading. It is these cycles that underpin the geopolitical model described in the next section.

The fractal nature of history and geopolitics

One of the most powerful branches of technical analysis has developed around the Elliott Wave principle, originally proposed by the prescient American accountant R. N. Elliott in 1928. Many modern scientific concepts were embedded in his work long before becoming established, including the fractal nature of the universe. Fractal theory holds that a complex process can be understood by identifying the smaller, simpler processes it contains, each of which is identical to the whole, only smaller. A common example of the many fractals found in nature is broccoli: each floret of the vegetable echoes the whole. Elliott identified repetitive cycles in market upturns and downturns (measured in "waves"), and was further able to classify the emotional character of each distinctive sub-wave.

This breakthrough provided the intuition behind the second principle: human emotions and collective subconscious reactions are invariant to scale, thus producing exactly the same patterns of collective behaviour from the smallest indigenous tribes to the largest and most advanced empires. Thus, what the Elliott wave method did for market analysis, the Five Stages of Empire model strives to do for geopolitics: studying the ebb and flow of empires throughout history can enable us to pinpoint the mechanisms that cause civilisations to rise and fall; and these principles apply equally to regional powers, which are in effect smaller fractals engaged in the same process – to scale – as empires.

The term "fractal" was coined by the late mathematician Benoît Mandelbrot in 1975, when he solidified hundreds of years of thought and mathematical development and laid the ground for a new branch of mathematics called "fractal geometry". Mandelbrot himself defined it as "the study of roughness, of the irregular and jagged." He went on to demonstrate how it applied to multiple natural and man-made phenomena, which in hindsight was not all that surprising, given that roughness is omnipresent in nature and human affairs. Mandelbrot explained that the objective of fractal analysis was to "spot the regularity inside the irregular, the pattern in the formless." He went on to say: "Consider social science: the devastating rhythm of war and peace, the unequal distribution of wealth in society, the dominance of big companies in an industry – all can be analysed as irregular fractal constructs that have more regularity to them than was first assumed...Fractal structures have been observed even in the frequency and intensity of warfare over five centuries of European history...[Fractal geometry] accurately describes some fundamental principles of how people often think and behave: in hierarchies, with repetition and scaling." (Mandelbrot and Hudson, 2008).

The asymmetry of slow build-up and fast release of geopolitical risk

As a former geophysicist and seismologist, this author has more than a passing acquaintance with the dynamics of earthquakes. They represent one of the best analogies from the natural world to describe the asymmetry in how risks can slowly build up in a system, in the same way that tension between tectonic plates builds underneath the surface over many years and decades; and how then, all of a sudden, the pressure can be released in a matter of minutes, bringing total destruction and utter chaos in its wake. The financial market equivalent of such asymmetry would be the slow build-up of hidden risks during the development of a speculative asset bubble, which can take many years, followed by a spectacular collapse over a very short period of time, typically within just a few days.

The nature of geopolitical risk is precisely like that: it builds up in a slow, almost imperceptible way over many years and decades, but once it reaches the critical point, the ensuing collapse is swift and all-encompassing. As an amateur historian with a lifetime interest in military history, this author has also studied the growth and declines of past empires, large and small, and has found such asymmetric pattern manifesting itself in each and every case – this constitutes the third principle.

Thus, the Five Stages of Empire model described in the next section is based on the following three basic premises.

- ❑ Recurring and recognisable collective behavioural patterns, which manifest themselves in financial markets and in other areas of human activity, also drive geopolitical cycles.
- ❑ These collective behavioural patterns repeat and replicate themselves, not only through time, but also on different scales – tribes, nations, regions and empires.
- ❑ The nature of geopolitical risk is asymmetric: slow build-up and fast release; correspondingly, the shape of the growth and decline curve of an empire is skewed: it takes a longer time to grow and mature than to overstretch and decline.

THE FIVE STAGES OF EMPIRE

Below we present a model of growth and decline of civilisations, which can assist in understanding history's "big picture" and in accurately assessing current and future geopolitical environments. To illustrate the influence and power projection of an empire, Figure 8.1 uses a graphical representation of the five stages in the shape of a bell curve. Empires are not all the same, of course, but the majority of them exhibit a similar distribution, peaking at about 60–70% along their lifecycles. The Five Stages of Empire are as follows.

1. Regionalisation.
2. Ascension to empire.
3. Maturity.
4. Overextension.
5. Decline and legacy.

As an empire grows, the world around it tends towards unipolarity, until at its peak it comes to dominate its surroundings. Then, as it declines, there is a trend towards multi-polarity as it weakens and its

Figure 8.1 The power curve of the Five Stages of Empire

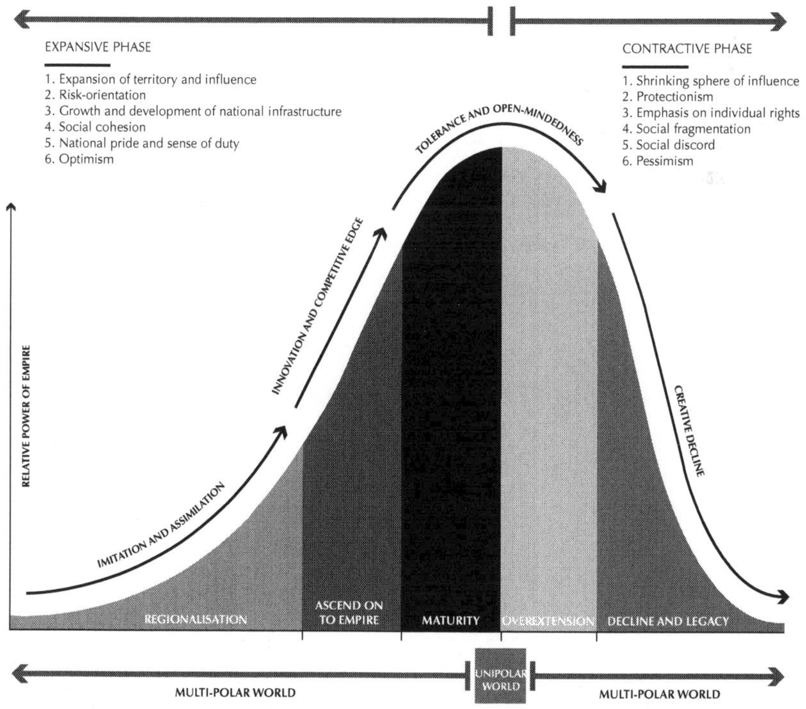

neighbours strengthen. Demographics lie at the heart of an empire's growth, and they provide a measure of its energy, predisposition to risk and value system. Moreover, all empires display a social composition divided between the core population and the workforce that has freed it to focus on expansion. In ancient times, slaves and serfs filled this role. Since the abolition of slavery in the West, they have been replaced by indentured labour, colonial subjects and the working classes.

The first three stages of an empire are associated with: the qualities of expansion; optimism; appetite for both individual as well as collective risk; investment in national infrastructure; a sense of cohesion and national duty; social cooperation; pride in national achievements and values; and, as the limitations of material world comfort are experienced, the search for fulfilment and a better future. During the expansive phase, growth is not linear but occurs in spurts interspersed with pauses for consolidation. As the region or empire becomes more economically powerful, it seeks to extend its influence as far and wide as possible.

There are no cases in history in which a wealthy country with strong demographics has not chosen to militarise its economic wealth, justifying such action by trade protectionism, access to natural resources, territorial control, political influence and domination of the widest possible economic sphere. With industrialisation, the size and power of empires have increased, along with the destructive potential of their war-making capacity. Nations must now carefully consider the cost/benefit analysis of war. As a result, they may commit hostile acts that are economic rather than military by nature. However, it would be a grave mistake to be lulled into a similar false sense of security as were the nations of the world prior to World War One, who erroneously believed that the close linking of global trade mechanisms would prevent war. All global trade does is to raise the threshold for all-out war; it does not render it obsolete.

The last two stages of empire are governed by the process of decline. Its hallmarks include: a lack of social cohesion and cooperation; an emphasis on the rights of the citizen as opposed to a sense of duty to the nation; protectionism; the inability of the empire to use foresight to invest in vital infrastructure for its future survival; unhappiness and a sense of exclusion; the fracturing of society into social sub-groups; social discord; and pessimism. We shall now consider each individual stage of the empire cycle in turn.

Regionalisation: The first stage of empire

Early in the growth of a regional power, a struggle occurs between various states within the same geographical vicinity, with the victor amalgamating all of the others (Ancient Rome, for example, absorbed other city-states before going on to control the whole of the peninsula and its surroundings). This enlarged state then becomes a player in the game of nascent empires, aiming to expand further until it attains imperial status. The key driver prompting this behaviour is a growing population, which both needs to be fed and provides extra "risk capital." The wealth of a new regional power increases through conquests, the spoils of war and the development of new trade relationships.

The regionalised entity's political and military establishments then take root, along with the society's core values. The military would, by this point, have developed a well-honed edge, making it a formidable opponent – although it would still be a long way from becoming the dominant force in its sphere of influence. Plans for expansion would continue to take into account the asymmetry of the regionalised power base in contrast with the local hegemon. The regional power would seek to make gradual and incremental gains until enough strength had been accumulated for a direct confrontation.

The catalyst propelling a nation from regional power to empire is the point at which it can no longer sustain its economy internally, particularly with respect to the acquisition of natural resources, so it is forced to look outside its borders. The crystallising moment comes when its military becomes strong enough to take on the powers around it with a good chance of success.

As an empire's core population increases, so does its demand for an enlarged menial workforce to match its growing economy and to focus the core population's energies on expansion. Traditionally, the army drove this demand: as the need for it to expand became more urgent, manpower was redirected from the maintenance of an agrarian economy. Additional labour was then required in the fields to grow and harvest crops. The Spartan solution was to annex other lands and rededicate the subjugated populations to food production, thereby freeing the Spartans to form one of the first large and permanent armies.

Civil war often attends rising empires that are approaching the end of their regionalisation stage. For the regional power in question – assuming it survives its civil war intact – the conflict can act as a

PANEL 8.1 THE FRACTAL OF REGIONALISATION

Understanding the relationship between a regional power and an empire is essential to grasping one of the most critical drivers for change in geopolitics at any one time. At what stage do regional powers become empires? What happens to regional powers that bid for empire but fail? The regionalisation stage is a fractal of the Five Stages of Empire. There are early and late stages of regionalisation, followed by maturity, overextension and decline. The inflection point – at which a nation either remains a regional power or ascends to empire – occurs at the maturity stage within the regionalisation cycle. If the demographic trend at this point exhibits momentum and continues to grow, it will force the regional power to expand as a result of an ever-pressing need for resources. The more forceful the demographic surge, the more likely the shift from regional power to empire. (Figure 8.2 is the Five Stages of Empire graph, but this time showing the fractal of regionalisation and the inflection point.)

However, the success of a regional power in its challenge will directly relate to the status of others situated within or near its domain. If it has no competitors, the regional power will certainly become an empire. However, if other potential empires of the same order exist in the vicinity, the challenger will only have a reasonable chance of success if one of those powers has reached the overextension stage in its own cycle, thereby creating a power vacuum. Timing is therefore crucial as to whether or not a new empire comes of age.

Failure by the challenger could result in its absorption by the victor, but might also result in the challenger's rapid overextension and decline. It will then subsequently reorganise itself to repeat the cycle. Thus, Rome's triumph as a regional power was also about Carthage's failure as a mature, overextended state. France built a limited continental empire in the 18th century, yet failed to successfully challenge British power in the race towards a global maritime empire. It was therefore limited to the status of regional power in a struggle that lasted for a hundred years. France did make two further challenges during this time, as a revolutionary and then later an imperial power, but ultimately failed in both attempts. Similar examples include Germany's challenge to the British Empire in 1914 and 1939, and Japan's offensive against the Asian and Pacific territories of the Western powers in World War Two. All resulted in the collapse of the regional challenger, which subsequently underwent a new regional cycle.

coalescing agent, preparing the nation for the quantum leap to ascension to empire. Examples include the English Civil War (1642–51), the American Civil War (1861–65) and the Chinese Civil War (1927–37 and 1945–49).

Ascension: The second stage of empire

When a regional power successfully absorbs a number of similar rivals, it then spreads out, projecting its power further. This process marks the ascension stage. Once again, smaller entities are amalgamated and absorbed (eg, Macedonia and Greece, Rome and Carthage). The algorithm of growth, given a simple model consisting of nothing but regional powers, operates as follows. When one entity conquers another, it becomes twice as powerful as the next entity it takes on; all things being equal, it will therefore succeed in half the time. This stage of growth is the most heady and dynamic, as the wealth and power of the new empire increase exponentially. Income from expansion is vastly greater than expenditure.

Figure 8.2 The fractal of regionalisation and the challenge for empire

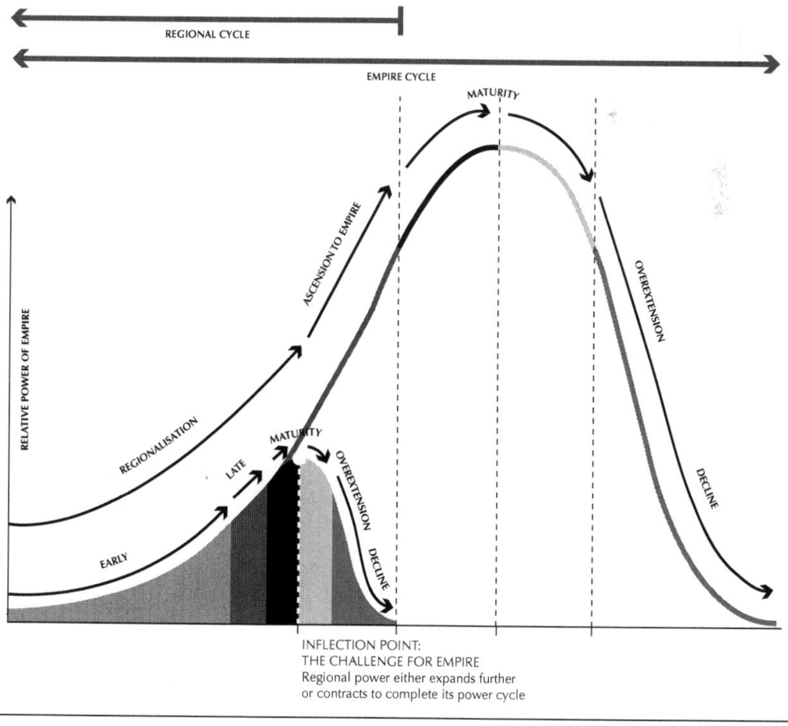

Demographic expansion is once again the key, pushing regional powers to expand their influence and bring in raw materials to sustain their economies. The population will be highly risk-orientated, which constitutes a big advantage in confrontations against rivals in a mature, overextended or declining phase of the empire cycle. The ascension phase is characterised by clear strategic planning and execution, along with an extensive degree of confidence that is expressed as a sense of collective destiny.

Britain entered its ascension stage early in the mid-16th century. It had ample supplies of wood, bronze and iron with which to build ships, but its economy was underdeveloped. It opted to acquire a share of Spain's wealth through privateering and freebooting, and in the process obtained the financial resources (gold and silver) to allow it to ascend to empire. American imperial evolution began with the early 20th century oil boom and the motor industry. China began its latest ascension in the mid-1990s, rather quietly, without anyone paying much attention at the time.

An ascending power seeking to supplant an established, mature one can only do so when the hegemon begins to decline. During the ascension stage, the core population of the ascending civilisation swells with a high concentration of people aged 30 years old or younger. Imbued with the qualities of youth, it is therefore expansive, risk-orientated, resilient and flexible. This risk-positive factor is further pronounced in cultures where males predominate significantly over females. China's population today, for example, is 56% male, and therefore has 5% extra "risk capital" to deploy during its ascension stage.

Maturity: The third stage of empire

In the cycle of empire, a phase of equilibrium and stability naturally follows a period of conquest and expansion – assuming the borders of the new empire are well defined and well defended, and the administrative system highly organised: this is the maturity stage of empire. Without gains from conquest, a stable economy is required to generate enough revenue both to sustain a defensive army and to maintain civil harmony. Over time, income and expenditure become balanced during this stage. In its mature stage, Rome restricted the size of its army under Augustus to 300,000–400,000 men in order to balance the budget. Even more extreme was the Western Jin

Dynasty's attempt to generate a huge peace dividend in China in the 3rd century AD, after attaining supremacy over all of its challengers: the entire army was disbanded. However, neither the Roman nor the Chinese strategy was ultimately successful in forestalling the eventual decline of their respective empires.

The beginning of imperial maturity is often witness to sweeping social changes within the empire. Population growth slows, and the ratio of young to old becomes more balanced. The drive to expand decelerates, and the empire enters a period of unmatched prosperity. The core population grows wealthy, achieving a high standard of living, which blunts the tougher qualities that drove previous generations during the regionalisation and ascension stages. When new wars erupt, the empire finds itself beset by a manpower shortage for the first time – which can only be solved by inducting the menial workforce into the military. Once such wars are over, the returning soldiers from this class reject their former lowly status and demand equal rights of citizenship. The core population begins to integrate with the awakening menial workforce, but the reins of power are still held by the former. Significant internal power shifts by the end of the (subsequent) overextension stage usually result from the social changes initiated during maturity.

A frequent characteristic of empires near the end of the maturity stage is the advent of peak internal conflict. Without an external target to act as a focus for an empire's aggression, its leaders turn inward and a power struggle results. Such conflicts can weaken the empire significantly. The distraction may also provide a strategic opening for any up-and-coming regional power awaiting the right opportunity to strike. Such critical moments can be particularly explosive in the case of rigid power structures, such as dictatorships and monarchies. On the other hand, democratic empires may witness a more subtle internal struggle between competing groups. In Britain, the decade that followed the Boer War saw a great deal of political upheaval that, according to Winston Churchill, took the empire to the brink of civil war. In more recent times, the US has seen the radical politics of the Bush-era neo-Conservatives come into play, representing a dramatic swing away from traditional American values and producing a backlash with tumultuous political consequences.

Overextension: The fourth stage of empire

Overextension signifies the onset of gradual decline, initially apparent only to the most astute observers, and ending in financial disasters and military challenges.

At some point, an empire's success induces complacency, arrogance, corruption and other manifestations of decay, as the comforts of civilised society give rise to expectations that the status quo will be maintained. The transformation of an empire from "barbarian" to "civilised" is now complete, and over time it will become ripe for domination by another aspirant. In the early stages of overextension, the cost to the economy of running an empire is no longer compensated for by revenue. The empire then begins to grow its debt burden, which increasingly limits its ability to raise military expenditure precisely at a time when it is most threatened by new challenges.

It also becomes increasingly difficult for an overextended empire to motivate its people to fight once they have attained a high and comfortable standard of living. Since the Vietnam War, the US has become increasingly reliant on its technology to ensure that American wartime casualties remain low. However, in wars where there is no alternative to having soldiers on the ground, considerable public outcry over fatalities occurs.

Wars are expensive, more so as technology bleeds from the hegemon to the challengers, making it very costly to maintain the military edge. In the overextension stage, a dominant empire will not reduce social or defence commitments, nor increase taxation. It moves rather into financial deficit, which saps its strength. Financial market peaks take place past the pinnacle of the empire cycle, as the system finds ways to increase spending by raising debt. During these periods, there is always talk of reducing costs, but doing so proves consistently unsuccessful. One way in which an empire can attempt to reduce defence costs is by building new alliances to spread the load – although doing so only delays the inevitable at best. However, it is worth noting that, when an empire overextends and then goes into decline, it is forced to scale back its influence in terms of both military presence and financial holdings. This spells the beginning of its end.

The social integration that began during the maturity stage with the demand for full rights by disenfranchised citizens now progresses rapidly during the overextension stage. The composition of society by the end of this phase of the empire cycle will have dramatically altered. Formerly low-status classes can now gain entry to the empire's power core. The barbarian auxiliaries drafted into the Roman legions, for example, gained leverage and ultimately control over Rome. The British Empire's reliance on its colonies in both world wars helped to accelerate its break-up after World War Two as they demanded independence. In the US, African Americans experienced a transition from slavery in the regionalisation stage to underclass in maturity. Black soldiers have served in US wars since the American Revolution, but, following the Vietnam War – in which they fought in greater numbers and in greater capacity than ever before – they pressed for validation as the civil rights movement intensified, and entered the middle and power classes. This increasing degree of social integration is perhaps most effectively symbolised by the 2008 election of the first black US president.

As the former underclass rises, a new wave of people from poorer nations fills the roles they have left behind. The problem of manning the armed forces continues, and the social makeup of the military continues to evolve as a result. The core of the problem lies in the fact that society now has a greater proportion of older citizens than younger ones. As a result, its decision-makers become more conservative and less adaptive in solving the growing challenges of the empire's decline.

Decline and legacy: The fifth stage of empire

For an empire in the final throes of overextension, the cost of power vastly outweighs its economic benefit. Imperial sustainability becomes increasingly unfeasible, and the system rapidly begins to disintegrate. Although the signs would have been present during the overextension stage, other great powers would, for the most part, not have begun to recognise the waning empire's vulnerability until the final stage of decline and legacy, when external and internal dynamics deteriorate at an alarming rate. Enemies on the periphery then awaken to this progressive ebbing of vitality, and become emboldened by incremental successes that can soon escalate. The old empire is now prey for other regional powers in the ascendant. The rate of decline surprises the world as a formerly iconic empire collapses.

This stage of decline and legacy can be described as the evolution of multi-polarity. The unipolar world dilutes as the hegemon grows feebler, while challenging nations grow stronger and begin to exert a new-found influence. Characteristic of this stage is the empire's collective denial that it is declining, expressed by the body politic and by the people themselves. Some major symbolic event then becomes the catalyst that shatters the illusion of the status quo. The response by the leadership is to attempt to more deeply embody the perceived – "original" – values of the empire. When their actions fail, a path is opened to new leadership, reflecting the new social order. This process can appear as if hope has been renewed; yet often it is, in effect, the beginning of the end of the empire, leading to the final phase – legacy. This endures to some degree after all empires have declined, in the form of a collective value system that persists in the region in which the empire was formerly active, suffusing its smaller units and remaining until they are, in turn, subsumed by the next ascending empire.

In the modern world, the advent of nuclear weapons and the accompanying threat of mutual assured destruction (MAD) may well have altered the dynamics of decline, as borne out by the Cold War. Whereas, in the past, empires in decline and legacy were often swallowed up, those wielding the nuclear advantage have the privilege of being protected by it as they re-form into their next incarnations. Europe and Russia have certainly benefited from this new model, as will the US, particularly as its missile shield defence system is developed further.

Europe is an example of a region in legacy. Following the collapse of its empires post-World War Two, it has gradually been trying to rebuild itself into the European Union (EU). However, as regionalisation is typically driven by expanding demographics, the current forced construct is unstable, as it has not taken place by a process of demographic attraction (ie, having a core nation with expanding demographics to which other nations are drawn voluntarily or by force of arms). Instead, it has been built around the core of "old Europe," which has negative demographics, by attracting peripheral nations with more positive demographics.

However, without greater benefits to the subsumed nations (eg, being part of a much stronger and growing larger entity), it is unlikely that this forced regionalisation will work: it does not have the characteristics of an entity that could manifest a strong regional power base, and as such we are unlikely to see Europe become an essential force in the world once more. Instead, it will more likely end up with a foreign policy akin to that of a greater Switzerland.

PANEL 8.2 THE COST OF EMPIRE

Empires cost enormous amounts of money to build and maintain. As such, their success is highly correlated to prosperity. History has seen evolution in the complexity not only of empires, but also of the financial systems supporting them. With the Renaissance came the concept of government debt, which could finance a nation's expansion. Britain was but one empire that benefited from this novel fiscal principle. Its empire's debt-to-GDP ratio clearly followed the Five Stages of Empire model (see Figure 8.3).

In stages 1 and 2, the cost of the empire's expansion is clearly shown by a dramatic increase in the ratio, with the debt funded domestically. In stage 3, the benefits of peace and profitable trade produce a massive empire dividend that returns the ratio to a low point. In stage 4, the cost of the empire's social structures and the defence burden required to fend off challengers increases, and so does the ratio, with the debt funded from the broader empire, to levels slightly higher than the previous peak. In stage 5, eventually the empire breaks up and the spending required to maintain it decreases dramatically, ultimately returning the ratio to a low point. While government debt during the early stages of empire was owned by British subjects, in the last two stages it was owned predominantly by the US, which then used this hold over Britain to force it to withdraw during the 1956 Suez Crisis, effectively ending Britain's imperial age.

Figure 8.4 illustrates the evolving debt burden of the US, which appears to follow a very similar pattern. During the previous debt-to-GDP peak, and throughout US history prior to that point, the debt was predominantly owned by the American public. In contrast, the current mountain of debt is owned by foreign powers, and particularly by China, which is clearly a geopolitical rival in ascendancy.

PRACTICAL IMPLEMENTATION

Geopolitical risk is driven by the motivations and actions of a small group of powerful national actors. A good model should be able to pinpoint where each of them is situated within the geopolitical cycle and relative to each other. In turn, this allows one to identify potential future geopolitical fault lines: areas with heightened risks of political confrontation and military conflict that may have potentially "game-changing" consequences.

The influence of Europe and Russia as geopolitical actors has

Figure 8.3 The British empire, 1702–1991: Ratio of government debt to GDP

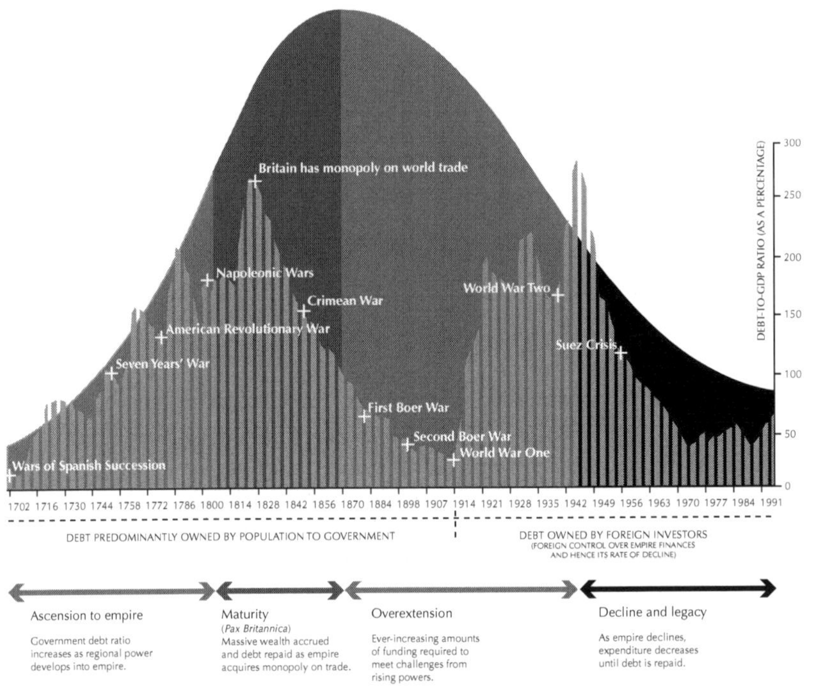

diminished significantly, as both regions are currently in the late legacy/early regionalisation stage. Given their unfavourable demographics, neither is expected to be in a position to mount a serious geopolitical challenge and ascend to empire any time soon. The US is exhibiting the tell-tale signs of late decline, which is expected to accelerate given its debt situation, low economic growth, increasing social inequality and polarisation of domestic politics. For the foreseeable future, the US political establishment will be fighting a rear-guard action to protect and preserve as much of America's waning power and influence as possible.

The Middle East is clearly in a late regionalisation stage: the Sunni/Shia rivalry can be viewed as the modern-day equivalent of the protracted regional civil wars of empires past. Whoever manages to ascend to dominance in the region will most likely be led by a strong polarised Islamic leadership that will refuse to have close ties with the Western world, unless the dynamics of China's expansion force them closer together.

Figure 8.4 The US debt burden as a function of its empire cycle

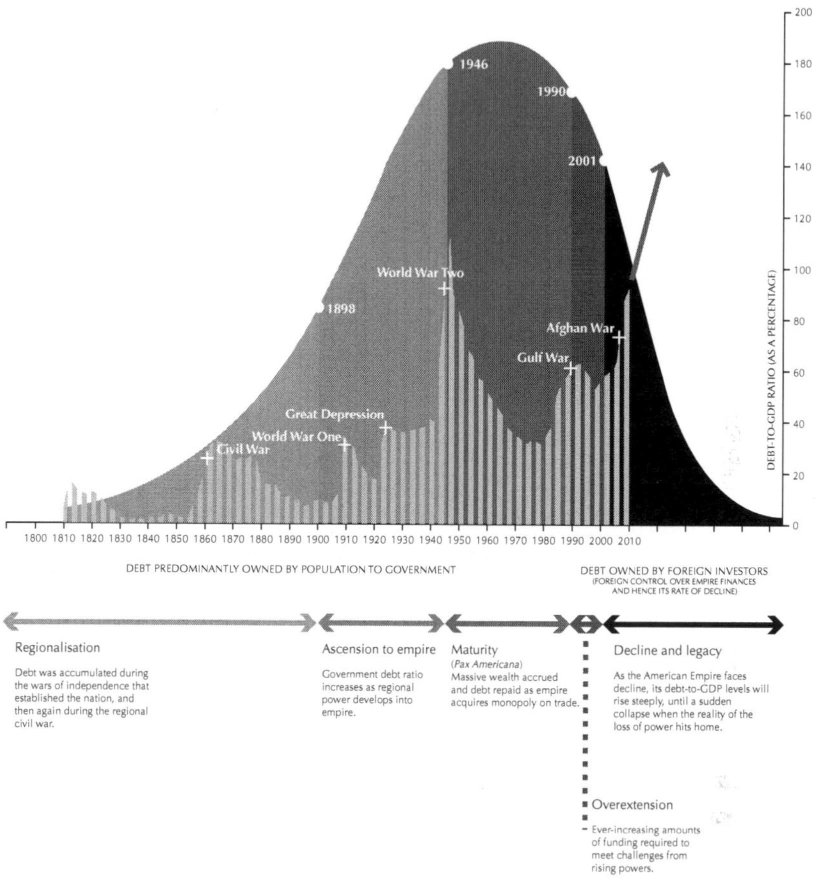

Brazil and India are also both in the later stage of regionalisation, but they are unlikely to move into the next stage of empire and expand further, due to the absence of a power vacuum to move into, and thus they are likely to follow the trajectory of France, who managed to become a very strong regional power, yet never succeeded in challenging the hegemon.

Finally, there is China, which is clearly in ascension – ever since the late 1990s, when it made a conscious decision to expand into the world to acquire resources to feed its growth. As with all empires at this stage, it has been propelled by very strong demographics: not only does it have the largest population in the world, its age and gender composition have also been conducive to further expansion, suggesting a higher risk tolerance. But there is a caveat: favourable demographics are expected to peak around 2025. Thereafter, China will start to age quickly, with the older population slowing down growth and leading to a much more conservative posture. This observation famously prompted analysts at Goldman Sachs to ask whether China will be able to get rich before it grows old.[2] The geopolitical equivalent of this question is: "Will China be able to mature as an empire before it overextends and starts declining?"

Two complications exert additional pressure on China's leadership. First, the world is in the ascending part of the Kondratiev Wave cycle and will be until 2025, which typically results in intensified competition for resources and increased geopolitical friction.[3] Second, explosive population growth in developing countries, which is occurring in the context of rapid industrialisation and urbanisation, is putting a relentless squeeze on global natural resources and climate. Thus, as China concentrates all of its efforts in the 12–15 years (from the time of writing in 2012) on breaking into the big league and becoming a full-fledged empire, it is bound to face tremendous cyclical and secular headwinds with respect to resource availability, with potentially serious geopolitical implications and risks of a major conflict.

So how can a global macro manager use this analysis in practice? It may be helpful to make a distinction between two different types of macro practitioners: short-term traders and long-term investors. For the former, our earlier earthquake analogy may be instructive. People living in seismically active areas go about their daily lives in much the same way as everyone else, with one important exception: there is a constant awareness of the danger. Companies and local communities organise regular training drills and exercises; households have pre-packed emergency bags with first aid kits, drinking water, flashlights, portable radios and warm clothes; individuals mentally prepare by visualising their actions in case of a major earthquake (eg, hiding under a table or standing inside a door frame at the first signs of serious tremors). People may end up living their whole lives without ever encountering the "Big One," but they constantly prepare for it to maximise their chances of survival.

By analogy, a global macro trader may spend long periods of their career operating in a stable environment, punctuated by a few defining major geopolitical "earthquakes."[4] Thus, they should always be aware of the dangers; they should map out and think through various geopolitical stress scenarios; and they should visualise their actions in case of a geopolitical emergency. The hallmark of truly outstanding discretionary macro traders has always been "the ability to imagine configurations of the world different from today and really believe it can happen."[5] Such ability must extend to the realm of geopolitics, albeit with a clear understanding of the long-term nature of the risks involved.

In terms of day-to-day trading activity, this situation is not that dissimilar to a global macro manager who is living through a speculative asset bubble: they know it will come crashing down at some point and they need to be fully prepared when it does. But it can take many years, and in the meantime it would be foolhardy and expensive to fade the bubble. So, instead, the manager consciously rides the bubble, but they do so very carefully – with the eventual collapse in mind – by maintaining maximum flexibility (eg, highly liquid instruments) and downside protection (eg, asymmetric trade construction).[6]

In the case of long-term institutional investors, the arguments for explicitly incorporating geopolitical risk as part of their analysis are even more compelling. First, given their inter-generational investment horizons, they are much more likely to face a geopolitical "earthquake" at some point in the future. Second, because they see themselves as "patient money" – unleveraged and unconstrained – and thus able to withstand interim shocks and illiquidity, based on their top-down macro analysis they are more likely than short-term traders to put on less liquid, relative value positions, with a view to normalisation over the medium to long term. But it is precisely these positions that are bound to suffer the most if the slowly accumulating geopolitical risks suddenly materialise.

While a group of so-called "extra-financial" risks – usually referred to as ESG (environmental, social and governance) – have become recognised, if not fully priced into markets effectively, geopolitical risks are not yet well understood by the markets and hence are not really priced in. Indeed, if the Five Stages of Empire model is correct, then over the next 12–15 years we are bound to see the full implications of the decline of the Western world and the rise of the East led by China, which is about as big as a geopolitical shock can be, given that such power shifts only occur every four or five centuries. The medium-term financial consequences of this will likely be:

- highly inflationary policies (ie, excessive printing of money) in America and Europe;
- stagflation in the West, leading to destruction of wealth in the middle classes;
- "militarised Keynesianism" in the US (ie, massive defense spending as fiscal stimulus);
- increasingly protectionist stance towards foreign government investments;
- America's "Suez Moment" in its relations with China;
- the end of the US dollar's monopoly as the world's reserve currency; and
- the loss of "safe haven" status by the US and European government bonds.

Most importantly, as we undergo the geopolitical shock of not just one but many lifetimes, with enormous ramifications for our societies and lifestyles, the economic and financial consequences, along with the potential national policy responses, cannot be understood properly without a geopolitical model that is internally consistent and that can effectively explain both historical and current events.

This chapter is an amended and updated version of a chapter that first appeared in *Breaking the Code of History* (Self-published, 2009).

1 For example, Michael Marcus, one of the first global macro traders and a legend in the industry, recounted in his interview with Jack Schwager how he had taken a massive long position in Hong Kong gold futures immediately following a breaking-news report on the Soviet invasion of Afghanistan in 1979. His ability to understand the significance and market implications of this geopolitical event, and to react swiftly and decisively, resulted in remarkable profits. Yra Harris, another global macro pioneer and a renowned CME futures floor trader, remarked in an interview with Steve Drobny: "Global macro is really a new term. It used to be called 'geopolitics.'" (Schwager, 1989; Drobny, 2006).

2 See Qiao, 2006.

3 In the mid-1920s, the brilliant Soviet economist Nikolai Kondratiev developed his Wave Theory, which proposed that alternating cycles of rising and falling commodity prices (plotted as sinusoidal K waves) follow a predictable pattern in economics, averaging approximately 53 years each. In practical terms, a K wave represents around 25 years of mounting commodity prices, followed by a downward cycle lasting another 25 years. The current ascending phase started around the turn of the century.

4 For example, the near collapse in 2008 of the over-leveraged Western financial system was precipitated by America's imperial overextension during the previous decade.
5 Bruce Kovner interview in Schwager (1989).
6 For an excellent discussion of managing a global macro fund through a speculative bubble, see Colm O'Shea's interview in Schwager (2012).

REFERENCES

Mandelbrot, B. and R. L. Hudson, 2008, *The (Mis)Behaviour of Markets: A Fractal View of Risk, Ruin and Reward* (London, England: Profile Books).

Murrin, D., 2010, *Breaking the Code of History: Past, Present, Future* (Fernhurst, England: Apollo Analysis).

Qiao, H., 2006, "Will China Grow Old before Getting Rich?" Global Economics Paper No. 138, Goldman Sachs, February 14,

Schwager, J. D., 1989, *Market Wizards: Interviews with Top Traders* (New York, NY: New York Institute of Finance, 1989

Schwager, J. D., 2012, *Hedge Fund Market Wizards: How Winning Traders Win* (Hoboken, NJ: Wiley)

9

Global Macro: A Prime Broker's Perspective

Barry Bausano

Deutsche Bank Securities

The traditional prime brokerage model was originally designed to service the classic equity long/short hedge fund manager. Global macro strategies developed largely outside that model, and prime brokers were typically confined to supporting just the equity portion of macro portfolios. However, in response to the evolution of trading styles, increasingly globalised markets and the changing regulatory environment, over time the traditional equity prime brokerage model has evolved into a sophisticated multi-asset, multi-product prime brokerage and prime finance offering. This chapter will examine the history of these developments, the role of prime brokers in supporting global macro managers and the changing regulatory environment that will likely shape prime services and impact trading strategies for years to come.

A BIT OF PERSONAL HISTORY

This author began his career in finance in 1985, and very early on was privileged to work for three legendary global macro managers: Julian Robertson at Tiger Management, Michael Steinhardt at Steinhardt Partners and Louis Bacon at Moore Capital Management. Although all three shared the "macro" label, their investment styles were materially different. But what they all had in common was a willingness to pursue opportunities across the globe, in developed and emerging markets, extending their investment theses and trade expressions across the full spectrum of asset classes and financial products. This author's experience of working for these luminary managers for over a decade mirrored the development of the "global macro" category of hedge funds more broadly. Each invariably approached the market from the initial perspective of their own core product or stylistic competency; however, as the investment landscape morphed, macro managers would courageously "style drift" towards what they perceived to be the optimal geography, asset class, product and trading strategy.

The strategies employed by the managers included directional, relative value, fundamental and technical; some of them also put on longer-term strategic positions alongside short-term tactical trades and hedges. Fund structures also adapted: while most macro managers maintained the traditional flagship fund housing all the strategies, others shifted towards a multi-strategy format, with independent portfolio vehicles for each individual strategy. Irrespective of these changes in the global macro hedge fund model, one fundamental principle remained irrevocably consistent. The art and science of remaining true to the core investment principles and risk management discipline, while continuously adapting to market conditions, is what distinguishes these and other best-in-class macro managers. As the global macro hedge fund model evolved over time, it became increasingly complex and challenging to service and support, putting a premium on the ability of executing brokers and prime service providers to innovate and adapt.

During this author's involvement with the three legendary macro funds, one of the biggest practical challenges was the requirement to dynamically shift portfolio exposure by effectively manoeuvering across different markets and products: bonds, swaps, repos, futures, options, equities, indexes, foreign exchange spot and forward contracts, commodities and new products, as they emerged. Each trade was constructed within the context of a specific investment idea, but one also needed to take into account its incremental impact on the overall portfolio characteristics. To further complicate matters, this process was executed across different geographies, trading jurisdictions, exchanges and over-the-counter (OTC) markets.

To facilitate these transactions, macro funds look to the executing dealer who provides market access, execution services and often commits capital to enhance the available liquidity. After overcoming all of the above challenges to assume the desired economic and market risk for the portfolio, major operational and financial control risks and challenges emerge post-transaction, as each trading environment exhibits a disparate range of settlement, clearing, custody, accounting, regulatory and tax regimes. In the equity asset class, the role and service model of a hedge fund's prime broker has been long established. However, in later years, and particularly since the turn of the century, the prime brokerage model has evolved significantly to accommodate the broadening requirements of other hedge fund types, especially global macro and multi-strategy hedge fund clients.

PRIME BROKERAGE AND FINANCE

Prime brokerage, in its original and most basic form, was a set of specialised services offered to top equity hedge fund clients, allowing them to execute cash equity transactions with several brokers while maintaining a single centralised "prime" brokerage account to settle, clear, margin and report those equity trades. The prime broker would provide so-called "locates" for potential short sales, lend shares to deliver against shorts and finance long positions to create leverage, in addition to general trade reconciliation, cash management, reporting, corporate actions processing and operational support services. This equity-focused, single prime broker-based model dominated the industry until the early 2000s, after which major changes in the investment landscape and hedge fund manager behaviour dramatically altered the game.

First, hedge fund portfolio investments became much more global in scope. Second, a much broader range of assets was financed in prime brokerage facilities. Third, leverage availability increased through the use of synthetic financing techniques. Finally, in the aftermath of the global financial crisis of 2007–09, a fourth dynamic emerged that further shaped the relationship between leveraged investors and their financiers: namely, an intense focus on the size and stability of a prime broker's balance sheet, along with a much more careful assessment of their operational and financial risk management.

Globalisation

Hedge funds generally, and global macro managers in particular, started to deploy capital on a much more global basis, as they increasingly sought to apply their investment expertise not only across developed, but also emerging and frontier markets. They were doing so with the hope of achieving better absolute returns as well as diversification benefits. This naturally presented new risks and operational challenges for their prime brokers, as the new and exotic markets often had peculiar trading rules, liquidity characteristics, settlement conventions and foreign exchange exposures. All of these new elements had to be incorporated into the consolidated service offering, while all the new risks, which added considerable complexity, had to be accurately measured in order to appropriately margin the portfolio.

A prime broker's ability to accommodate the geographic breadth of a client's portfolio was necessarily dependent on the underlying footprint of the parent franchise. To the extent that the core broker franchise already had trading operations, credit lines, foreign currency capabilities, exchange memberships, custodial arrangements and other necessary infrastructure in a given market, the more easily the prime services function could support their hedge fund client activities. Thus, the global operational footprint and international transaction capabilities of a broker became an important consideration in the selection of a prime financier.

Product expansion

The second new source of complexity and risk was the increasing breadth of assets and products that hedge fund managers wanted to trade and finance in their prime brokerage accounts. While they have always been early adopters of new investment techniques and innovative financial products, since the turn of the century hedge fund managers have been increasingly crossing asset class boundaries, while the new financial instruments they employed were scaling new heights of complexity.

For example, a global macro manager seeking to express a view on the outcome of the European sovereign debt crisis might choose to trade currencies, sovereign debt, credit default swaps on the financial sector debt or options on shares of European companies in the export sector, among many other alternatives. In another well-publicised example, during the global financial crisis of 2007–09, many macro managers expressed negative views on the US housing market through positions in synthetic CDO tranches. These complex products allowed them to efficiently tailor their portfolio exposures to precisely match their investment views.

Along with the obvious benefits, this development brought with it the requirement to consider the prime financier's product trading capabilities. Hedge fund managers needed to be sure that their prime broker had the core competency in a new product's trading, valuation and settlement conventions. Many hedge fund operations and finance teams seek to settle and finance transactions with the executing broker whenever possible. This procedure reduces unnecessary operational settlement risk and also limits the otherwise multiplied credit counterparty risk. A by-product of this procedure is the high correlation between a hedge fund's top execution counterparts and top financing relationships, which is completely consistent with the increasing concentration in the global banking and brokerage industry. Unsurprisingly, as the ever-smaller group of truly global banks and brokers with demonstrated multi-asset and multi-product expertise capture a higher proportion of total execution volumes, their associated prime brokerage and financing units have a correspondingly high and concentrated market share.

Leverage availability

Several market developments conspired to increase the leverage available to hedge fund managers, also resulting in a fundamental shift in the relationship between prime brokers and their clients. Important among these were the emergence of synthetic equity financing, the broad development of derivative trading products and the capital efficiency generated by cross-product margining. The end result of these changes was to transform prime brokerage and finance from a collateral-based agency lending business into a risk-based portfolio margin business. For macro and multi-strategy managers, this commenced a long-awaited consolidation of the multiple points of single product prime brokerage and financing relationships.

Synthetic equity finance

Historically, leverage in the traditional equity prime brokerage model was limited by the 50% margin prescribed by the so-called "Regulation T"; however, with the advent of "synthetic equity" or "arranged financing", managers were able to achieve much higher leverage ratios. The basic trade structure was that the financier would own the physical asset and simply swap the economic return to a client via an OTC derivative contract. There are numerous financial and operational efficiencies for the client in this arrangement, including the ability to achieve greater leverage. This development opened up a whole range of "micro" arbitrage strategies, such as statistical arbitrage, where the market inefficiency being exploited was so small that adequate portfolio returns could only be realised through the multiplier effect of greater leverage. A variety of equity market-neutral strategies became feasible with managers striving to isolate very narrow slices of risk, highly leveraged, to generate portfolio alpha independent of broader equity market performance. These strategies have generally profited the macro and multi-strategy portfolios to which they were added. However, when things go awry, as they did in the "quant quake" of August 2007, seemingly small moves in the "gross" exposures can have a dramatic impact on the net asset value (NAV) of the leveraged portfolio.

Derivative product usage

An additional source of leverage that has impacted hedge fund portfolios and the risk in prime brokerage accounts is the inclusion of International Swap Dealers Association (ISDA) governed derivatives contracts with a range of interest rate and credit underlying exposures. With these positions, margin is calculated by estimating the expected volatility of the position and the consequent impact on the value of the portfolio. Additionally, the estimated liquidity of the position is measured as a function of the potential market moves that could transpire in the time required to exit the risk. Initial margin is posted by the client, and variation margin is transferred to reflect the changing market value of the trade on a daily – and sometimes intraday – basis. The added complexity of calculating the range of possible valuations on derivative positions, their potential correlation to the rest of the portfolio, along with the projected liquidity to exit, presents challenges for hedge fund managers and the prime brokerage risk departments. The most successful prime brokers and financiers have adopted rigorous control environments, transparent valuation validations and sophisticated risk analytics to carefully assess the characteristics of portfolios with these products. This was the genesis of the cross-product margining approach.

Cross-product margining

If synthetic equity provided the leverage required for managers to pursue more isolated and narrow risk opportunities within the equity asset class, then the advent of cross-product margining opened the door to multi-asset arbitrage. Capital structure arbitrage and convertible bond arbitrage are excellent examples of strategies that benefit from the capital efficiency generated by cross-product margining. For example, assume a manager buys a convertible bond with implied volatility cheap to their expectation of realised volatility and they would like to isolate and monetise just that risk. After selling a delta-weighted amount of the issuer's equity, they may further hedge their rate risk with an interest rate swap, and their residual credit risk with a credit default swap. The net risk resulting from the total package of securities and derivatives may be far less than a cursory examination of all the notional trade legs might suggest. It is this ability to measure the offsetting and correlated risks and assign margin to the net exposure that defines cross-product margining. When judiciously used, the capital efficiency generated from cross-margining can be a powerful tool to manage liquidity and maintain a broader diversity of portfolio risks.

COUNTERPARTY RISK MANAGEMENT

One of the significant results of the 2008 credit crisis was a new-found focus on counterparty credit risk. The prosperous and benign decade that preceded the crisis, devoid of broker–dealer failures, generated an emphasis on market risk to the exclusion of credit risk. Simply described, if a manager bought a security from dealer A and sold the same security onwards to dealer B, they would judge themselves market "flat" and give little consideration to the residual credit risk of their open and off-setting positions. The failures and near failures of 2008 resulted in substantial losses and uncertain counterparty exposures.

This was reminiscent of the lessons of the 1998 Russian financial crisis: a hedge was only valuable if the counterpart performed on their obligation. In the days leading up to that crisis, many hedge funds, including global macro managers, had purchased high-yielding Russian Treasury bills (GKOs) and hedged their currency risk by purchasing put options on the Russian rouble. Unfortunately, at the height of the crisis, many option writers declared *force majeure* and did not honour their obligations. This led to catastrophic losses for hedge fund managers, whose losses on the defaulted GKOs were no longer offset by expected gains from the currency put options. This was a classic instance where the counterparty credit risk exposure overwhelmed the market risk of the trade.

As a result of the 2008 market events, and driven in large part by institutional hedge fund investors, hedge fund managers began to assess carefully the liability side of their balance sheets. Decisions to award prime brokerage and financing mandates had historically rested on firm reputations, pricing, operations efficiency, security supply, quality of reporting, etc. Suddenly, the criteria of safety, soundness and diversification emerged as critical. Prime brokerage and financing counterparts that had the structural advantages of multi-currency deposit bases, statutory access to central bank liquidity facilities, economic size and strength in their home countries and, often as a consequence of the preceding factors, low credit default spreads were hotly sought after as financing partners. An additional premium was ascribed to firms that had navigated the financial crisis with minimal damage. This wholesale re-ordering of the competitive landscape of the prime brokerage and financing business persists at the time of writing almost five years after the crisis.

ALTERNATIVE PRODUCT CLEARING AND FINANCE

Before we proceed to consider the future of the prime brokerage industry, let us review some other clearing and financing products and platforms that have developed contemporaneously with traditional prime brokerage. Most of them have evolved around non-equity products, and as such they were of direct relevance to those global macro funds that traded primarily fixed income and foreign exchange markets. Such products and platforms include foreign exchange prime brokerage (FXPB), listed futures, bond repo financing and derivatives intermediation businesses, all of which provided a centralised clearing, margining and reporting function for their respective products. Analogous to equity prime brokerage, they could provide these functions in conjunction with, or independent of, trade execution. We now briefly consider each of these services.

Foreign exchange prime brokerage

The floating exchange rate system that developed in the wake of the breakdown of the Bretton Woods system offered monetary policy flexibility to central banks, but it also introduced new risks to international trade. Multinational corporations and money centre banks could maintain foreign currency deposits in various countries as required to maintain their business activities. However, it was cumbersome for global investors and traders to maintain numerous deposit accounts and collapse offsetting trades. By the early 1990s, as money managers more commonly employed foreign exchange hedging and trading strategies, centralised clearing became very important and FXPB was born.

While traditional equity prime brokerage provided leverage via financing long stock positions and lending shares to cover short positions, FXPB went a step further. Clients actually transacted directly on the credit lines of the FXPB. Consequently, the client could benefit from multiple execution relationships, while maintaining consolidated legal and credit risk through consistent governing documents. Margin requirements were reduced and financing risks mitigated as positions and collateral were consolidated with the FXPB. Additional operational efficiencies were delivered through consolidated settlement and reporting, with consistent service and valuations. The FXPB service included execution and was typically housed within the FX division of a bank or broker. Indeed, the primary rationale for providing this service was to capture the FX execution and financing business of the client. Eventually, as the FX trading market developed, electronic trading, direct market access and algorithmic execution became part of the FXPB product suite.

FXPB continues to evolve, and barriers to entry in the FX market as well as transaction costs have fallen considerably. The huge growth in volumes experienced by the FX market since the early 2000s have been largely driven by the buy-side, which is trading FX as an independent asset class. While this has been influenced by a number of factors, notably electronic trading and globalisation, a huge impetus has come from the provision of FXPB services.

Listed futures and options

Futures clearing merchants (FCMs) served similar functions for listed futures traders as equity prime brokers did for their equity trading hedge fund clients. These entities are registered with the National Futures Association (NFA) and authorised to solicit and accept orders to execute futures and options transactions on futures exchanges. They would centrally clear and settle trades, accept margin from clients, centrally report executions from multiple executing brokers and manage collateral postings to the exchange. The primary clients were systematic macro and commodities managers that focused narrowly on trading futures. These commodity trading advisors (CTAs) and commodity pool operators (CPOs) were also registered with the NFA, and the entire industry was regulated by the Commodity Futures Trading Commission (CFTC). Outside the regulated community of users, the next major participant in futures markets are the corporate and commercial hedgers – which can range from grain-elevator operators to arable and cattle farmers and owners of oil refineries. One of the important nuances that differentiate FCMs is the ability to service these types of clients, including their requirements for the physical delivery of hard commodities. Although dwarfed in size by the FX market, many futures market trading developments paralleled the FX market. The highly leveraged products and often-volatile price action necessitated disciplined trading strategies and risk controls; several of the world's premier global macro fund managers developed out of this arena.

Fixed income repurchase agreements (repo)

There is a long history of leveraged fixed income securities trading, financed through repo. In these transactions, a client purchases a bond from a dealer, and then lends the bond back to the dealer that generates the cash, less a "haircut" (margin), to pay for the bond. The financing is achieved by selling the bond today with a pre-arrangement to repurchase the bond at a future date. The price differential between the sale and repurchase, less the accrued interest on the bond for that period, represents the implied interest rate paid by the client for the money borrowed, and the leverage is determined by the size of the required haircut. In the case of a client selling short a bond, the opposite process is followed, called a "reverse repurchase agreement" where the cash is re-lent to the dealer in exchange for borrowing the security to make delivery.

While this process bears some similarities to the various prime brokerage facilities, especially inasmuch as one can finance bond trades through repo transactions independent of the executing broker, there are still some significant differences. Primary among these is that the financing, margin, settlement and reporting of these transactions is on a trade-by-trade basis rather than a portfolio basis, as in the prime brokerage model. Additionally, the post-execution functions – settlement, margin, service, reporting – tend to be processed and serviced by the operations department of the dealer on an individual transaction, rather than aggregate portfolio, basis.

In the early 2010s, multi-strategy and global macro funds, accustomed to the operational and capital efficiency of the prime brokerage model, approached their equity prime brokers requesting they extend their service offering to include fixed income products. Fortunately, a few of the sophisticated providers utilised their cross-product margining capabilities and adapted their systems and service infrastructure to accommodate fixed income products. This consolidated the offering of streamlined client business requirements, including human capital, operational support, systems infrastructure and technology usage. Importantly, this also created capital efficiencies for global macro funds, as the more diversified portfolios often generated offsetting risks, resulting in lower overall margin requirements.

Derivatives intermediation

Over time, global macro funds became active traders in OTC derivatives, including credit default swaps and interest rate swaps. While appreciating the bespoke investment features of these products, managers quickly determined that they were complicated to handle operationally. The OTC derivative products were typically longer dated, with bilaterally negotiated terms, nascent procedures and governed by the ISDA trading conventions and documentation. As a result of these factors, large funds and dealers quickly developed large concentrations of counterparty credit and operational risk. A new service quickly emerged on Wall Street: *derivatives prime brokerage*, also known as OTC intermediation, which macro funds, especially those in the relative value space, embraced. This mirrored many features of FXPB, including centralised reporting, consolidated operations and portfolio-based margining. Perhaps most importantly, all of the offsetting positions and consequent counterparty credit exposures were collapsed for clients. This product was popular with hedge fund clients, and often led to significantly enhanced execution relationships with the providing dealers.

Unfortunately, this product was actually a credit enhancement transaction masquerading as an operational function. Essentially, a client would trade on the credit lines and in the "name" of their derivatives prime broker. Thus, the executing broker had the benefit of capturing the bid–offer spread on the client trade, while accepting the credit counterparty risk of a major bank or broker. This too-good-to-be-true product fell victim to the balance sheet stresses of the 2008 credit crisis, and many banks withdrew or severely curtailed the offering.

INDUSTRY IN TRANSITION

This chapter has described in some detail a variety of financing vehicles, clearing services and operational products that would be required to adequately support the full breadth of strategies deployed by the global macro hedge fund community. Historically, these various facilities operated independently within institutions in close vertical alignment with their respective product "silos"; for example, equity prime brokerage was housed within the broader equity division and bond repo financing was a subset of the larger rates trading business. Occasionally, nearly adjacent products would be cobbled together into a combined offering; however, the prospect for a broadly unified risk, margin and financing approach across assets, along with centralised client service and reporting, was a distant hope.

This author twice launched or participated at the inception of new global macro hedge funds, once in 1993 and again in 1999. In both instances, it was necessary to form multiple product-specific clearing and financing counterpart relationships, one each for listed futures and options, bond repo financing, foreign exchange, etc. This was both operationally cumbersome and capital inefficient, as several legs of offsetting trade strategies were often margined and reported independently. The funds executed individual ISDA trading documents across multiple banks, posted margin requirements with each bank individually and managed separate position reconciliation and operational processes. This, of course, had a direct impact on the capital usage and operational efficiency for the macro funds in question.

From the turn of the century, prime brokers began to adapt, as many hedge fund clients, beyond just the macro subset, became increasingly multi-product users in their portfolios. The first and most common business adjacency was in the listed futures and options clearing business, and several major providers combined these two divisions. Other products were occasionally bolted onto the prime brokerage offering; however, more typically informal agreements of cooperation were reached to accommodate the needs of the most important clients. The credit crisis of 2008 and the subsequent regulatory mandate have significantly raised the bar with regard to the breadth of clearing services that Wall Street would be required to provide in the future.

CREDIT CRISIS AND REGULATION

The 2008 global financial crisis resulted in massive government interventions, uncovered major frauds and caused uncertainty among investors, intermediaries and regulators. The failures of several significant financial institutions resulted in a greater scrutiny from investors, regulators and auditors on the important role that prime brokers play in the primary capital markets and the importance of enhanced transparency, strong custody and internal risk controls at prime brokerage operations.

These dynamics instigated G20 regulatory initiatives, which have been codified into several streams of regulation, such as the Dodd–Frank Act in the US, the European Markets Infrastructure Regulation (EMIR), the Markets in Financial Instruments Directive (MiFID) and Basel III. In broad terms, this regulation aims to: bring more transparency to the system through increased reporting requirements; introduce centralised clearing for the majority of derivatives; impose higher capital costs on those derivatives that cannot be cleared; and regulate execution. These acts, for which some of the specific implementation rules are still being drafted, will have a profound impact upon market structure and consequently the behaviour of hedge funds and the services that prime brokers offer.

OTC derivatives will be most impacted by the regulatory mandate. Clients trading OTC products, such as interest rate swaps, credit default swaps and non-deliverable foreign exchange forwards, will be required to clear through a central counterparty. Each hedge fund will be required to appoint a derivatives prime broker, who will clear their trades with the central counterparty, thus reducing bilateral counterparty risk concentration and duplication. These rules will facilitate more transparency, but will also increase the cost of market participation (eg, trade processing, collateral, custody).

Furthermore, all transactions mandated for clearing will be independently collateralised, which many anticipate will represent a significant drain on aggregate market liquidity. Clearing houses will only accept high-quality sovereign debt or cash as collateral, placing addition burdens on market participants to hold eligible collateral or on prime brokers to swap clients into eligible collateral. This will inevitably generate money market distortions until market forces and secured swap techniques balance the increased demand for government bonds as collateral. Other regulation, notably Basel III, will increase capital costs. Products that are less liquid, or that require longer duration and term financing, will all become more expensive to leverage. These changes will inevitably lower the degree of leverage in the system, change valuations for these assets and alter return expectations for strategies that utilise term finance and less liquid assets.

EXECUTION "ARMS RACE"

These regulations, particularly Dodd–Frank and MiFID, will also have an impact on execution and are expected to lead to a further integration of execution and financing services in both liquid and less liquid markets. There are many different methods to execute a liquid transaction, with algorithmic trading increasingly coming to the fore. The spectrum stretches from virtual artificial intelligence programmes (where an algorithm will learn and adapt to a respective trading situation) to the basic plumbing and connectivity of exchange-supported order types. Algorithms have become a service that systematic macro funds in particular rely on to help them seek liquidity across a range of financial markets, including listed derivatives.

Another distinguishing element of liquid market execution for the managers that employ high-frequency trading strategies is the transaction "latency", or speed. Aggressive firms for whom speed is an important success factor go to some lengths to achieve small advantages. For example, one such firm outfitted their entire trading infrastructure with gold-plated cables in order shave off a thousandth of a millisecond in trading speed. Another rented office space in buildings adjacent to an exchange in which a high-frequency strategy was being deployed so that their servers were a few hundred feet closer to the exchange's gateways.

Consequently, one differentiating factor of a broker's product offering is a low-latency trading environment, particularly in a co-location centre (where rack space is shared with a market centre in order to reduce round-trip times for orders). Enabling clients who want to trade directional strategies around the globe in a low-latency environment is a service only the largest broker–dealers can offer. Time scales to implement new strategies are often very aggressive to exploit market anomalies before they shrink or are noticed by other firms.

On any exchange where liquidity is challenging, global macro funds look not only for basic connectivity, but also for their brokers to commit capital in order to facilitate business. Contracts eligible for clearing will be required to be traded on a more automated basis with the creation of swap execution facilities (SEFs) – or the equivalent organised trading facilities (OTFs) in Europe. Possible effects of the new market structure on execution may include new dynamics around block trades and capital commitment to illiquid products, as platform disclosure requirements increase hedging risk for the executing dealer. With some other products, such as interest rate swaps, liquidity may increase as price and volume transparency lowers bid–offer spreads and facilitates automated trading.

The new regulatory regime will redefine market dynamics with a focus on capital efficiency and the cost of financing: the explicit cost of execution, along with the liquidity premium for illiquid transactions, will inevitably alter the profitability of some strategies. For instance, more complex and leveraged relative value arbitrage strategies between structured and basic instruments may become more difficult to execute and finance. This may lead to more opportunities as competition exits the market, but the successor strategy will likely be low leverage and low turnover by nature. Conversely, liquid flow products and newly listed instruments, such as interest rate swaps, will likely benefit from higher volume and price transparency. Trading strategies such as systematic macro, managed futures and those with a tactical trading bias will become more prominent.

THE FUTURE OF PRIME BROKERAGE

All of this will once again transform the prime brokerage business, making it even more dependent on superior technology and infrastructure. There will be a strong emphasis on scale and efficiency; success will come to those who can innovate and bundle together tools across markets, between cleared and non-cleared products, and who can link together agency and principal execution. Many of the tremendous technological advancements that were developed to accommodate higher frequency trading may be adapted to a broader product mix. For example, many clients have evolved from confirming locates daily to intra-day, with some requests coming every 10 seconds. Corporate actions as well as cash management is now completely automated, with SWIFT messages going directly into prime broker systems, which also then flow seamlessly through their internal networks, often with no human intervention involved. All this requires the prime broker to be able to generate intra-day updated inventory data and excess cash availability data, and to maintain reporting infrastructure for genuine online instant reconciliations, all of which is light-years ahead of where the industry was even at the start of the century.

There are a host of additional services that most of the top-tier prime brokers have developed and offered since the early 1990s: start-up consulting services, capital introduction, executive search and placement, technology and communications consulting and support, dedicated on-boarding and client service teams, customised reporting, risk measurement and analysis, etc. These are all very important services, which can provide tremendous advantages to a macro fund's finance and operations teams, and in the case of consulting and capital introduction, substantive strategic value to the hedge fund manager and the portfolio.

While the market structure that will ultimately emerge from the regulatory changes is not yet set in stone, a number of key features and requirements that will define a successful prime broker are already clear. The following six criteria will be critical for any prime brokerage platform to be counted among the small and concentrated group of dominant execution, financing and clearing players.

- Broad geographic coverage, including emerging and frontier markets.

- A broad product suite across the full spectrum of assets.
- Large and diversified balance sheet, with a multi-currency deposit base and statutory access to central bank liquidity facilities.
- Top-tier equity prime brokerage and finance business.
- Top-tier listed and OTC derivatives clearing business.
- Strong transactions banking franchise (ie, custody, cash management, etc).

This is a tall order, and the number of prime brokers who can be held to this standard is very small. Nonetheless, for global macro hedge fund managers who require the flexibility to trade and invest wherever the market opportunities take them, there is no other choice. These managers will need to balance considerations of operational efficiency with the safety and diversity of their service providers, to arrive at the minimal number of counterparts that provide maximum safety and coverage. This trend is already underway, as the world's largest and most sophisticated global macro managers increasingly concentrate their prime brokerage and financing business with the top two or three counterparts, who often account for more than 80% of their business. Global macro managers will continue to rely on large and sophisticated prime brokers to support their trading activity across multiple geographies and asset classes, even as the prime brokerage business model itself continues to evolve through regulatory changes, advances in technology and product innovation.

10

Understanding Global Macro Leverage

John Casano
Financial Diligence Networks LLC

Since the latter half of 2007, a number of significant macroeconomic factors have dominated the global investment landscape. What started out as a bursting of the housing bubble in the US turned into a cascade of events that eventually threatened the entire global financial system in 2008. During that period, many fundamental investment strategies based on micro-level analysis of company-specific situations were challenged by highly correlated, volatile and downward-trending markets. At the same time, many global macro funds differentiated themselves from other hedge fund strategies by producing positive absolute returns and diversifying risk in institutional portfolios.

Global macro strategies typically do well in times of a sustained increase in the volatility of currencies, interest rates, commodities and equity markets. They also tend to outperform when markets are driven by overall macroeconomic themes rather than by the fundamentals of individual securities. It is therefore not surprising that institutional investors have shown an increased interest in global macro hedge funds since 2009. Additional attractions of these strategies include good liquidity, uncorrelated return streams and transparent asset pricing and valuation.

One of the key concerns typically raised by institutional investors who are relatively new to hedge funds is the nature and extent of leverage embedded in the funds, and its potential impact on the risk profile of their portfolios (not to mention the reputational "headline risk" of potential blow-ups due to excessive leverage). However, an uninformed, negative knee-jerk reaction on the part of allocators to the use of derivatives and leverage by portfolio managers can result in missed opportunities to strengthen and diversify their portfolios. Different hedge fund strategies apply leverage differently, and this can be a source of some confusion. This chapter will focus on the nature and mechanics of leverage in global macro funds as compared to the more straightforward case of leverage in a typical long/short equity fund. It will particularly discuss why gross notional leverage is a flawed risk indicator when it comes to analysing global macro funds, and attempt to provide the reader with a better understanding of how leverage is used by global macro portfolio managers.

DIFFERENT TYPES OF LEVERAGE

Allocators who focus their research primarily on hedge funds that employ fundamental long/short equity or credit strategies may find it difficult to understand how global macro funds source and use leverage. This confusion typically stems from their attempts to apply traditional frameworks for analysing balance sheet and margin leverage to the analysis of derivatives-based leverage.

Balance sheet and margin leverage

Hedge funds that purchase equities, bonds and other non-derivative securities generally pay the full price of those securities in cash with investment capital in the fund's account. However, portfolio managers of such funds may also utilise balance sheet and/or margin leverage. Balance sheet leverage refers to the financing of long positions in a portfolio with the cash proceeds from short sales. Margin leverage refers to the utilisation of margin financing provided by the prime broker. Both balance sheet leverage and margin leverage are a means by which a portfolio manager can increase their gross long exposure in excess of 100%. In fact, selling any security short could itself be considered a form of leverage, since the fund is borrowing the security in order to sell it. Allocators accustomed to monitoring fundamental long/short strategies can quickly identify a fund's risk profile due to its overall short exposure, balance sheet leverage and margin leverage by looking at the fund's long, short, net and gross exposures.

Derivatives-based leverage

The leverage used by global macro funds is typically derivatives-based – that is, leverage inherent in the derivative instruments which the funds trade. The notional amount or exposure of a derivative refers to that of the underlying security that the derivative contract references. Examples of derivatives include futures, forwards, swaps and options. Futures instruments are exchange-traded and standardised; they are netted and settled daily, mitigating counterparty risk via the mechanism of daily margin adjustments. Forwards and swaps are traded over-the-counter (OTC), so counterparty risk is a consideration, but it is typically addressed through careful credit analysis and diversification. The principal (notional) amount of the derivatives is not exchanged, and, if needed, collateral can be posted and periodically adjusted for changes in the value of the underlying, based on mutually agreed terms. Options can be traded on exchanges or OTC, but in both cases only a fraction of the notional amount is used to purchase an option (referred to as the option premium). Consequently, the cash deployed by global macro managers who primarily trade in derivatives markets tends to be a fraction of the fund's total cash position, and is used to fund margin and collateral requirements.[1]

The traditional analysis of balance sheet leverage is generally not applicable to a portfolio of derivatives. In contrast to long/short equity funds, global macro managers generally do not borrow money or securities to put on trading positions, because the total amount required to establish such positions in the derivatives markets is only a small fraction of the fund's assets. In order to magnify their returns, all the manager needs to do is simply increase the amount of the fund's capital deployed as margin.

Unlike the profit and loss (P&L) calculations from investing in portfolios of cash securities, P&L calculations from investing in a portfolio of derivatives can be presented in different ways: as return on the notional exposure; as return on the portfolio's investor capital or net asset value (NAV); or as return on the cash in the margin account. For an investor in a hedge fund, the return on the portfolio's NAV is the most relevant and representative measure. The return on the notional amount and the return on the cash used for margin are potentially helpful in understanding the fund's use of cash and how the portfolio manager trades in general.

CASE STUDY: LONG/SHORT EQUITY VERSUS GLOBAL MACRO

We shall now compare and contrast two cases of applying leverage in the hedge fund context: one illustrating the example of a generic long/short equity hedge fund and the other an example of a generic global macro fund.

The long/short equity case

Let us assume that a long/short equity portfolio manager has positioned their fund at 145% gross long exposure and 65% gross short exposure by utilising balance sheet leverage. Therefore, the portfolio's total gross exposure, calculated by adding the gross longs and shorts, is 210%, and the portfolio's net exposure, calculated by subtracting the gross short from the gross long, is 80%. In this scenario, one can say that the portfolio is levered 2.1x (two-point-one times). If we assume that the prime broker has transferred to the fund all of the cash proceeds from the short sales, then the fund has a final cash position equal to the original capital of the fund, plus the short exposure and minus the long exposure. In our example, the fund has a cash position equal to 20% of assets under management (AUM).[2]

If the portfolio manager were to make further long investments in excess of 20% of AUM without making additional short sales, the fund would have to borrow capital from the prime broker (ie, use margin leverage). For example, if the portfolio manager in this scenario were to increase their gross long exposure to 215% without making any further short sales, they would have to borrow more from their prime broker by utilising margin leverage in addition to their use of balance sheet leverage. In this scenario, even if they choose to increase the fund's short exposure from 65% to 100%, then they would still have to borrow 15% through margin leverage. In the end, they would be left with no cash and a 3.15x levered portfolio (215% long + 100% short).

The global macro case

Let us assume that a global macro portfolio manager has a US$50,000 portfolio, and they buy a 10,000-ounce generic metal contract at US$10 per ounce (worth US$100,000). The margin requirement is US$3,000, leaving US$47,000 in unencumbered cash. The purchase of a second identical metal contract will require an additional US$3,000 in margin, for a total cash outlay of US$6,000, thus leaving US$44,000

Table 10.1 Long/short equity leverage scenarios

	Long-only	Market-neutral	130/30 product	Case study part I	Case study part II
Long	100%	100%	130%	145%	215%
Short	0%	100%	30%	65%	100%
Net	100%	0%	100%	80%	115%
Gross	100%	200%	160%	210%	315%
Cash	0%	0%	0%	20%	0%
Leverage	1x	2x	1.6x	2.1x	3.15x
Type of leverage	None	Balance sheet	Balance sheet	Balance sheet	Balance sheet and margin leverage

in unencumbered cash. This results in US$200,000 of total notional exposure. If the portfolio manager holds these two contracts, a 1% increase in the price of the metal will create a total notional exposure of US$202,000 and the margin account will be credited US$2,000, which represents a 33% return on the trade if measured against the cash outlay, and a 4% return on investor capital or NAV.

Because this portfolio manager is not borrowing more money to invest in the second contract, they are not leveraging the fund in the traditional sense. Instead, they are doubling the volatility of their portfolio and increasing the total embedded leverage via the margin-to-equity ratio, or the ratio between the amount of capital used to fund the positions and the fund's NAV. A market movement against their positions may require additional margin deposits from the remaining cash in the portfolio. As the overall margin requirements for the fund near the size of the fund's NAV, the portfolio becomes increasingly risky: for a given price drop in the underlying assets, more and more equity is wiped out and less cash is available to fund the invested instruments. The balance sheet and margin leverage

Table 10.2 Global macro leverage scenarios

No. of metals contracts	1	2
Portfolio net asset value	US$50,000	US$50,000
Total notional exposures	US$100,000	US$200,000
Unencumbered cash	US$47,000	US$44,000
Margin	US$3,000	US$6,000
Leverage	2x	4x
Margin-to-equity ratio	6%	12%

that the long/short equity manager used to magnify their returns relied on the fund's prime broker to facilitate and finance these transactions. In contrast, the global macro manager was able to increase their leverage simply by increasing the notional amount of derivatives they traded, without any need to borrow securities or capital.

Typically, the average global macro fund uses around 20% of their NAV as margin; the remainder is invested in government-backed cash securities held at the custodian's account in the fund's name. As a result, extensive use of derivatives-based leverage has implications for cash management. Because global macro managers typically have a huge chunk of their portfolio in the form of cash versus a relatively small cash position in the case of a long/short equity manager, there is a larger responsibility on them to ensure proper management of cash balances. Not only does the creditworthiness of the custodian holding the cash play a bigger role, interest rates are also an important factor in the manager's decision.

Long/short equity funds typically have agreements with their prime brokers that set out the terms of their cash management arrangements. Depending on the supply and demand for prime brokerage services, the agreements prime brokers have in place with their clients may have additional clauses that allow the brokers to increase the amount of margin the funds must remit in order to maintain their trading positions. If a fund does not have this cash available and the portfolio manager wishes to maintain those positions, they will be forced to raise additional cash. Global macro funds trading derivative contracts on exchanges may have more control over their cash, given the nature and source of their leverage.

EVOLUTION OF GLOBAL MACRO AND LEVERAGE

Unlike most of their peers in more recent times, some of the largest and most famous global macro managers of the past used to run large and successful long/short equity books alongside their macro trading operations. This was partly for historical reasons: global macro evolved from two separate streams – the equity stream and the commodity stream. The former comprised legendary equity managers such as George Soros, Julian Robertson and Michael Steinhardt, who by the mid- to late 1980s had reinvented themselves into macro managers. While they started actively trading bonds, currencies and commodities, they also continued to run their long/short equity portfolios. Not to be outdone, in the 1990s some of the larger and more famous global macro managers from the commodity stream (eg, Tudor and Caxton) also hired talented equity traders to run dedicated and sizable long/short equity allocations.

Consequently, these managers used different types of leverage within different parts of their portfolios: balance sheet and margin leverage in their long/short equity strategies, derivatives-based leverage in their macro books. They understood very well the different sources and mechanics of leverage, as well as the various issues and challenges arising from them. Below is an extended quote from George Soros's seminal book, *The Alchemy of Finance*, where he explains his approach to leverage as practiced at Quantum Fund in the mid-1980s:

> The best way to understand the role of leverage is to think of an ordinary investment portfolio as [two-dimensional] and loose ... Leverage adds a third dimension: credit. What was a loosely held together, flat portfolio becomes a tightly knit three-dimensional structure in which the equity base has to support the credit used.
>
> Leveraged funds usually employ their borrowed capital in the same way as their equity base. That is not the case in Quantum Fund. We operate in many markets, and we generally invest our equity in stocks and use our leverage to speculate in commodities, [which] in this context include stock index futures as well as bonds and currencies. Stocks are generally much less liquid than commodities. By investing less than our entire equity capital in relatively illiquid stocks, we avoid the danger of a catastrophic collapse in case of a margin call.
>
> Quantum Fund combines some of the features of a stock market fund with those of a commodity fund. Historically, Quantum Fund operated at first almost exclusively in stocks... In the last few years macroeconomic speculation has become paramount. The degree of leverage we employ is much more modest than in pure commodity funds, and the exposure in various markets serves to balance as well as to leverage the portfolio.
>
> One needs a safety margin over and above the [regulatory] margin requirements. The safety margin can be quantified by looking at the uncommitted buying power, but it is not a reliable measure because different types of investments carry widely divergent margin requirements ... Where to limit one's exposure is one of the most difficult questions in operating a leveraged fund, and there is no hard and fast answer. As a general rule, I try not to exceed 100% of the Fund's equity capital in any one market.[3]

As a side note, it is interesting to observe how discretionary macro managers, certainly in the early days, tended to describe their leverage as a percentage of assets under management, which can be clearly seen in the quote above. In contrast, managed futures strategies always tended to view leverage in margin-to-equity terms. As will be discussed later, more recently the concept of capital utilisation ratio has come to the fore – very similar to margin-to-equity, but with the added benefit of accounting for option net premium costs.

One final point on the implications of different types of leverage in the old macro business model: in one way, the relationship between macro and equity analysts in organisations like Soros and Tiger was mutually supportive and symbiotic, but in another way it was often competitive and strained. For example, in many cases, global macro trades – which typically used significantly less of the firm's capital – would prove much more profitable within a shorter timeframe than straight long or short equity plays. Such considerations of capital efficiency, which was directly related to the type and amount of leverage available to each business line, often impacted individual traders' P&L and year-end bonuses.[4]

GROSS NOTIONAL LEVERAGE: A FLAWED RISK INDICATOR

Those accustomed to evaluating long/short equity funds may be tempted to use a global macro fund's gross notional exposure as a comparative proxy or a sort of high-level gauge of overall risk. However, without properly taking into account all the other dimensions of financial risk, this framework applied in isolation is conceptually flawed and potentially misleading. There are at least four reasons for this.

Notional exposure is not directly tied to volatility

First, gross notional exposure of two different instruments may not necessarily indicate how risky the positions are because of the differences in their inherent volatility. For example, George Soros was asked in an interview many years ago about the amount of leverage he was applying in his fund: "For a US$100 million, how much are you borrowing on average?" To which he replied, "This is a meaningless figure because US$100 million invested in Treasury bills has a much different risk factor than US$100 million invested in 30-year bonds."[5] To complicate matters further, low volatility is not always the best indicator of a low-risk investment, while high volatility is not always a negative characteristic.

One could easily point to the return patterns of event-driven or statistical arbitrage strategies as evidence that investments with stable return streams in normal times often exhibit massive left-tail risks during market stress, leading to occasional experiences of drastic drawdowns. The returns of these hedge fund strategies have similar characteristics to writing options: they tend to have a short truncated right tail, a concentration of positive returns just above 0% and the occasional dramatic left-tail event. Although a specific event causing massive drawdowns may not yet have occurred, statistically it is only a matter of time before it does. Therefore, volatility – or lack thereof – does not necessarily capture the inherent risks in these strategies. To some extent, the same may be true for those global macro hedge funds that specialise in relative-value investing.

On the other hand, a fund with a highly volatile return stream should not be automatically discounted. Assuming there has not been a dramatic "style drift" or any other major changes to the strategy, an increase in volatility from an unexpectedly high positive return is surely a welcome development. Also, if correlations are sufficiently low, adding a highly volatile fund to a portfolio of hedge funds may reduce the overall level of portfolio volatility.

Portfolio managers use leverage differently

Second, global macro funds implement different strategies. Although there are many ways to split up the global macro universe, one distinction is between funds that are primarily directional in nature, betting on outright market moves, and funds that implement primarily relative value trades, betting on convergence between two similar instruments. The amount of notional leverage used by these relative-value funds can vary widely. At one end of the spectrum was a fund like Long Term Capital Management (LTCM),[6] which ran gross notional leverage of 100-times equity and owned liquid and illiquid securities. At the other end of the spectrum could be a fund that runs gross notional leverage of, say, three to five times its AUM, invests almost solely in highly liquid sovereign bonds and usually runs unencumbered cash levels of approximately 90%.

Which is more risky: a market-neutral equity fund with a 300% gross exposure and a 0% net exposure, or a long/short equity fund with a directional bias, holding a portfolio with 100% gross exposure and 100% net exposure? Based on this data alone, it is difficult to determine which fund is more risky. The market-neutral fund is using much more leverage, but the directional fund carries a lot of equity market risk. The same is true for global macro funds that implement directional and relative-value trades. Generally speaking, while the relative-value managers may have larger notional exposures than managers with directional strategies, they are not necessarily "riskier." Understanding exactly how the portfolio manager trades and manages their portfolio is at least as important as understanding the total notional leverage being utilised.

Leverage does not necessarily account for liquidity

Third, not all notional exposure is the same due to differences in the liquidity of the underlying positions. For example, it can be easily argued that a global macro fund invested with two-times notional leverage in illiquid emerging market credit instruments should be viewed as more risky than a global macro fund invested with four-times notional leverage in highly liquid G7 interest rate instruments, simply because of the available liquidity in these markets. Assuming that the volatility of these positions was consistent across the two funds, the illiquidity in the emerging market focused fund may prevent the portfolio manager from redeeming and exiting quickly. Historically, liquidity in emerging markets tends to dry up in times of uncertainty, as investors all rush to the exits in a flight to quality. What was once liquid can dry up quickly, and a portfolio manager may have to face the difficult choice of covering the positions swiftly at the expense of a massive write-down or holding them on their books indefinitely.

Leverage does not necessarily account for correlations

Fourth, a global macro fund may increase its notional leverage to invest in negatively correlated positions. For example, consider a portfolio manager who is leveraged and positioned long equities and long government bonds in an environment where equities and bonds are negatively correlated: although the notional portfolio exposure may exceed 100% of NAV, it can be "less risky" than implied by the optics of leverage. Needless to say, in this scenario, the macro manager's ability to measure and track cross-asset correlations accurately and in a timely manner becomes absolutely critical.

CONCLUSION

Allocators are often afraid of leverage because they tend to think that it is going to hurt them in some way. Leverage certainly has the potential to magnify losses; in some scenarios, losses can be incurred on leveraged positions in excess of the original capital allocated to the trade (eg, an investor may be required to commit additional capital to meet a margin call). As a result, this fear often makes allocators leery of strategies that employ relatively high levels of gross notional leverage. However, a more nuanced point of view is necessary if one does not want to ignore what could be a tremendous portfolio construction benefit. Derivatives are often used as risk mitigators: a portfolio manager using a call option to obtain a US$5 million long equity exposure in lieu of an outright purchase of US$5 million of stock will have reduced risk by protecting the fund on the downside.

Allocators and their consultants tend to look at different risk measures across all of the hedge funds in which they invest in order to gauge the overall portfolio risk and to compare individual funds: there is no one single measure that can capture risk in its entirety. While using the various risk measurements and tools for monitoring the portfolio and evaluating individual hedge funds is a vital and necessary part of an allocator's job, care must be taken not to put too much emphasis on just one or two specific risk indicators.

While gross notional leverage may help describe the risk of a portfolio of traditional securities with homogenous risk characteristics, the capital utilisation ratio – or the ratio of the margin requirements plus the net option premium costs over the total equity of the portfolio – is a much more relevant metric for describing a global macro fund's leveraged status. Nevertheless, some market practitioners may argue that the capital utilisation ratio is also flawed, because some positions require very little margin, yet can be quite volatile.

While leverage is an extremely powerful tool, it should not be viewed as the tell-tale indicator of the "riskiness" of a global macro fund. To comprehend and appreciate the total risk in a global macro portfolio, with all of its nuances and multiple dimensions, a holistic approach is required. This should consider, among other things, the portfolio's value-at-risk (VaR), changes in value due to a one basis point change in the interest rate (DV01), the capital utilisation ratio, instrument types, stress test results, liquidity profile and the overall risk management function of the global macro fund in question. The nature and mechanics of leverage used by funds investing in traditional securities are dramatically different from the nature and mechanics of leverage used by funds that implement a global macro strategy and invest mostly in derivatives.

When analysing leverage and other risk indicators of a global macro fund, it is very important not to treat them as static measures: the evolution over time of the fund's notional leverage, margin-to-equity, capital utilisation ratio, DV01, VaR, stress test results and other measures offers useful insights into how the macro manager trades and manages the fund. For example, if, over the course of four months, the margin-to-equity ratio of a global macro fund goes from 10% to 12% to 9% to 25%, that would seem to indicate a dramatic change in the way the portfolio was managed. At the very least, this should prompt the allocator to seek a meeting with the manager to investigate the reason behind the jump in the ratio.

If one were to define risk as total notional exposure over a portfolio's NAV, then examining the aggregate risk of a portfolio of hedge funds with different strategies would be misleading because each strategy acquires leverage differently. The concept of leverage as a risk metric only works in a homogeneous portfolio, a portfolio with nearly identical assets. All methods of defining leverage have their issues, but if one consistently applies the same methodology through time, then at least one would have a better understanding of the dynamics of leverage in a given fund.

This chapter is partly based on a paper written by the author at NEPC LLC in 2011.

1 The margin required to trade derivatives or to enter into a contract is traditionally set by the exchanges on which these instruments are traded, and the amount is often much smaller when compared to the margin requirements set by prime brokers.
2 100%+65%–145%=20%.
3 Soros (1987).
4 For a more detailed discussion, see Strachman (2004).
5 Soros (1995).
6 It should be noted that LTCM was not a global macro fund, but a fixed income relative value fund which, prior to its spectacular blow-up, had expanded into other relative-value strategies (eg, volatility and risk arbitrage). However, it did trade in many of the same markets that would be considered the mainstay of global macro funds (eg, G7 interest rates, government bonds and related derivatives).

REFERENCES

Casano, J., 2010, "Global Macro Leverage Confusion", *NEPC*, LLC report, October.

Soros, G., 1987, *The Alchemy of Finance: Reading the Mind of the Market* (New York, NY: Simon & Schuster).

Soros, G., 1995, *Soros on Soros: Staying Ahead of the Curve* (New York, NY: John Wiley).

Strachman, D., 2004, *Julian Robertson: A Tiger in the Land of Bulls and Bears* (Hoboken, NJ:Wiley).

11

Global Macro: An Investment Consultant's Perspective

Simon Fox

Mercer

As a global investment consultant, Mercer has experience of working with clients from a variety of backgrounds. While some of our clients would recognise the term *global macro*, many others will have originally invested in what was called global tactical asset allocation (GTAA). In this chapter, we will review the history of investing in global macro strategies by many of our clients, before considering the role that these strategies have played over time and the rationale behind them. We will conclude with a discussion of how we see them being used by investors over the coming years.

HISTORICAL BACKGROUND

For some of our clients, global macro exposure has always been part of their hedge fund allocation, often in the form of a sleeve in a broader fund of hedge funds portfolio. In this way, the exposure to macro has been part of a general "alternatives" exposure that has sought to diversify traditional equity and, in some cases, fixed income allocations.

For many in the US, however, the macro allocation evolved from a more traditional tactical asset allocation (TAA) mandate. While investors would set the broad strategic direction for their portfolio (ie, their mix between equities, bonds and cash), most investors were not in a position to make informed tactical tilts relative to their strategic asset mix through time. A tactical asset allocation manager would therefore be used to make shorter-term tactical adjustments to a client's strategic stock and bond allocations, reflecting the manager's expectations for future market movements. When they started, TAA mandates adjusted the domestic stock and bond allocations, usually based on some form of fundamental analysis. These strategies tended to be limited to taking tactical positions relative to the investor's actual investments and, as such, the strategies had relatively little breadth. As pension plans and other large investors increased their international allocations in the 1990s, tactical overlays followed suit and became known as GTAA strategies. In later years, GTAA managers have included assets not in an investor's strategic benchmark, such as commodities.

Some of the same ideas were also used in the UK– due to a desire to incorporate a degree of flexibility to a strategic asset allocation that was otherwise fixed by the investor. However, the macro allocations started life as active currency management. Indeed, GTAA strategies emerged in the UK in the early 2000s as institutional investors began to increase their exposure to overseas equities and related foreign currency risk. With the currency markets seen as a ripe source of alpha opportunities, active currency management was seen as an attractive source of returns. Broader strategies, which also incorporated skill in equity market and bond market selection, became the logical evolution of a sole focus on currency, making GTAA an attractive diversifying investment.

Whatever the original genesis of these exposures, over time the GTAA mandates in both the US and the UK have decoupled from the underlying strategic asset mix by adopting absolute return benchmarks rather than scheme-specific ones. This change, combined with an increasing use of non-benchmark assets and markets, and in particular commodities, has led to the blurring of lines between traditional GTAA mandates and global macro strategies from an investment perspective. Importantly, the "institutionalisation" of global macro space, particularly after the global financial crisis of 2007–09, has brought hedge funds closer in line with the more "institutionally friendly" GTAA descendants.

TYPES OF GLOBAL MACRO STRATEGIES

Before considering the attributes of global macro generally, it is important to realise that the universe of managers in this category is not homogenous. To help provide an initial framework for exploring this category, it can be useful to consider two approaches of global macro managers: fundamental macro and managed futures. In addition, there are specialist managers focused on particular asset classes – for example, commodities, interest rates and foreign exchange. Figure 11.1 shows how the universe of managers can be readily mapped on two axes.

Interestingly, the origins of our clients' investments in global macro (as discussed above) have themselves influenced the types of managers used. Strategies evolving from TAA or active currency management often adopted a fundamental and systematic (or model-driven) approach to identifying the trades to place, so a manager with a GTAA heritage is more often than not located in the top-left quadrant of Figure 11.1.

These fundamental systematic macro managers, which represented the largest type of exposure across our client base at the end of 2011, attempt to identify over- and under-priced markets through economic modelling. They typically use a wide variety of inputs, such as interest rates, trade flows, earnings, etc. Insofar as it can be expressed mathematically, they may also use judgement from analysts as to the fundamental value of a market or instrument. They will input these return assessments, as well as risk assessments, into

Figure 11.1 Styles of global macro investing

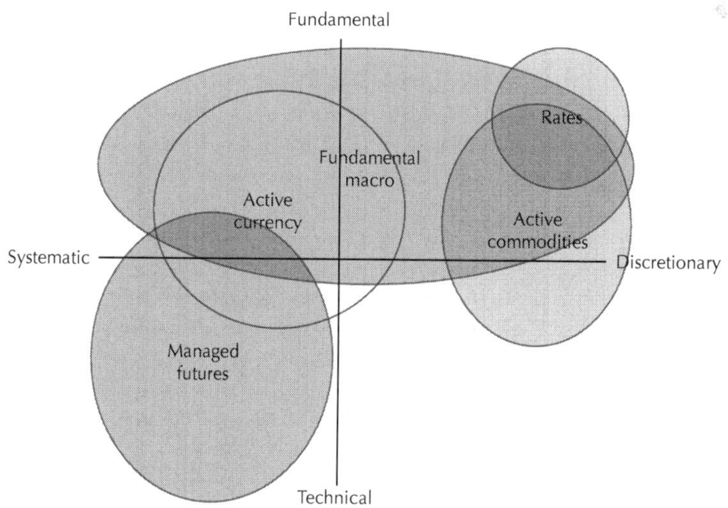

some type of optimisation system to identify the most efficient portfolio to express their model's views.

Managed futures managers, which represented the second largest type of exposure across our client base at the end of 2011, developed from the commodities trading markets.[1] These managers use technical analysis, which focuses on price movements – and in particular momentum – as the primary determinants of which instruments to buy and sell. Their highly structured and systematic approach has increasingly gained acceptance among institutional investors; their often low correlation to both fundamental systematic managers and the equity markets has been an additional attraction.

Fundamental discretionary macro strategies have been the most elusive for institutional investors with direct allocations to hedge funds. Historically less "institutionally friendly," harder to pin down in terms of where they make their money and often more expensive, these strategies have been more common as investments made through a fund of hedge funds rather than as direct allocations in a client's portfolio. Nevertheless, their ability to generate some of the richest return profiles in the broad hedge fund universe makes them a compelling opportunity for an increasingly savvy institutional investor base.

In addition to these broad types of mandates, many investors still retain more narrowly focused active currency mandates, taking advantage of the ability of specialists to add value to their portfolios. Specialist commodity mandates have also emerged, both as sources of uncorrelated returns and also to provide exposure to long-term commodity price appreciation. Global macro managers with a distinct rates focus represent the final piece in the puzzle – a strategy that to date seems somewhat under-utilised by institutional investors.

As an aside, we note that in practice there are few global macro managers who operate on a purely discretionary technical basis (ie, in the bottom-right quadrant of Figure 11.1). As such, we tend not to focus on this as a core area for categorisation purposes.

RATIONALE AND SOURCES OF RETURNS

At its simplest, global macro is a label given to investment strategies in which the manager seeks to add value through asset allocation and currency management decisions rather than through security selection, which clients access via their long-only equity and bond mandates.

In this sense, global macro involves tactically going long those markets that the manager's process suggests are attractive and shorting the less attractive markets. This can be done on a relative value basis (such that, if the manager's view is correct, the attractive markets will only need to outperform the unattractive ones, and value will be added) or with a directional component. Global macro managers, especially those with a GTAA heritage, will therefore typically seek to add value through:

- country selection within equities;
- country selection within bonds;
- equity/bond/cash allocation decisions, taken either on a global basis or separately within each country;
- currency management decisions; and
- commodity market positions.

Clearly, the way in which a manager seeks to determine the relative attractiveness or otherwise of positions in any given market, currency or commodity will vary depending on the manager's style, with technical/fundamental and systematic/discretionary delineators being key metrics in this. Moreover, the use of instruments other than futures and forwards (eg, some direct equity and credit instruments, options, swaps) are all possible within this universe and can nuance the exposures set out above. Indeed, the more discretionary global macro managers may consider more complex trade structures, including options – for instance, to try and enhance the positive asymmetry of the likely payout profile. Moreover, for those managers, the *Greeks* – a trading position's gamma, delta, vega and other option sensitivity parameters – also then become a potential source of risk and return.

For the managed futures specialists, who rely primarily on technical analysis and particularly trend following, we see the main value proposition stemming from the market inefficiencies generated by behavioural finance. Trends themselves can be explained by investor behaviour: markets responding slowly to new information because of anchoring and cognitive dissonance biases, for example, then overshooting fundamental value because of fair weather investing and fear and greed. Looking at the commodity markets alone, Miffre and Rallis (2007) provide an analysis of the profitability of momentum strategies applied to over 20 US commodity futures markets during a 25-year history. They use a combination of various time periods to identify momentum and find a number of combinations with significant positive returns. A similar analysis can be found in Baltas and Kosowski (2012). Active managers are well aware of this tendency and exploit it as a common tactic. Given the fundamental basis for most investors' portfolios and the typical focus on fundamentally driven active management for the implementation, the incorporation of technical signals can provide a natural offset to some of the biases inherent in many institutional investment portfolios.

Fundamental managers focus instead on the implications of economic analysis to understand the likely future movements in the markets, currencies and commodities. Simple factors, such as *value*, *carry* and *investor sentiment* may all contribute to the managers' returns, particularly for systematic managers. More discretionary managers will likely blend these niche betas with more esoteric insights about politics, economics and their understanding of the markets. Some may even seek to build up their picture of the world from a "bottom-up" perspective – for example, counting the kernels of corn in the field to assess likely future corn prices. Relative to most market participants, high-quality fundamental macro managers will have a clear informational advantage.

More importantly, many of these markets include large groups of price takers – ie, participants who are less sensitive to the market price. Currency markets include significant trade from central banks, multinational corporations and even tourists, who are all fairly price insensitive when buying foreign currency; similarly, commodity markets include producers, hedgers and index investors. It is quite likely that these inefficiencies will continue to exist for the foreseeable future.

Even among fund managers, we note that there are fewer strategies investing with a top-down macro view of the world than there are managing investments within asset classes (eg, traditional long-only equity managers), thus arguably giving more scope for managers operating in the global space to exploit market inefficiencies and add value than in traditional selection in equity and credit investing. Overall, we believe that the inefficiencies between markets are at least as significant and exploitable as inefficiencies within markets.

However, there are important caveats that investors need to keep in mind: markets can remain irrational for significant periods of time and fundamentals are constantly evolving, particularly in light of the increased government intervention in the wake of the global financial crisis of 2007–09. As such, high-quality portfolio construction and risk management can be as important as getting the initial insights right. Indeed, for an investor to exploit this opportunity, manager selection and portfolio construction remain vital parts of the process for achieving long-term success.

OTHER ATTRACTIONS OF GLOBAL MACRO

While we believe that skilled global macro managers have the potential to produce long-term positive returns through different market environments, other features of the global macro universe are also attractive to institutional investors:

- low correlation with equity markets (ie, portfolio diversification benefits);
- reasonably good liquidity relative to other alternative asset classes; and
- reasonably good transparency into the underlying exposures.

Global macro strategies are structured to implement a set of views on the direction of a broad array of global markets and instruments. They can profit from either up or down movements in markets or the divergence or convergence of specific markets. Moreover, as the instruments traded are typically futures contracts and currency forwards, the markets for which tend to be very liquid even in times of stress, managers can rotate their portfolios more easily than other types of hedge funds. In this way, they have the potential, at least theoretically, to make money in any market environment. The liquid nature of the trading instruments also prevents the strategies from being caught in liquidity squeezes that can seriously undermine other types of hedge fund strategies. Indeed, history suggests that this combination of features can help protect returns through periods of crisis, such as in 2008.[2]

Taking this a step further, we note that through periods of extreme risk aversion, when volatility spikes and when risk appetite indexes turn sharply negative, global macro styles of investing still, on average, deliver positive returns. Our analysis of these risk aversion indexes since 1993 highlights that approximately 10% of months can be broadly classified as "risk averse," and that in such months the only hedge fund indexes to deliver positive returns are managed futures, global macro and dedicated short-bias indexes.[3] In contrast, all other broad styles of hedge funds mirror the performance of the equity markets in delivering negative returns through these periods.

An added benefit of the use of forwards and futures is that these strategies can often provide more frequent liquidity to investors than other hedge funds, or even other types of alternative asset classes more generally. Similarly, these instruments are easily priced and widely traded and so most managers are willing and able to disclose their underlying market exposures to investors on a frequent basis, offering reasonable reporting transparency. Given the institutional lineage of many GTAA strategies, these types of global macro strategy are often broadly "institutionally friendly."

COMMON INVESTOR CONCERNS

While there are compelling reasons for investing in this space, this is not to say that there are no unique risks or issues that institutional investors often need to understand and address before attaining a sufficient level of comfort with global macro strategies. Some of the key concerns typically raised by institutional investors include perceptions of high volatility, embedded leverage, high fees and the general fear of hedge fund investing.

Use of leverage and high volatility

Global macro returns are typically more volatile than the returns of the overall hedge fund industry, and in particular multi-strategy funds of hedge funds, which historically have been one of the more common routes to building a diversified hedge funds exposure for institutional investors. To achieve high volatility and – hopefully – commensurately high returns, global macro strategies can incorporate a fairly high degree of embedded leverage.

For most allocators, the volatility of any strategy can simply be addressed as part of the overall risk budgeting process for the investor's portfolio – moderating the size of the overall exposure to reflect the higher volatility of the strategy. Where there has been a relatively high allocation to equity – for example, in countries such as the UK – this has enabled investors to gain comfort with allocations of 5–10% of total assets to a portfolio of different global macro strategies. Allocations of this size are justified by the expected long-term low correlation of the strategy to the equity markets. In such exposures, however, manager diversification is very important.

Institutional investors have gained comfort explicitly with the use of leverage in global macro strategies in two ways. First, the liquid nature of the instruments used means that the leverage itself does not leave these strategies vulnerable to a liquidity squeeze of the kind that impacted other hedge funds in the crisis of 2007–09. Second, to provide reassurance that the leverage could not expose other parts of the asset portfolio to potential losses, investors have found comfort in the typical limited liability status of the investment vehicles used. This structure means that the maximum *theoretical* loss that an investor can suffer is limited to the value of the assets allocated to the fund. In practice, there are usually a number of controls in place – both internal and external, including those imposed by trading partners and exchanges – that make it extremely unlikely that a global macro manager could incur losses of that magnitude, let alone in excess of its available capital. This formal backstop has, however, proved particularly reassuring to some investors.

Relatively high fees

The investment management fees charged by global macro managers are often in line with the broader hedge fund industry, in the order of 1–2% annual base fee, plus a performance-related fee of 20%. This is significantly higher than for traditional long-only equity and bond mandates, and many institutional clients who are relatively new to the hedge fund industry have questioned whether such fees are appropriate in principle. On a more pragmatic note, they have also questioned whether the managers genuinely have the ability to consistently generate returns in excess of such fees. In the end, however, high fees have been accepted by many investors as a simple fact of life and ultimately in the view that the evidence strongly points to the value of these strategies on a net-of-fees basis. Managers who have been more flexible and innovative in the structuring of their fees, to better reflect the long-term partnership approach desired by institutional investors, will have seen benefits in fundraising. We also expect institutional investors to continue to challenge all of their managers, including global macro managers, on the fees they charge.

Hedge fund fears

Hedge funds often suffer from a bad press, and probably always will: they are an easy target for politicians and journalists, especially during crises, and tend to only make headlines when things go wrong. No matter how much due diligence and care goes into a hedge fund investment by an institutional investor, they will always retain an element of "headline risk" that hedge funds in general, or even some of their selected managers in particular, find themselves mentioned in the press, whether fairly or unfairly. This risk is compounded for investors by the tendency for hedge funds to be domiciled offshore, and to have limited regulatory oversight. Investing in hedge funds therefore carries fewer investor protections and rights than most traditional investments. Hedge funds, including global macro strategies, can also implement complex trading strategies, sometimes revealing little in terms of their "secret sauce," which can be particularly frustrating with some of the "black box" managed futures strategies. All this adds to the general fear of investing in hedge funds. To the degree that some global macro strategies have been able to demonstrate a more "institutionally friendly" nature than others, it has served them in good stead in gaining institutional assets over the last 10 years.

ROLE IN INSTITUTIONAL PORTFOLIOS

We have noted the potential for global macro strategies to generate positive long-term returns, their potential diversification benefits given the low correlation to equity in particular, and also the decent liquidity and transparency that they offer investors. Given all these benefits, it is not surprising that global macro strategies have emerged as common investments in institutional investment portfolios. But how will their role develop in the future, as their GTAA heritage fades into the past?

The decade following the early 2000s saw significant changes in institutional asset allocations, especially from pension funds. There was a strong trend to diversify out of traditional public equities into alternatives. Mercer has encouraged this trend, as we believe portfolios have better risk–return profiles when the opportunity set is expanded to include high-quality alternative strategies, in the same way as with good active management of traditional assets (see Figure 11.2).

In the early 2000s, there were only a few accessible alternative strategies for institutional investors, including GTAA strategies, funds of hedge funds, private equity funds of funds and local real estate. All this has changed as new strategies have emerged, managers have "institutionalised" and investors have sought to be more opportunistic in their investing, especially after the global financial crisis of 2007–09. Faced with this increasing choice and complexity with respect to alternative asset classes, a common question investors ask has been: "How do I build a coherent alternative investment allocation?"

A useful starting point is to look at the total portfolio and divide it into a *base* portfolio and a *growth* portfolio. The split between base and growth will depend on the investor's long-term objectives, risk appetite and market opportunities. The base portfolio is designed to match liabilities, if any, and to be defensive in general. It will therefore consist of high-quality sovereign debt, inflation-linked bonds, high-quality credit, and cash equivalents. In contrast, the growth portfolio is designed to generate long-term returns through a

Figure 11.2 Enhancing the efficiency of investment portfolios

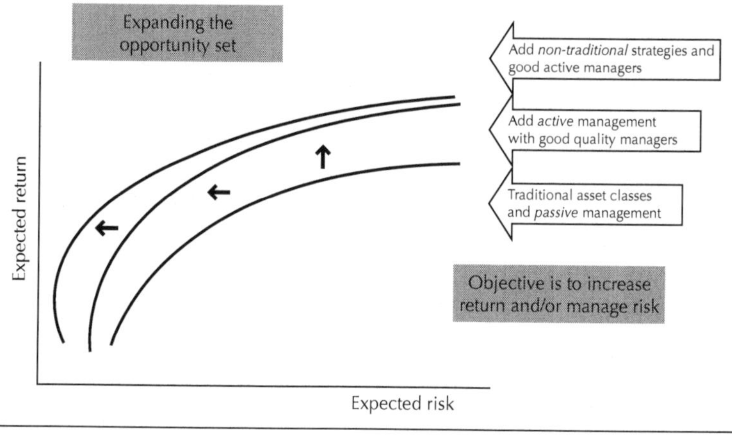

combination of beta and alpha sources from both traditional and alternative asset classes. It is intended to be the risk-seeking engine of the overall fund. For most investors, we would expect the general approach to building a growth portfolio to be similar, with the weights put on "base" and "growth" components ensuring the overall portfolio risk is appropriate to the investor's particular risk tolerance.

The cornerstone for most growth portfolios has historically been an allocation to public equity. For many clients it remains the sole exposure. While we continue to believe that a significant public equity allocation makes sense for investors (given the economic rationale for long-term returns, the historical evidence for value creation, the liquidity of markets, etc), we see a significant role for alternatives as well. Global macro strategies are part of that mix.

Alternative asset classes can be used to supplement an exposure to equities with three broad aims: to help diversify the growth portfolio; to increase expected returns from the growth portfolio; and to introduce greater inflation sensitivity. Commodities and other real assets are typically used to achieve the third of these goals, and will naturally also provide some diversification. Private equity strategies are most often used as return enhancers. Importantly, we believe that hedge funds – including global macro strategies – can add the most value when they are used as a risk-reduction tool in the growth portfolio, reducing risk by increasing diversification but without compromising long-term expected returns.

Hedge funds provide exposure to non-traditional risk factors that naturally diversify the risks that dominate a traditional growth portfolio, and equity risk in particular. By introducing new risk factors, the portfolio carries additional return drivers and relies less on the direction of capital markets, resulting in a lower-risk growth portfolio. Importantly, this risk-reduction capability does not necessarily come at the cost of lower expected returns, making hedge funds one of the more compelling parts of a broadly diversified growth portfolio.

Within this framework, we see global macro strategies adding value by exploiting investor behaviour risks (eg, managed futures capitalising on market trends), capturing *value* and *carry* premia across different markets (typical of the more systematic fundamental managers) and market timing. In addition, associated with this will also be significant manager skill.

Therefore, looking to the future, we would expect global macro strategies to remain a material part of institutional investors' portfolios. Along with other hedge funds, they provide access to differentiated sources of returns that help provide diversification within growth portfolios, where it is often lacking. Global macro strategies themselves historically have provided two extra characteristics that set them apart from other broad hedge fund styles: they have remained highly liquid in the face of severely stressed market environments (eg, the global financial crisis of 2007–09) and they have proved less correlated with equity than many other styles. We expect our institutional clients to increasingly use alternatives, to have an increasingly diversified mix of strategies within their alternatives allocation and to have global macro strategies as a core part of that allocation.

ONE, TWO OR MANY?

Global macro strategies share a number of common characteristics and, in aggregate, provide a recognisable pattern of returns. However, as already discussed, this remains a relatively heterogeneous group of investments with significant variations in investment process, manager styles and levels of manager skill. Moreover, individual strategies often have relatively high volatility. This has two key implications for investors.

First, the identification of high-quality managers is critical. No matter how much one can generalise from the historical performance of these strategies in aggregate, underlying it are some outstanding successes and some major failures. As noted earlier, these are highly volatile investments that rely on a manager's insights and skills. There are no real shortcuts around this; manager research requires experience, judgement and a fair amount of "elbow grease," but it is a critical part of the overall puzzle.

The second implication is that position sizing is important and blending managers can create a far more robust exposure than picking a single manager. Indeed, the heterogeneity of the space means that it is possible to find high-quality managers operating with a range of styles and approaches that can enable investors to build a compelling portfolio of global macro strategies.

The benefits of diversification typically outweigh the additional governance burden for a number of reasons. Even with good manager selection, hedge funds are small businesses and are heavily dependent on maintaining their people, culture and market niche to continue to add value; not all managers will perform as expected, particularly over the short term; and, most importantly, hedge fund investors have few ways to limit the risks taken by a manager – the most effective measure is position size. Given this, we believe that investors give themselves the best chance for success by building out a portfolio of managers or by balancing active management risks with other exposures in their portfolio (eg, by constructing a broader portfolio of hedge funds).

CONCLUSION

Global macro strategies, whether they have emerged in investors' portfolios from a GTAA heritage or as part of a pure hedge fund allocation, have had – and will continue to have – a role in institutional investment portfolios. Institutional investors continue to rely on equity markets as the primary source of "growth" within their investment allocations; alternative asset classes, such as hedge funds, can offer access to other types of risk premia, thus providing diversification benefits within a growth portfolio. Global macro strategies are one of the more attractive diversifying alternative investment opportunities available.

Operating in a space that provides access to recognised "niche betas," as well as market inefficiencies that provide a rich opportunity set for skilled active management, global macro managers can partake in a compelling range of potential investments. In addition to their ability to provide positive expected long-term returns, their other characteristics also make them attractive to institutional investors. In aggregate, they have historically been able to provide a lower correlation to equity than other hedge fund styles and often a de-correlating exposure in periods of extreme risk aversion; they have offered investors good liquidity and had no need to restrict redemptions during the last market crisis; and many provide institutional levels of service and transparency.

But the universe of global macro managers is not homogenous – it does not fulfil the criteria of an "asset class." Having examined the opportunity set, we can identify some broad styles of management: fundamental versus technical and systematic versus discretionary. This classification can help investors think about how to build and tilt a portfolio of global macro managers. However, even this categorisation can mask the heterogeneity of individual managers underlying it. Some will be asset class specialists, others generalists; some will seek directional exposures, others relative value trades; and the list goes on. Moreover, while the space provides some great opportunities for asset managers, manager skill will remain a key criterion for success. This highlights the importance of robust manager selection and also illustrates the potential diversification benefits within a blend of global macro managers.

Overall, we believe that global macro has an important role to play in our clients' portfolios. While there are challenges with any alternative investment, global macro strategies have proved more accessible than most and have delivered strong, diversifying returns for institutional investors.

1 The industry also uses the term "commodity trading advisors" (CTAs) to describe these managers.

2 As the S&P 500 index declined 37%, the Dow Jones Credit Suisse Global Macro index was down only 5%, while the Dow Jones Credit Suisse Managed Futures index was *up* 18%.

3 For all the analyses in this chapter, we use the Dow Jones Credit Suisse Broad Hedge Fund indexes; for risk aversion, we use the Credit Suisse Global Risk Appetite index.

REFERENCES

Baltas, A. and R. Kosowski, 2012, "Momentum Strategies in Futures Markets and Trend-following Funds," working paper, June (available at http://ssrn.com/abstract=1968996).

Miffre, J. and G. Rallis, 2007, "Momentum Strategies in Commodity Futures Markets," *Journal of Banking and Finance*, (31)6, pp 1863–86.

12

Global Macro: a Fund of Hedge Fund's Perspective

Omar Kodmani and Andrew Rozanov

Permal Group

This chapter will consider global macro strategies from the point of view of a fund of hedge funds (FoHF). While Permal Group runs one of the oldest and largest funds of global macro funds in the industry, the authors have made a conscious effort *not* to use it as the basis for the ensuing discussion. Instead, we have opted to use standard hedge fund industry benchmarks to make a more generic case, while drawing on the collective experience of our firm to highlight various issues and challenges that we believe are relevant for FoHF practitioners and their institutional clients.

In the first section, we will consider global macro in the context of a multi-strategy FoHF portfolio. Specifically, we review the background to the renewed institutional interest in these strategies post-crisis, and focus on how they compare to other hedge fund strategies in terms of long-term return, risk and diversification potential. We make a particular point of looking at how global macro has performed historically during and immediately after major financial crises.

The next section shifts from a multi-strategy to a single-strategy perspective: we consider some issues and challenges involved in constructing and running a portfolio of global macro funds. We do so from three different angles – sub-strategy allocation, manager selection and risk management. There is an important caveat that must be clearly stated upfront: throughout this discussion we omit or mention only in passing various aspects of FoHF management which are mission-critical, but which are not necessarily unique to global macro in that they equally apply to portfolios running other strategies. In this chapter, as indeed in the whole book, the focus is exclusively on what makes global macro unique and different.

In the third section, we contextualise the discussion by challenging a widely held view: that there is such a phenomenon as a "typical" global macro investor experience. While most investors and commentators would usually acknowledge that macro is a highly heterogeneous space, they would often fail to make the logical connection: different combinations of macro managers can produce very different results, especially in the short term, thus leading to very different investor experiences. For example, someone who had invested in the HFRX Macro/CTA index after the global financial crisis of 2008 would have seen vastly different results – and would probably have a very different opinion of global macro – compared to someone who during the same period had invested in a portfolio similar to the Dow Jones Credit Suisse Global Macro Broad Hedge Fund index. The point here is not that one index is necessarily better than the other, but that asset allocators and institutional investors must develop a more nuanced view before making definitive judgements about the role of global macro in their portfolios.

The final section concludes with some thoughts on the current state and prospects of the FoHF industry and the potential role of global macro strategies in shaping its future.

GLOBAL MACRO IN A MULTI-STRATEGY PORTFOLIO

Global macro has a long and storied history. It has always been one of the core hedge fund strategies, attracting considerable investor interest and assets. In the early 1990s, it accounted for more than 40% of all assets invested in hedge funds,[1] which were heavily concentrated in just a handful of firms (such as Soros, Tiger, Steinhardt, Caxton and Tudor). At the time, most of the money came from funds of hedge funds or directly from ultra-high-net-worth individuals, family offices and private banks. While there were some early allocators among institutional investors, generally they tended to shy away from hedge funds in those days.

However, in the late 1990s and especially in the first decade of the 21st century, institutional money increasingly flowed into hedge funds, as they proved their worth by preserving and growing capital in the wake of the technology bubble collapse. But institutions did not favour all strategies equally: the relative weight of global macro steadily declined, reaching a historical low of approximately 15% of total assets just before the global financial crisis of 2007–09, as institutional funds flooded into long/short equity and various arbitrage strategies.[2] There were at least three reasons underpinning this preference.

First, most of these strategies tended to be asset class based and focused on "bottom-up" security selection, which was fairly straightforward and easy to understand in the institutional context. Second, the overall macroeconomic and policy backdrop was very benign: experts incessantly talked about the era of "Great Moderation," of central banks being fully in control, of emerging market economies implementing responsible monetary and fiscal policies. The global economy appeared stable and prosperous, and there just did not seem to be sufficient opportunities for consistently profitable "top-down" macro trading.

Finally, if one were to look at risk only through the prism of volatility, CTAs and systematic macro strategies in particular can at times appear riskier compared to many arbitrage-based strategies. But this is largely an illusion. For example, many arbitrage strategies have a so-called "short volatility" return profile: they produce very steady and attractive returns during stable periods, only to suffer devastating losses during crises and dislocations. Also, many of these strategies operate in less liquid markets, which can lead to artificial smoothing of returns – ie, returns appear more stable than they are in reality, underestimating volatility and overestimating risk-adjusted return indicators (eg, Sharpe ratio). When the global financial crisis hit in 2007–08, many of the hidden risks of these strategies came to fore, while global macro flourished, leading to renewed institutional interest.

With this backdrop, let us now consider how global macro, both discretionary and systematic, stacks up against other hedge fund strategies. We will start by looking at long-term returns, risk and diversification benefits. Figure 12.1 shows the cumulative performance of all the Dow Jones Credit Suisse Broad Hedge Fund indexes since inception in January 1994 up to June 2012; it also includes the MSCI World index for global equities.

Two observations immediately stand out. First, over most of the

Figure 12.1 Cumulative performance by strategy (Jan 1994 – Jun 2012)

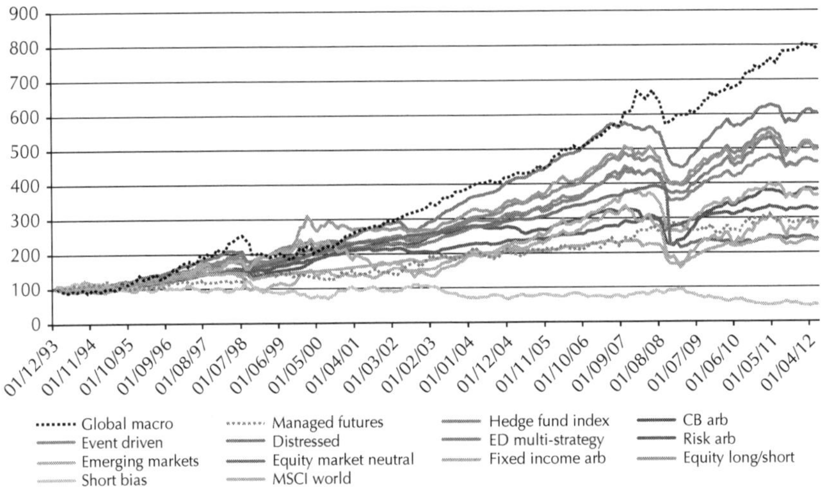

Source: Dow Jones Credit Suisse Hedge Fund Index and MSCI data; calculations by the authors

18½ years covered by the chart – and certainly since the turn of the century – global macro has beaten all other hedge fund strategies and global equity markets hands down. Second, systematic macro managers, as proxied by the Managed Futures Index, have not done anywhere near as well in either absolute or relative terms; however, they did perform in line with global equities, delivering similar long-term returns, but at a fraction of equity volatility. As we shall see, they also performed extremely well during the financial crisis of 2008, effectively de-correlating from other strategies and thus offering tremendous diversification benefits. Table 12.1 provides summary statistics for all the strategies over the entire period.

Table 12.2 rearranges the data to present hedge fund strategy rankings by Sharpe ratio,[3] skewness, excess kurtosis and correlation to global equities.

All else being equal, a higher Sharpe ratio is desirable as it means higher risk-adjusted returns. This is a measure of efficiency of an investment strategy: how many units of excess return are produced per each unit of risk taken (where risk is defined as volatility). Discretionary and systematic macro are distinctly different on this measure: while the former is among the top three hedge fund

Table 12.1 Summary performance statistics by strategy (Jan 1994 – Jun 2012)

	Global macro	Managed futures	Hedge Fund Index	Convertible arbitrage	Event-driven	Event-driven distressed	Event-driven multi-strategy
Cumulative returns	686.4%	181.3%	360.2%	281.5%	404.2%	503.5%	361.6%
Annualised returns	11.7%	6.3%	8.6%	7.5%	9.0%	10.0%	8.5%
Annualised volatility	9.7%	11.7%	7.6%	6.9%	6.3%	6.6%	6.9%
Sharpe ratio (3.12%)	0.88	0.27	0.72	0.63	0.93	1.03	0.79
Skewness	0.02	0.03	–0.18	–2.68	–2.22	–2.14	–1.73
Kurtosis	3.89	–0.02	2.47	16.16	10.59	10.76	7.47
Equity correlation	0.22	–0.04	0.59	0.43	0.68	0.65	0.64

	Risk arbitrage	Emerging markets	Equity market-neutral	Fixed income arbitrage	Equity long/short	Dedicated short bias	MSCI World
Cumulative returns	225.3%	264.1%	139.7%	134.3%	397.4%	–51.7%	182.1%
Annualised returns	6.5%	8.1%	5.4%	4.8%	9.2%	–2.5%	6.9%
Annualised volatility	4.2%	14.9%	10.3%	6.0%	10.0%	17.0%	15.7%
Sharpe ratio (3.12%)	0.81	0.34	0.22	0.28	0.61	–0.33	0.24
Skewness	–0.98	–0.75	–11.86	–3.81	–0.01	0.66	–0.73
Kurtosis	4.59	5.10	162.63	24.26	3.18	1.37	1.45
Equity correlation	0.56	0.60	0.30	0.46	0.71	-0.74	1.00

Source: Dow Jones Credit Suisse Hedge Fund Index and MSCI data; calculations by the authors

Table 12.2 Strategy rankings by performance statistics (Jan 1994 – Jun 2012)

Sharpe ranking		Skewness ranking		Kurtosis ranking		Equity correlation ranking	
Distressed	1.03	Short bias	0.66	Managed futures	–0.02	Short bias	–0.74
Event-driven	0.93	Managed futures	0.03	Short bias	1.37	Managed futures	–0.04
Global macro	0.88	Global macro	0.02	MSCI World	1.45	Global macro	0.22
Risk arbitrage	0.81	Equity long/short	–0.01	Hedge fund index	2.47	Equity market-neutral	0.30
ED multi-strategy	0.79	Hedge Fund Index	–0.18	Equity long/short	3.18	CB arbitrage	0.43
Hedge Fund Index	0.72	MSCI World	–0.73	Global macro	3.89	Fixed income arbitrage	0.46
CB arb	0.63	Emerging markets	–0.75	Risk arbitrage	4.59	Risk arbitrage	0.56
Equity long/short	0.61	Risk arbitrage	–0.98	Emerging markets	5.10	Hedge Fund Index	0.59
Emerging markets	0.34	ED multi-strategy	–1.73	ED multi-strategy	7.47	Emerging markets	0.60
Fixed income arbitrage	0.28	Distressed	–2.14	Event-driven	10.59	ED multi-strategy	0.64
Managed futures	0.27	Event driven	–2.22	Distressed	10.76	Distressed	0.65
MSCI World	0.24	CB arbitrage	–2.68	CB arbitrage	16.16	Event-driven	0.68
Equity market-neutral	0.22	Fixed income arbitrage	–3.81	Fixed income arbitrage	24.26	Equity long/short	0.71
Short bias	–0.33	Equity market-neutral	–11.86	Equity market-neutral	162.63	MSCI World	1.00

Source: Dow Jones Credit Suisse Hedge Fund Index and MSCI data; calculations by the authors

strategies, the latter is among the bottom three (we exclude MSCI World, which is not a hedge fund strategy). And if one were to eliminate a single huge outlier data point for the equity market-neutral strategy (a loss of –40.5% in November 2008), it would take its Sharpe ratio from 0.22 all the way to the top of the ranking at 1.16, leaving managed futures as the second worst strategy after dedicated short bias.[4]

Skewness and kurtosis – the higher statistical moments of a return distribution – can offer unique insights into the risk signatures of individual hedge fund strategies which cannot be captured by volatility alone. Both measures need to be considered together in order to draw meaningful inferences. For example, a combination of strongly negative skewness and large kurtosis is often indicative of a "short volatility" type strategy – making steady returns in normal times, but suffering dramatic losses in crises and dislocations. Distressed and event-driven strategies, which looked so attractive in terms of their Sharpe ratios, actually have some of the worst risk profiles in terms of higher moments.

By contrast, global macro is only marginally less attractive in terms of Sharpe ratio, but considerably less risky in its higher moments, with practically normal skewness and only slightly fatter tails. But it is managed futures strategies that really shine in this comparison: their returns exhibit a normal distribution with no hidden risks lurking in the left tail, which is a rare and valuable feature among hedge funds. As can be seen from the rankings, most strategies have strongly negative skewness and very fat tails and, while the exact order of the rankings may differ, these tend to be the same kinds of less liquid, arbitrage-type strategies (even when we correct for the outlier data point, equity market-neutral still exhibits strong negative skewness and fat tails: –0.98 and 5.11, respectively).

Finally, we look at strategy rankings by correlation to equity, where again global macro, and managed futures in particular, come out close to the top. All hedge fund strategies that had strong negative skewness and very fat tails also happen to be strongly positively correlated to global equities, underscoring their limited diversification potential, especially in times of crises and dislocations. Interestingly, equity long/short strategies, which scored very close to global macro on skewness and kurtosis and exhibited a decent long-term Sharpe ratio, fail completely on the correlation score: at

0.71 they have the highest correlation to global equity of all hedge fund strategies.

One way of illustrating the long-term benefits of discretionary and systematic macro is to plot annualised returns since inception for all hedge fund strategies against their long-term correlation to global equities. In Figure 12.2, the more a strategy plots in the "north-western" direction, the more desirable it would be for an equity-heavy institutional portfolio.

Another way of highlighting the long-term diversification potential of global macro strategies is to re-map traditional asset classes onto "correlation clusters" based on how tightly or loosely they are interlinked with the broad categories of equity, fixed income and commodities. In Figure 12.3, we reproduce the results of such analysis as presented in Welton Investment Corporation's 2011 paper, "Diversification: Often Discussed, but Frequently Misunderstood."

As can be seen in Figure 12.3, out of the 24 traditional asset class benchmark indexes used in the analysis, US government two-year

Figure 12.2 Annualised Returns versus Correlation to Equity (Jan 1994 – Jun 2012)

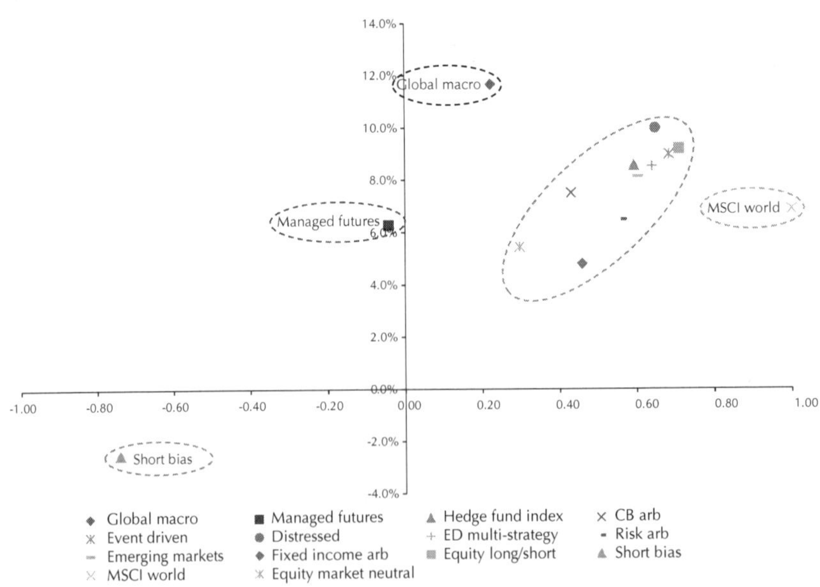

Source: Dow Jones Credit Suisse Hedge Fund Index and MSCI data; calculations by the authors

Treasuries, the Dow Jones Credit Suisse Managed Futures Index and, to a lesser extent, the Dow Jones Credit Suisse Global Macro Index appear to offer the greatest diversification potential to a multi-asset class institutional portfolio.

It is clear that, in terms of their long-run risk–return profiles and diversification potential, both discretionary and systematic macro have unique characteristics that can add considerable value to a multi-strategy FoHF portfolio. Interestingly, this conclusion holds if we carry out a similar analysis on HFRX indexes (see Figures 12.A1–12.A2 and Tables 12.A1–12.A2 in the appendix to this chapter). This suggests that while there may be striking differences between the

Figure 12.3 Traditional asset class-based allocation framework versus a diversity-based allocation framework (Jan 1999 – Jun 2010)

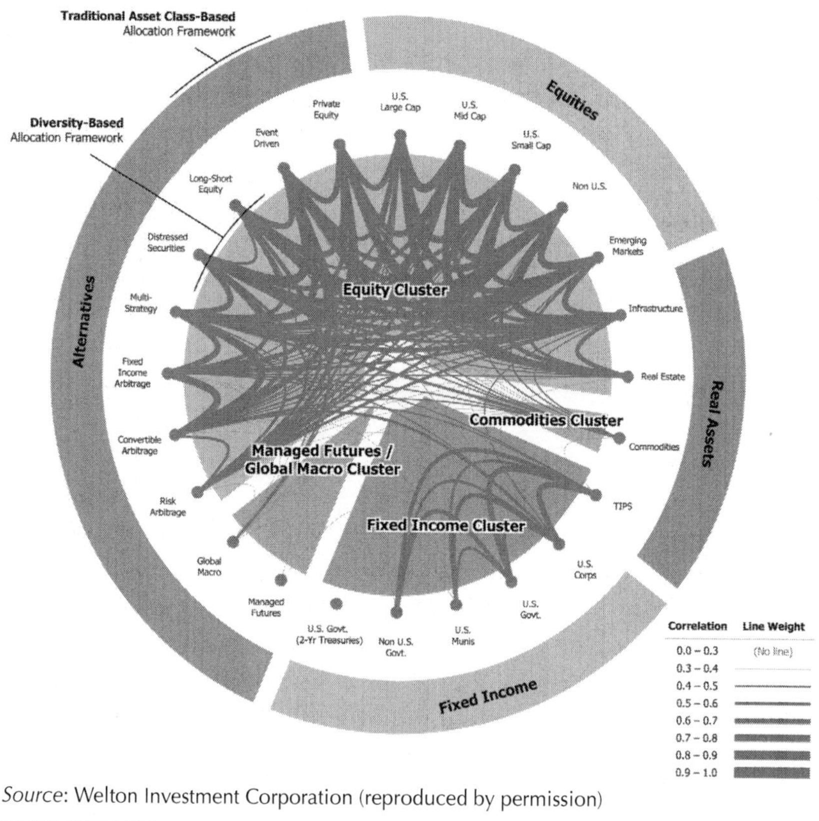

Source: Welton Investment Corporation (reproduced by permission)

two "macro experiences" in the short term – a topic we cover in some detail later in the chapter – over the long run allocations to global macro tend to bring similar benefits to investors irrespective of which index family is used in the analysis.

We now turn to the question of global macro performance in times of stress and dislocation, which is often invoked as one of the most compelling arguments in favour of adding these strategies to the hedge fund mix. Figure 12.4 depicts the cumulative performance of the Dow Jones Credit Suisse Broad Hedge Fund indexes and the MSCI World index during the recent global financial crisis (August 2007–February 2009).[5]

As the equity index halved in value, the majority of hedge funds declined in concert: all but four strategies registered massive double-digit losses, ranging from –14% to –41%. Risk arbitrage was flat, and only three strategies produced meaningful positive returns: dedicated short bias (+24.4%), managed futures (+21.8%) and global macro (+5.3%).[6]

And while the short bias strategy registered the highest return in the crisis, as a long-term allocation in a multi-strategy FoHF portfolio it is prohibitively expensive: from its inception in January 1994 to

Figure 12.4 Cumulative performance by strategy (Aug 2007 – Feb 2009)

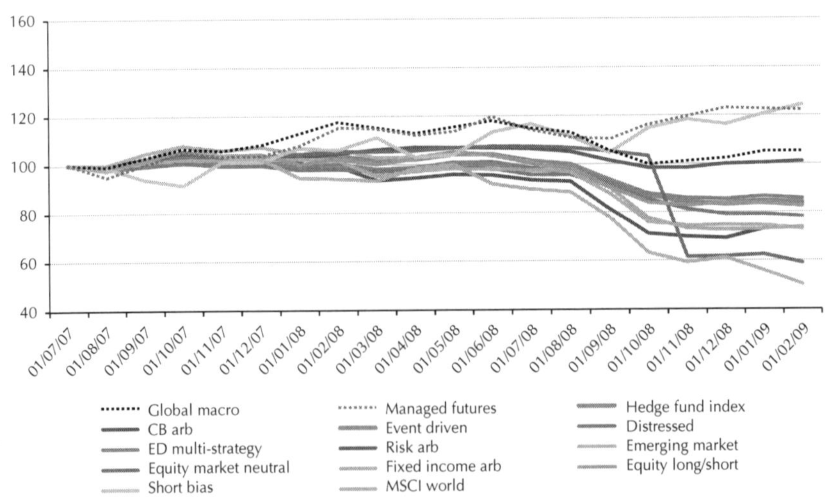

Source: Dow Jones Credit Suisse Hedge Fund Index and MSCI data; calculations by the authors

June 2012 it lost almost 52%. Against this backdrop, systematic and discretionary macro strategies stand out as genuinely unique in their ability to de-correlate and add value in a crisis, while maintaining a positive expected return and earning their keep over the long run.

Such outstanding performance during the global financial crisis was certainly not a fluke. Below we illustrate the superior performance *on average* by global macro strategies during and immediately following financial crises and market dislocations. We adopt the same methodology as used by Credit Suisse analysts in their 2009 white paper, "Global Macro – A Bridge over Troubled Water?" but extend the analysis in three important ways, by:

- including data for the global financial crisis, which was still unfolding when Credit Suisse released their report in the first quarter of 2009;
- including the months when the actual dislocation events happened, as we believe they contain important information on how various hedge fund strategies responded; and
- running the same analysis using HFRX indexes to check the robustness of our conclusions (see Appendix).

We look at the one-year, two-year and three-year annualised returns for all Dow Jones Credit Suisse Broad Hedge Fund indexes and the MSCI World index over eight different crises since 1994, starting from each respective dislocation event:

- February 1994 – bond market rout following the Fed's surprise rate hike;
- December 1994 – Mexican Tequila Crisis following the peso devaluation;
- July 1997 – Asian financial crisis following the Thai baht devaluation;
- August 1998 – Russian default/LTCM blow-up;
- March 2000 – technology bubble collapse;
- September 2001 – terrorist attacks on September 11;
- June 2002 – Fallen angels crisis following accounting frauds and corporate defaults; and
- August 2007 – global financial crisis following the sub-prime debacle in the US.

Figure 12.5 compares the *average* annualised performance over one year, two years and three years after a dislocation event, as registered by global macro, managed futures, the average hedge fund and global equity as proxied by MSCI World.

Discretionary and systematic macro managers tend to significantly outperform both the average hedge fund and the equity market during the first post-crisis year. In subsequent years, discretionary macro continues to outperform by a wide margin, while managed futures underperform other hedge fund strategies. Still, systematic managers comfortably outperform equities in the second and third year.

Table 12.3 drills down to a more granular level of detail, looking at relative performance rankings of global macro and managed futures versus other hedge fund strategies and global equity over the same time horizons. The message is clear and consistent: *on average* both types of macro funds tend to outperform other hedge fund strategies during the first post-dislocation year. In years two and three, however, *on average* it pays to reallocate assets away from trend-following CTA managers to discretionary macro managers. Our conclusions favouring global macro strategies during and immediately following crises and dislocations are broadly supported by the same analysis applied to the HFRX family of hedge fund indexes (see Figures 12.A3–12.A4 and Table 12.A3 in the appendix).

From a FoHF practitioner's perspective, global macro managers not only tend to make money and outperform other hedge fund strategies during crises and dislocations, typically they also represent the most liquid part of a multi-strategy portfolio. As a crisis

Figure 12.5 Average annualised performance through eight crises

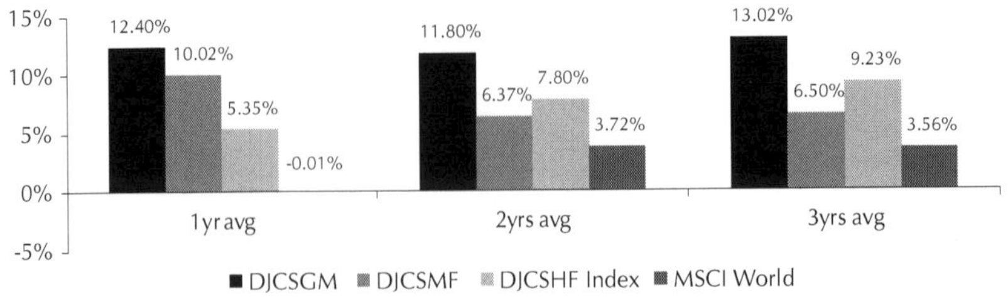

Source: Dow Jones Credit Suisse Hedge Fund Index and MSCI data; calculations by the authors

Table 12.3 Hedge fund strategy and global equity performance through eight crises

Rank	1	2	3	4	5	6	7	8	9	10	11
One-year average performance	Global macro 12.40%	Managed futures 10.02%	Equity market-neutral 9.63%	Event-driven distress 7.01%	L/S equity 6.15%	Event-driven 5.98%	CB arb 5.94%	HF Index 5.35%	Event-driven multi 5.11%	Fixed income arb 4.21%	MSCI W –0.01%
Two-year average performance	Global macro 11.80%	Event-driven distress 10.27%	L/S equity 9.35%	Event-driven 8.49%	CB arb 7.98%	HF Index 7.80%	Event-driven multi 7.43%	Equity Market Neutral 6.64%	Managed futures 6.37%	Fixed income arb 4.39%	MSCI W 3.72%
Three-year average performance	Global macro 13.02%	Event-driven distress 11.60%	Event-driven 10.00%	L/S equity 10.00%	CB arb 9.37%	HF Index 9.23%	Event-driven multi 9.19%	Equity Market Neutral 7.69%	Managed futures 6.50%	Fixed income arb 5.79%	MSCI W 3.56%
Average ranking post-dislocation	Global macro	Event-driven distress	L/S equity	Event-driven	CB arb	Equity market-neutral	HF Index	Managed Futures	Event-driven multi	Fixed income arb	MSCI W

Source: Dow Jones Credit Suisse Hedge Fund Index and MSCI data; calculations by the authors

unfolds and markets collapse, rendering many arbitrage-type hedge funds illiquid, the relative weight and importance of a global macro allocation increases commensurately: as liquidity becomes scarce, profits generated by macro managers can be quickly monetised and reallocated as necessary – for example, to satisfy investor redemptions or to take advantage of opportunities presented by the crisis.

From our experience, a global macro allocation in the context of a multi-strategy FoHF portfolio should be viewed not only in terms of its return-generating capacity, but also as an insurance policy. In times when investors seek protection from extreme left tail risks, it is logical to approach global macro and trend-following CTAs in particular as a tail risk mitigation tool, which has the added benefit of paying for itself in the long run.

PORTFOLIOS OF GLOBAL MACRO FUNDS

Now that we have demonstrated the highly attractive risk–return and diversification properties of global macro in the context of multi-strategy FoHF portfolios, we turn our attention to the challenges of managing single-strategy *portfolios of global macro funds*. We look at sub-strategy allocation, manager selection and risk management.

The most important decision from a top-down perspective is to achieve maximum diversification across different sub-strategies, individual trading styles and approaches, and investment horizons. As we saw in the previous section, historically discretionary managers tend to provide the best long-term returns, while systematic managers offer de-correlation and the best downside protection in times of crises and dislocations, often with a considerable degree of convexity. In line with this experience, it is logical to put a significantly higher strategic weight on discretionary macro relative to systematic macro (in our experience, a ratio of 2-to-1 is a good starting point).

In addition to these two core sub-strategies, FoHF managers often make satellite allocations to specialist funds that can add meaningful diversification while being complementary to global macro (commodities, foreign exchange, volatility, etc). For example, given the increasing prominence of emerging markets in global macro, some FoHF managers may have chosen to include dedicated emerging market fixed income and currency specialists. Similarly, those allocators who at the turn of the century held a strong conviction in long-term commodity price appreciation, and who thought their existing managers were not offering sufficient directional exposure, may have added dedicated commodity managers to the mix. For the larger and better-resourced FoHF managers, the level of granularity was often even more precise, as they shifted from generalist commodity traders to specialists focusing on particular sectors (oil and gas, metals, agriculture, etc). The increased level of granularity put a premium on the FoHF manager's ability to analyse and tactically shift exposure across different sub-strategies and market sectors.

Diversification is important not only *across*, but also *within* sub-strategies: allocators need to be able to mix different trading styles and investment horizons in their sub-portfolios. For example, with discretionary macro, one should include both long-term thematic managers and short-term tactical traders. Similarly, with systematic macro, one should be able to cover the whole spectrum of styles and horizons – long-term trend followers, short-term trend followers and non-trend funds.

There are two reasons why it is beneficial to achieve maximum diversification. First, and self-evidently, it makes for the most efficient portfolio with robust long-term returns. Second, for FoHF managers with good tactical positioning and timing skills, it provides the maximum breadth of opportunities to add value. Let us consider how a skilful allocator might have added value during and immediately after the global financial crisis of 2007–09.

A good macro fund-of-funds manager would always "listen to the market": investing with some of the most talented and experienced macro traders provides them with unique access to the most up-to-date information flow and cutting-edge analysis. By late 2006 and early 2007, many macro managers were beginning to get cautious, if not downright uneasy, about the multiple bubbles and imbalances that had been building up in the system. Taking their cue from these traders, a good macro fund-of-funds manager would have started to gradually reposition their portfolio in anticipation of a major correction or dislocation: putting a stronger emphasis on systematic managers and especially trend followers; lowering exposure to directional commodity specialists who tend to be net long; shifting towards volatility funds with net long exposure and/or tail risk protection at the expense of relative value volatility specialists.

Above all, this fund of funds manager would have reviewed the liquidity profiles of the underlying funds, with a particular focus on those discretionary managers who during the good years may have exhibited some "style drift" towards the multi-strategy format or private equity-type investments.

After capitalising on multiple re-pricings in various asset markets during the global financial crisis, and seeing the recovery gain momentum in 2009, our FoHF manager would have reversed some of these shifts: moving back to the long-term 2-to-1 ratio between discretionary and systematic; adding some net long commodity exposure; rebalancing back to volatility specialists who are best positioned to capture relative value opportunities. Not all of these tactical shifts would have necessarily worked out: as discussed in more detail later in the chapter, the unique post-crisis macroeconomic and policy environment confounded many a macro specialist. But the breadth of sub-strategies and styles that comes with maximum diversification may have helped a macro fund-of-funds manager learn and adjust "on the fly." For example, in the discretionary sub-allocation, being able to tactically shift assets from long-term thematic traders to short-term tactical traders could have made a big difference in 2012 by allowing the fund to capture, among other things, the move in 10-year US Treasury yields from 1.8% to 2.4% and then all the way back down and lower. Similarly, being able to tactically shift assets from long-term to short-term trend followers, as well as to non-trend-following systematic programmes, would have helped in the choppy "risk-on/risk-off" environment of 2011 and 2012.

Tactical portfolio positioning is as much an art as a science. The same can be said of manager selection and risk management. While there are many rules and principles that are absolutely critical to successfully researching, selecting and monitoring individual managers, they apply as much to global macro as they do to any other hedge fund strategy.[7] Since our focus here is exclusively on global macro, we limit our discussion to the issues and challenges that, in our view, are particularly relevant to these strategies.

A global macro fund-of-funds analyst has to deal with a very broad universe of managers. In June 2012, according to estimates from *Hedge Fund Research (HFR)*, out of the total hedge fund universe of approximately 7,700 funds and US$2,100 billion of assets, global macro strategies – very broadly defined – accounted for approximately 1,800 funds and US$460 billion of assets. This encompasses all types of macro strategies as defined by *HFR*, including discretionary thematic, systematic diversified, multi-strategy, currency, commodities and active trading funds.[8] Alternatively, using the Dow Jones Credit Suisse universe of global macro and managed futures funds, which strives to represent at least 40% of the total, as of December 2011 there were approximately 240 distinct strategies in both categories, collectively managing just under US$227 billion in assets.[9] Whichever way one looks at it, the universe is large and complex, and it requires the FoHF analyst to apply some preliminary quantitative screens and a healthy dose of common sense to narrow it down to a manageable initial shortlist.

Inevitably, there are both "push" and "pull" elements in building up the shortlist: some funds will be "pulled" by the analyst as a result of screening the universe, while other funds will be "pushed" to their attention by industry contacts, service providers and placement agents. The analyst must have a healthy dose of scepticism to be able to see through the hype: after the global financial crisis, many managers want to get on the bandwagon and position their funds as having at least some elements of global macro.

Once the initial shortlist is ready, the analyst will then proceed to apply more elaborate quantitative screens and sophisticated analytical techniques to narrow it down further to those managers who will be contacted for further information. When the analyst is finally ready to visit them for face-to-face interviews, they will need to prepare a comprehensive set of questions that are directly relevant to the specific type of global macro strategy – discretionary or systematic – that is the specialty of each individual manager on the list.

At this stage, the analyst would do well to consult a very useful and authoritative resource produced in 2006 by the Education Committee of the Greenwich Roundtable, entitled "Best Practices in Hedge Fund Investing: Due Diligence for Global Macro and Managed Futures Strategies." This document provides a helpful template for asking – in a rigorous and comprehensive way – probing and insightful questions of global macro managers about: their strategies and investment process; team and organisation; fee structure and terms; risk management; fund structure and asset base; operations and transparency; third parties; and other matters. The interested reader will find many useful insights in this document, which is geared specifically towards global macro.

In this chapter, we focus on just three aspects of macro strategies that we believe deserve a closer examination. The first is *style drift*. With most hedge fund strategies, evidence of style drift would be viewed as a major early warning sign: if a US equity long/short manager or a European event-driven manager were to start dabbling in Asian currencies, soft commodities or variance swaps, alarm bells would go off. But with macro managers, style drift of this nature is to a large extent built into the strategy: their mandate typically gives them the freedom and flexibility to trade across different geographies, asset classes and financial instruments.

However, this does not mean that the question of style drift in global macro is an open and shut case. There are at least three relevant scenarios that present potential problems. First, there is a risk of *competence drift*: while it is perfectly acceptable for a macro fund to move into different areas, it must have the requisite expertise and infrastructure to trade the markets and instruments in question. For example, when a discretionary macro manager specialising in directional trading in G10 markets decides to expand into emerging markets, commodities or volatility trading, the FoHF analyst must be prepared to probe the manager's competence in these areas. Similarly, when a trend-following systematic manager decides to expand into short-term non-trend models or volatility trading models, the same questions must be asked.

Another potential problem has to do with *liquidity drift*. The whole point of global macro strategies is that they are nimble traders who can turn on a sixpence once market conditions change. If the FoHF analyst notices that a macro fund increasingly gets involved in the more esoteric and illiquid markets, "red flags" must be raised and hard questions asked of the manager. Finally, with systematic managers, there is another potentially dangerous drift, which involves discretionary overrides of the underlying quantitative models. While there will be times when such human intervention is justified, once it becomes less of an exception and more of the rule, the rationale for keeping the fund in the portfolio must be revisited.

The second aspect of manager selection and risk management in global macro that bears highlighting is the special challenge posed by *manager correlations*. It is a well-known fact that systematic managers tend to have more correlated returns among each other than discretionary managers. What is perhaps less well understood is that, statistically speaking, to differentiate between the performance of two different managers with a high degree of confidence it takes a much larger statistical sample when correlations are low. In other words, given the particularly heterogeneous nature of discretionary macro managers, it would normally take a much longer history of returns to reach the same level of confidence in their performance numbers as with the more highly correlated systematic managers. By being aware of this particular limitation of statistical analysis, a macro fund-of-funds analyst may wish to put more emphasis on the qualitative review of a discretionary manager with a relatively short track record.

The third challenge facing a macro fund-of-funds analyst worth highlighting has to do with the observation that global macro is probably the most difficult hedge fund strategy to analyse and explain using common risk factors. Unlike long/short equity and various arbitrage-type strategies, only a small part of the variation of global macro returns can be explained by risk factors – such as equity beta, duration, credit, style, size, momentum and carry. This remains true even after one applies sophisticated statistical methods to account for the time-varying nature of the risk-factor exposures taken on by macro funds. This presents our fund-of-funds analyst with a problem: how can they know for sure that the positive returns generated by a macro manager above and beyond the time-varying risk-factor exposures represent genuine and repeatable alpha?

As can be seen from just this brief discussion alone, the job of a global macro fund-of-funds analyst is enormously challenging and complex. It requires a uniquely broad skill set, which includes not just a thorough understanding of macroeconomics, capital markets, portfolio and risk management, and fundamental and technical analyses, but also elements of political science, financial history, sociology and behavioural psychology. To the extent that the analyst covers not only discretionary, but also systematic managers, a thorough grounding in a broad range of quantitative methods and disciplines is mandatory. On top of that, the analyst must be sufficiently personable, sociable and erudite to be able to develop strong personal networks with global macro practitioners and to cultivate relationships of trust that can be so vital to accessing timely market intelligence.

THE FALLACY OF A "TYPICAL" MACRO INVESTOR EXPERIENCE

We will now address some criticisms of global macro that appeared in a number of business and financial media reports in the years immediately following the global financial crisis of 2007–09. Specifically, there were suggestions that global macro managers *as a group* were struggling to perform, as they found themselves in an unfamiliar trading environment that was extremely difficult to navigate. Many reporters were backing their stories with anecdotal evidence and recent performance numbers for some of the largest and long-established funds in the macro space; others were pointing to the dismal performance of the HFRX Macro/CTA Index – one of the more popular and widely used benchmarks in the industry.[10]

It is true that, after the crisis, global macro managers have been navigating through unchartered territory: massive and persistent deleveraging by the private sector in the developed economies; zero lower bound and unorthodox monetary policies; government intervention and regulatory expansion on an unprecedented scale; acute sovereign debt and banking problems in the eurozone, to name just some of the bigger and newer challenges. It is also true that some of the mega-stars of the industry have failed to impress in terms of performance. And it is most certainly true that during the period in question the HFRX Macro/CTA Index dropped like a stone: it lost money every calendar year from January 2009 to December 2011, and continued to lose money during the first six months of 2012, resulting in a cumulative loss of 16.3%.

If, looking at this evidence alone, investors were to conclude that global macro did not fit in their portfolios and that they would be better off avoiding it altogether, it would be totally understandable – and totally wrong! Thankfully, an increasing number of institutional investors decided to look beyond these negative media reports and the performance of a single index, choosing to do their homework, dig deeper and develop a more nuanced and multi-dimensional view of the industry. They were not just expressing more interest and initiating more searches for global macro mandates,[11] they were actually allocating new money – and they were doing so in size.[12]

Why would institutional investors be so keen to increase their global macro exposure in the face of an extremely challenging macroeconomic environment and the widely publicised mediocre performance at some of the larger and better-known funds? The answer, in our view, has to do mainly with the fact that they were looking beyond the recent short-term performance to evaluate the long-term potential of global macro to add value to their portfolios in terms of returns, risk and diversification – which (as we saw earlier) is formidable. But there may also be another reason: lacklustre returns at some funds and negative short-term performance of the HFRX Macro/CTA Index may not necessarily be representative of a "typical" investor experience with global macro during the post-crisis years.

Figure 12.6 contrasts and compares the performance of the HFRX Macro/CTA Index against another popular and widely followed benchmark – the Dow Jones Credit Suisse Global Macro Broad Hedge Fund Index – from January 2009 until June 2012. The difference could not be starker: while the former index lost more than 16%, the latter had a cumulative gain of almost 35%.

Looking at Figure 12.6, the more perceptive reader will point out – correctly – that it may not be an entirely fair comparison: the HFRX index includes a sizable allocation to trend-following CTA programmes, which had a much more difficult time during this period, while the Dow Jones Credit Suisse index consists primarily of

Figure 12.6 HFRX Macro/CTA versus DJCS Global Macro (Jan 2009 – Jun 2012)

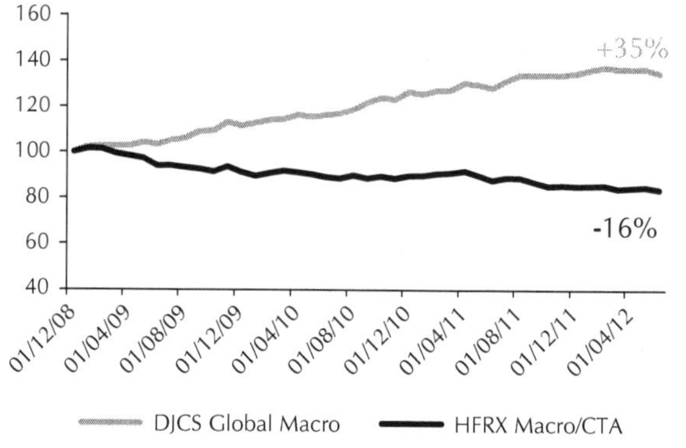

Source: Dow Jones Credit Suisse Hedge Fund Index and HFR data; calculations by the authors

discretionary macro managers. To correct for this mismatch and put the two indexes on a more equal footing, we create a synthetic benchmark comprising 50% Dow Jones Credit Suisse Global Macro Index and 50% Dow Jones Credit Suisse Managed Futures Index, the latter consisting predominantly of CTAs and systematic managers.

While Figure 12.7 offers a more balanced comparison in terms of index composition, it is still a tale of two diametrically opposite global macro experiences: at the end of June 2012, an investor in one index would have been up 16% since the crisis, while an investor in the other index would have been down 16%. It would be entirely understandable if their views of global macro resulting from these experiences would be radically different.

At first glance, it is baffling how two indexes purporting to represent the same segment of the hedge fund industry can be so divergent in their dynamics and outcomes. But there are at least three reasons that can help explain such divergences among hedge fund indexes.

First, different hedge fund managers may report performance to different indexes, and some may report to none at all. Given how heterogeneous global macro strategies are, the smaller the overlap in manager coverage, the larger the potential divergence. Second, different index providers often have different index construction methodologies. One of the more obvious sources of potential

Figure 12.7 HFRX Macro/CTA versus Synthetic DJCS 50/50 Index (Jan 2009 – Jun 2012)

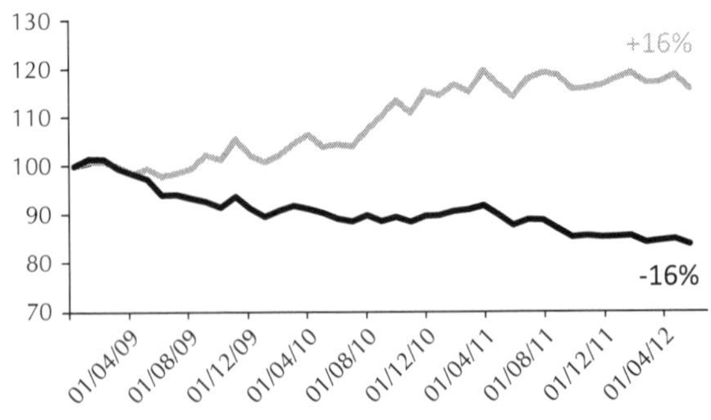

Source: Dow Jones Credit Suisse Hedge Fund Index and HFR data; calculations by the authors

divergence is the weighting scheme: some indexes weight managers based on their asset size, others go for equal weighting, yet a third group might apply a proprietary *representative optimisation* technique.

Finally, there is always a trade-off between investability and representation. An index that strives to be as representative of a hedge fund sector as possible will necessarily opt for the maximum number of funds, irrespective of their underlying capacity and whether they are open or closed to new investments. In contrast, an index designed to serve as the basis for investable products by definition must focus only on those funds that are open and that have sufficient capacity for new money.

The comparison between the two global macro indexes presented above is not meant to suggest that one is necessarily better than the other; rather, the point is that because these two indexes are effectively two very different representations of an investor's global macro "experience," they should be referenced and used in the appropriate context. If, for various regulatory, institutional or perceived reputational reasons an investor cannot access the underlying hedge funds either through a FoHF or directly, and has therefore no other choice but to go for an investable index like HFRX, any appeals or references to a non-investable index become a moot point. If, on the other hand, such access to the underlying hedge funds through a FoHF or directly *is* available, then using a more representative hedge fund index, even if it is non-investable, may be both more appropriate and illuminating.

Two more points are worth mentioning with respect to measuring and evaluating the performance of a global macro allocation against a benchmark. First, it is important to compare like-to-like: if the macro allocation guidelines call for a minimum of, say, 30% invested in CTAs and other systematic strategies, it would be inappropriate to use an index comprising only discretionary managers. A customised index consisting of 70% discretionary and 30% systematic would be more appropriate in this case.

Second, it is important to bear in mind that hedge fund indexes suffer from well-documented biases (backfill bias, survivorship bias, etc) that flatter index performance numbers. Neither FoHFs nor internally run hedge fund allocation teams have the same luxury – all of their mistakes and failures are fully reflected in their past performance. Also, while index performance data is net of fees charged by the underlying hedge fund managers, it does not take into account any fees or costs involved in actually running a hedge fund allocation, be it in the form of FoHF fees or costs associated with setting up and operating an in-house hedge fund investment capability.

When institutional investors consider the role and place of global macro strategies in their portfolios, they need to choose their global macro reference index carefully. It must be appropriate given their objectives, constraints and other specific circumstances, it must be representative and meaningful in terms of composition and its performance must be adjusted for biases and extra costs.

GLOBAL MACRO AND THE FUTURE OF THE FOHF INDUSTRY

Since the global financial crisis of 2007–09, the FoHF industry has been going through a painful, yet necessary and healthy process of consolidation and change. Many of the less experienced "me too" players who jumped on the bandwagon during the halcyon pre-crisis days were simply not of the appropriate quality and calibre. Charging a rich second layer of fees for the sole benefit of providing access to the underlying managers and constructing portfolios using backward-looking, off-the-shelf statistical packages was not a viable business model. Investing with fraudulent managers was a clear failure of due diligence and risk management. Liquidity mismatches between the underlying positions and what was promised to investors was another type of failure that came to light during the crisis.

As a result, many of the smaller players have been shaken out or absorbed by larger organisations; the bar has been raised dramatically and permanently in terms of critical mass and institutional-quality infrastructure and analytics. The largest and most dynamic players in the industry are in the process of reinventing themselves, developing and expanding their capabilities in managed accounts, customised solutions and institutional advisory. In this context, FoHF organisations with solid global macro skills and capabilities have an additional advantage: they can engage with large institutional investors on multiple levels – not just on the level of their alternative allocations and risk budgets, but also on the top-down, strategic and tactical asset allocation level.

Of all hedge fund strategies, global macro is unique in that its macroeconomic insights and risk-taking decisions have much in common with institutional practices of global tactical asset allocation and portfolio-wide risk management. The analytical frameworks and approach to risk by global macro funds can be meaningfully translated and incorporated in an institutional setting. Those FoHF players who have strong global macro franchises and capabilities, and who understand how to leverage them to up their institutional game, will be in a position to reinvent themselves into trusted advisers and partners to the chief investment officers and asset allocation committees of large institutional investors.

APPENDIX – HFRX INDEX-BASED ANALYSIS

FIGURE 12.A1

Figure 12.A1 covers the period since inception of HFRX indexes from January 1998 to June 2012. The Macro/CTA index was consistently

Figure 12.A1 Cumulative performance by strategy (Jan 1998 – Jun 2012)

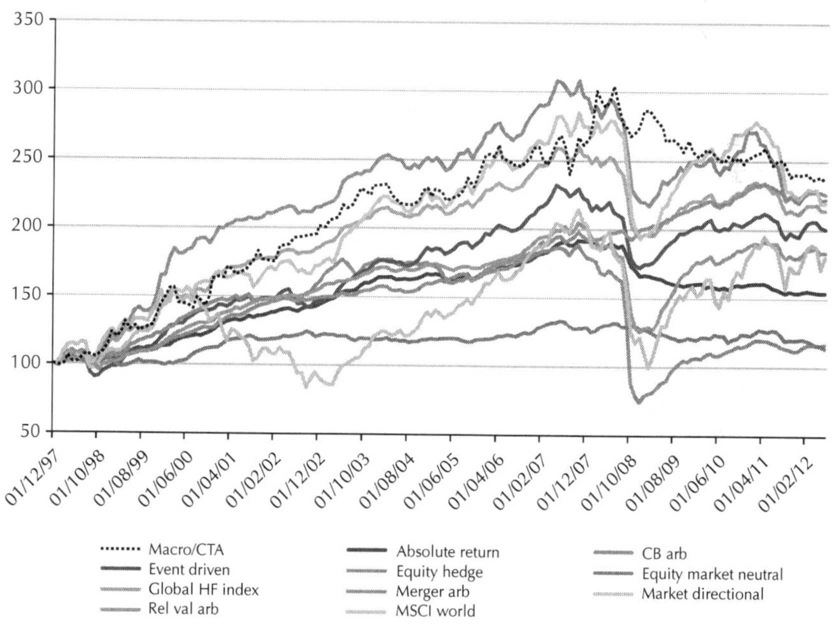

Source: HFR and MSCI data; calculations by the authors

Table 12.A1 Summary performance statistics by strategy (Jan 1998 – Jun 2012)

	Macro/CTA	Abs return	CB arb	Event-driven	Equity hedge
Cumulative returns	135.7%	54.3%	16.6%	100.7%	122.2%
Annualised returns	6.3%	3.1%	1.9%	5.1%	5.9%
Annualised volatility	8.9%	3.7%	11.9%	6.9%	8.7%
Sharpe ratio (2.61%)	0.42	0.12	–0.06	0.36	0.38
Skew	0.32	–1.20	–6.85	–1.45	–0.34
Kurtosis	1.11	3.19	63.87	4.56	3.07
Equity correlation	0.18	0.42	0.45	0.71	0.70

	Eq mrkt-neut	Global HF Index	Merger arb	Mrkt direct	Rel val arb	MSCI World
Cumulative returns	13.9%	114.0%	126.0%	119.3%	83.4%	80.3%
Annualised returns	1.0%	5.5%	5.7%	5.9%	4.5%	5.5%
Annualised volatility	4.1%	6.7%	3.7%	9.4%	7.3%	16.9%
Sharpe ratio (2.61%)	–0.40	0.43	0.84	0.35	0.25	0.17
Skew	–0.34	–0.66	–1.14	–1.34	–2.75	–0.68
Kurtosis	0.44	4.76	3.23	4.88	15.82	1.13
Equity correlation	0.02	0.62	0.46	0.73	0.53	1.00

Source: HFR and MSCI data; calculations by the authors

Table 12.A2 Strategy rankings by performance statistics (Jan 1998 – Jun 2012)

Sharpe ranking		**Skewness ranking**		**Kurtosis ranking**		**Equity correlation ranking**	
Merger arb	0.84	Macro/CTA	0.32	Equity market-neutral	0.44	Equity market-neutral	0.02
Global HF Index	0.43	Equity hedge	–0.34	Macro/CTA	1.11	Macro/CTA	0.18
Macro/CTA	0.42	Equity market-neutral	–0.34	MSCI World	1.13	Absolute return	0.42
Equity hedge	0.38	Global HF index	–0.66	Equity hedge	3.07	CB arb	0.45
Event-driven	0.36	MSCI World	–0.68	Absolute return	3.19	Merger arb	0.46
Market directional	0.35	Merger arb	–1.14	Merger arb	3.23	Rel val arb	0.53
Rel val arb	0.25	Absolute return	–1.20	Event-driven	4.56	Global HF Index	0.62
MSCI World	0.17	Market directional	–1.34	Global HF Index	4.76	Equity hedge	0.70
Absolute return	0.12	Event-driven	–1.45	Market directional	4.88	Event-driven	0.71
CB arb	–0.06	Rel val arb	–2.75	Rel val arb	15.82	Market directional	0.73
Equity market-neutral	–0.40	CB arb	–6.85	CB arb	63.87	MSCI World	1.00

Source: HFR and MSCI data; calculations by the authors

among the top performing hedge fund strategies throughout this period, producing the best cumulative performance (as of June 2012).

The HFRX Macro/CTA Index was among the top three performers in terms of the Sharpe ratio; it also exhibited highly desirable characteristics in its higher moments (ie, skewness and kurtosis), as well as its low correlation to equities.

FIGURE 12.A2

We run the same analysis on HFRX indexes as we did on Dow Jones Credit Suisse indexes for Figure 12.2 in the main body of the chapter; to illustrate the long-term benefits of discretionary and systematic macro strategies, we plot annualised returns since inception for all hedge fund strategies against their long-term correlation to global equities. The more a strategy plots in the "north-western" direction, the more desirable it would be for an equity-heavy institutional portfolio.

Figure 12.A2 Annualised returns versus correlation to equity (Jan 1998 – Jun 2012)

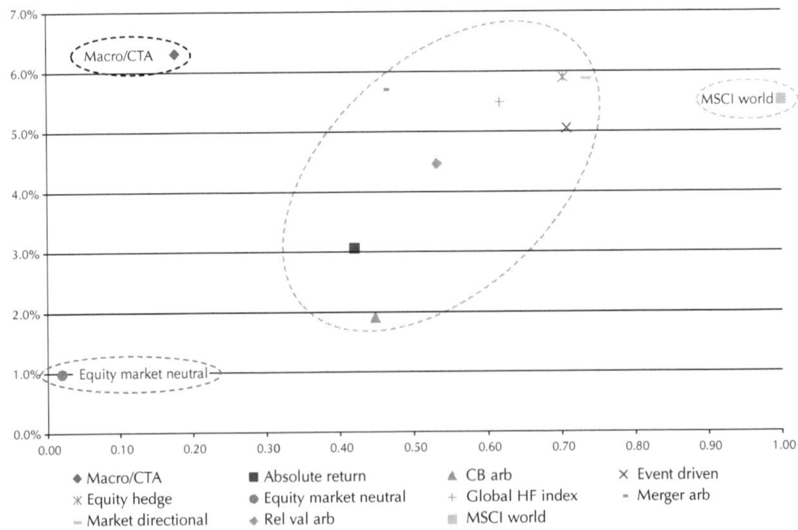

Source: HFR and MSCI data; calculations by the authors

FIGURE 12.A3

Figure 12.A3 covers the period of the global financial crisis from August 2007 to February 2009; in addition to the HFRX indexes used in the previous analysis, we include data series for the HFRX Systematic Diversified CTA Index, which was launched in 2005. This index demonstrates the highly desirable quality of systematic macro and CTA strategies in times of major crises and dislocations, namely their high degree of convexity: as equities and other risk assets decline, the outperformance of the index accelerates. Only three strategies produced positive absolute returns during this period: the Systematic Diversified CTA Index (+41.2%), the Macro/CTA Index (+10.0%) and merger arbitrage (+5.7%).

FIGURE 12.A4

Figure 12.A4 compares the *average* annualised performance over one year, two years and three years after a dislocation event, as registered by the HFRX Macro/CTA Index versus the average hedge fund and global equities, as proxied by the HFRX Global Hedge Fund Index and the MSCI World index, respectively. Given that the HFRX

Figure 12.A3 Cumulative performance by strategy (Aug 2007 – Feb 2009)

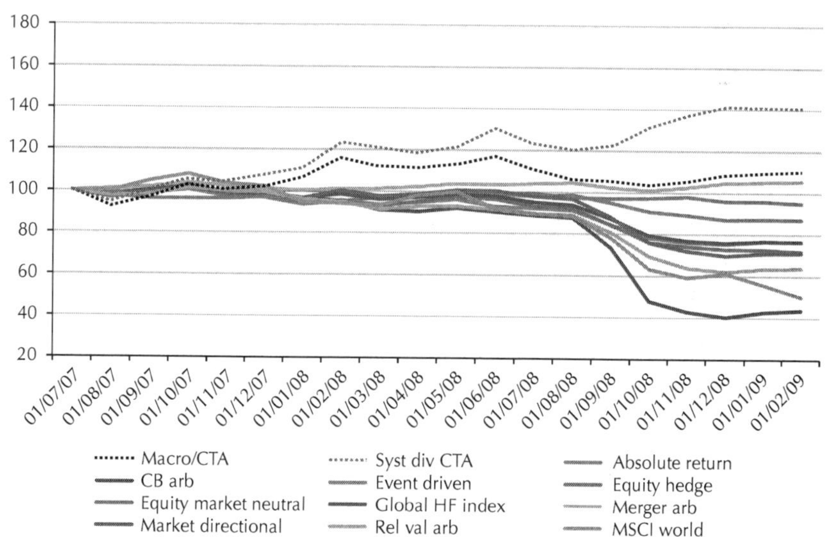

Source: HFR and MSCI data; calculations by the authors

Table 12.A3 Hedge fund strategy and global equity performance through five crises

Rank	**1**	**2**	**3**	**4**	**5**	**6**	**7**	**8**	**9**
One-year average performance	Macro/CTA 11.35%	Equity hedge 9.69%	HFRX global HF 7.23%	Equally weighted 6.22%	Distressed 6.11%	Conv. arbitrage 5.65%	Event-driven 3.71%	Equity market-neutral 3.28%	MSCI W –7.27%
Two-year average performance	Equity hedge 8.73%	Macro/CTA 8.47%	HFRX Global HF 6.29%	Event-driven 5.44%	Equally weighted 5.14%	Distressed 4.51%	Conv. arbitrage 1.52%	Equity market-neutral 0.84%	MSCI W –2.79%
Three-year average performance	Macro/CTA 7.39%	Equity hedge 6.73%	HFRX Global HF 6.07%	Distressed 5.81%	Equally weighted 5.25%	Event-driven 5.14%	Conv. arbitrage 3.07%	Equity market-neutral 1.61%	MSCI W –3.47%
Average ranking post-dislocation	Macro/CTA	Equity hedge	HFRX Global HF	Equally weighted	Event-driven	Distressed	Conv. arbitrage	Equity market-neutral	MSCI W

Source: HFR and MSCI data; calculations by the authors

Figure 12.A4 Average annualised performance through five crises

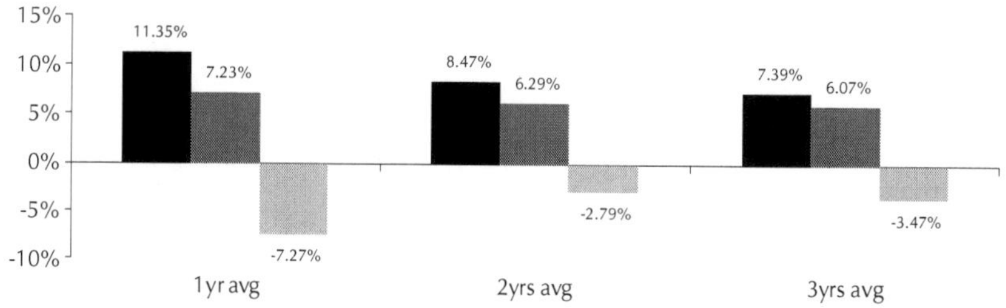

Source: HFR and MSCI data; calculations by the authors

indexes were launched in 1998, we are averaging annualised performance over five financial crises.

Table 12.A3 drills down to a more granular level of detail, looking at relative performance rankings of the HFRX Macro/CTA Index versus other hedge fund strategies and global equity over the same time horizons. The message is clear and consistent: *on average* macro funds tend to outperform other hedge fund strategies and global equity over one, two and three years post-dislocation.

The authors would like to acknowledge their colleagues Tommaso Ammendola and Lelia Wells for their support in researching and producing this chapter, and to thank the prime services and index teams at Credit Suisse for their help with the index data.

1 According to *HFR* estimates, in Q4 1990, macro strategies accounted for 39.3% of assets under management in the hedge fund industry. Based on Dow Jones Credit Suisse estimates, global macro accounted for 64.4% of the hedge fund universe in January 1994.

2 According to *HFR* estimates, at the end of 2007 macro strategies accounted for 15.4% of industry total. Based on Dow Jones Credit Suisse estimates, global macro registered its lowest point at 9.8% of industry total in April 2007 (note that managed futures accounted for 4.5% of industry total at the time; their lowest point was in March 1998, at 1.8% of hedge fund assets).

3 In calculating Sharpe ratios, we use the risk-free rate of 3.12%, which was the average annualised return on three-month US Treasury bills during the period in question.

4 There may be a data issue with the Dow Jones Credit Suisse Equity Market Neutral index, which recorded a huge loss of –40.5% in November 2008. This contrasts dramatically with all other indexes for the same strategy (eg, HFRX Equity Market Neutral index recorded a gain of 0.7% during the same month). This huge outlier has a significant impact on all our calculations for this strategy; we recalculate some of the statistics by assuming a return of 0% for that month and include the resulting information in our comments.

5 We acknowledge that different analysts may use different starting points for the financial crisis; we follow experienced global macro practitioners (eg, George Soros, Colm O'Shea) in dating the start of the crisis from August 2007, when the interbank funding market broke

down and central banks were forced to start intervening on a massive scale (see Soros, 2009, and Schwager, 2012). August 2007 was also the month when widespread deleveraging started spilling over to other asset classes (eg, quantitative equity funds).

6 When we correct for the November 2008 data outlier in the Equity Market Neutral index series, the latter registers a slightly negative cumulative return of –1%, ranking fifth after risk arbitrage.

7 For a comprehensive review of Permal's approach to manager research and selection, see Kodmani (2003).

8 Source: HFR, 2012, "Global Hedge Fund Industry Report," second quarter.

9 Source: e-mail exchange between the authors and the Credit Suisse index team (August 16, 2012).

10 For a representative sample of media reports, see the following links:
www.ft.com/cms/s/3/c234129c-5912-11de-80b3-00144feabdc0.html#axzz251rGyb5G;
www.ft.com/cms/s/0/f0a24fc0-404a-11df-8d23-00144feabdc0.html#axzz251rGyb5G;
www.ft.com/cms/s/0/ce04410c-a978-11df-a6f2-00144feabdc0.html#axzz251rGyb5G;
www.economist.com/node/17909807;
www.ft.com/cms/s/0/a18263e0-9c0f-11e0-bef9-00144feabdc0.html#axzz251rGyb5G;
online.wsj.com/article/SB10001424052970204555904577168973485319422.html;
www.ft.com/cms/s/0/1666ba56-e180-11e1-9c72-00144feab49a.html#axzz251rGyb5G.

11 In early 2012, a Credit Suisse report on hedge fund investor sentiment showed that out of 33 strategies investors were most keen on global macro (45% net demand) and CTA/managed futures (37% net demand). In December 2011, a Barclays Capital report showed that out of eight hedge fund strategies, macro was the only one that registered a growing investor preference across *all* investor types (ie, public and private pensions, endowments and foundations, insurance companies, private banks, family offices and FoHFs).

12 According to *HFR*, between Q4 2007 and Q3 2011, assets in macro strategies rose from 15% to 22% of industry total, while equity hedge fund strategies declined from 37% to 27% during the same period.

REFERENCES

Barclays Capital, 2011, "The Money Trail," Prime Services, December.

Credit Suisse Capital Services, 2012, "Mid-Year Survey of Hedge Fund Investor Sentiment," July.

Credit Suisse Liquid Alternatives, 2009, "Global Macro – A Bridge over Troubled Water?" Alpha Strategies white paper, Q1.

The Economist, 2011, "Macrobatics: To Make Money, Macro Hedge Funds Must Be Nimble," January 13.

Education Committee Report, 2006, "Best Practices in Hedge Fund Investing: Due Diligence for Global Macro and Managed Futures Strategies," Greenwich Roundtable, winter.

HFR, 2012, "Global Hedge Fund Industry Report," second quarter.

Jones, S., 2010, "Funds Left Struggling for Gains amid Volatility," *Financial Times*, August 16.

Jones, S., 2010, "Macro Funds Miss Out On Crisis," *Financial Times*, April 5.

Jones, S., 2011, "Big Name Hedge Funds Braced for a Rough Ride," *Financial Times*, June 21.

Jones, S. and D. McCrum, 2012, "Moore Capital Echoes Macro Funds' Woes," *Financial Times*, August 22.

Kodmani, O., 2003, "Manager Selection," in S. Jaffer (ed), *Funds of Hedge Funds* (London, England: Euromoney Books).

Lex Column, 2009, "Macro Hedge Funds," *Financial Times*, June 15.

Schwager, J. D., 2012, *Hedge Fund Market Wizards: How Winning Traders Win* (Hoboken, NJ: Wiley).

Shah, N., 2012, "Macro Hedge Funds Lose More Than 10% in 2011," *Wall Street Journal*, January 18.

Soros, G., 2009, *The Crash of 2008 and What It Means: The New Paradigm for Financial Markets* (Oxford, England: PublicAffairs).

Welton Investment Corporation, 2011, "Diversification: Often Discussed, but Frequently Misunderstood," January.

13

The Case for Global Macro in Institutional Portfolios

Arjan Berkelaar

KIMC U.S. Inc

Global macro strategies attempt to generate returns by investing globally in equity, interest rate, commodity and currency markets. These strategies often employ leverage and typically use futures and currency forward contracts, as well as options on futures contracts to implement bets. Global macro is typically classified as either discretionary (ie, managers use subjective judgement in assessing market conditions) or systematic (ie, managers use a quantitative or rule-based approach to investing). A subset of systematic global macro strategies are commodity trading advisors (CTAs), sometimes also called *managed futures*. CTAs tend to be trend-following or momentum traders and typically use very little discretion, instead relying on computer programmes to follow price trends. This chapter will analyse both discretionary global macro and managed futures strategies from the perspective of a long-term institutional investor, such as an endowment or a foundation.

Traditionally, such investors have allocated only a small portion of their overall portfolio or their hedge fund portfolio to global macro strategies, choosing instead to allocate the majority of their hedge fund portfolios to long/short equity hedge funds. However, this trend has gradually changed, and many investors are shifting their hedge fund portfolios towards global macro managers. According to Hedge Fund Research, assets in equity hedge fund strategies fell from 37% to 27% of the industry total between the end of 2007 and the end of the third quarter of 2011. Over the same period, assets in macro strategies rose from 15% to 22% of the industry total.

Part of the appeal of global macro, and in particular managed futures or CTAs, is that their returns were less correlated to equity markets and other hedge fund strategies during the 2008 global financial crisis. Some investors even go so far as to allocate to CTAs as a form of tail-risk insurance. An additional attraction is that global macro hedge funds tend to be quite liquid, unlike many other hedge fund strategies.

This chapter is organised as follows. In the next section, we consider the historical track record of global macro, before looking at how global macro strategies fit into an overall asset allocation. This is followed by a discussion of the fit of global macro as part of a hedge fund portfolio. We then investigate whether global macro strategies have tail hedging properties, and examine the risk factor exposures of different hedge fund strategies.

HISTORICAL PERFORMANCE OF GLOBAL MACRO STRATEGIES

We will first review the historical track record of global macro strategies relative to other asset classes and hedge fund strategies. The two most commonly used sets of indexes that track the performance of the hedge fund industry are the HFRI indexes and the Dow Jones Credit Suisse indexes. In this chapter, we use the Dow Jones Credit Suisse (DJCS) hedge fund indexes. They are weighted based on each manager's assets under management, while the HFRI indexes are typically equally weighted. Our conclusions would be broadly similar, however, if we were to use the HFRI indexes instead.

Figure 13.1 shows the performance of different asset classes over the period December 1993 to April 2012. The performance of global macro clearly stands out. It should be noted that hedge fund indexes are typically biased due to survivorship and backfill biases, but even if we were to account for these, the performance of global macro is still quite remarkable. Managed futures or CTAs also had a decent performance over this period, and were on par with the performance of equities, fixed income and commodities.

Figure 13.2 shows the performance of four different hedge fund strategies over the period December 1993 to April 2012. Again, global macro clearly comes out ahead, while managed futures or CTAs lagged behind, albeit with a lower level of volatility.

Figure 13.1 Performance of different asset classes (December 1993–April 2012)[1]

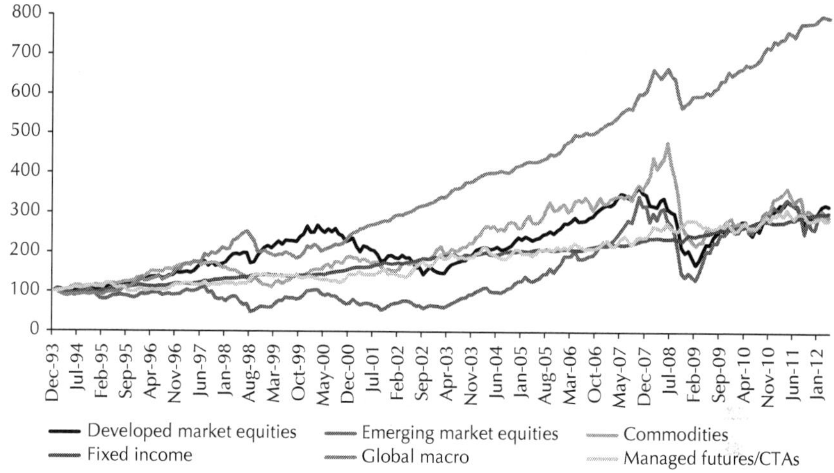

Figure 13.2 Performance of different hedge fund strategies (December 1993–April 2012)[2]

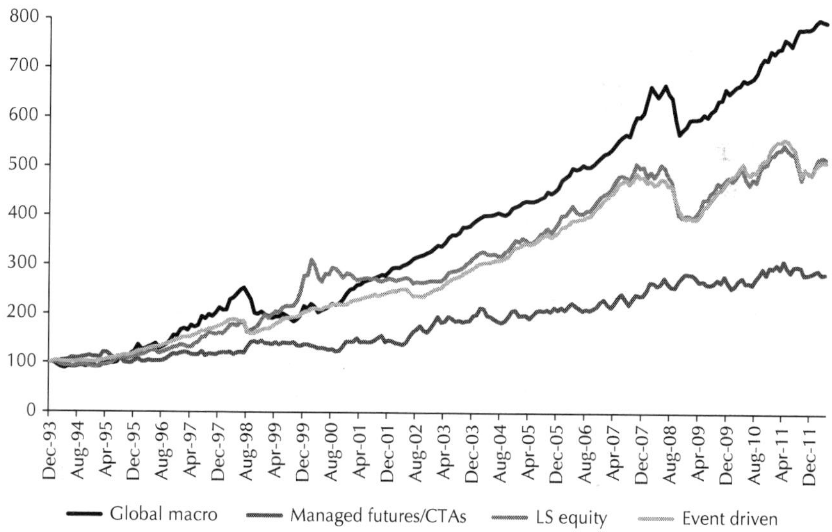

Table 13.1 exhibits a range of summary statistics for the asset classes shown in Figure 13.1. Global macro had the best annualised return (11.8%) and the highest Sharpe ratio (0.9), with a maximum drawdown of about 27%. Note, however, that the returns of global

Table 13.1 Summary statistics of various asset classes (December 1993–April 2012)[3]

	Developed market equities	Emerging market equities	Commodities	Fixed income	Global macro	Managed futures
Annualised mean	7.61%	9.01%	7.17%	6.14%	11.83%	6.40%
Annualised volatility	15.7%	24.5%	15.9%	3.7%	9.7%	11.7%
Sharpe ratio	0.28	0.24	0.25	0.80	0.89	0.28
Maximum drawdown	–53.7%	–61.4%	–54.3%	–5.1%	–26.8%	–17.7%
Skewness	–0.73	–0.71	–0.61	–0.28	0.01	0.02
Kurtosis[4]	1.54	1.75	2.34	1.01	3.88	0.00
95% value-at-risk	–7.96%	–10.50%	–6.36%	–1.34%	–2.89%	–4.82%
95% Expected tail loss	–10.7%	–16.4%	–9.9%	–2.0%	–6.0%	–6.3%
Serial correlation	0.19	0.19	0.09	0.05	0.17	0.06

macro exhibit excess kurtosis (ie, fatter tails than implied by a normal distribution). Managed futures, on the other hand, had a relatively low annualised return (6.4%, which was slightly better than fixed income) with higher volatility compared to global macro, a much lower Sharpe ratio (0.28), and a maximum drawdown of about 18%. The returns of managed futures seem to be more normally distributed compared to global macro, with virtually no skewness and kurtosis.

In addition to the typical statistics such as mean, standard deviation, skewness, kurtosis, maximum drawdown and value-at-risk (VaR), we also include in Table 13.1 expected tail loss and serial correlation. Expected tail loss – also sometimes referred to as conditional value-at-risk (CVaR) – captures tail risk beyond just the VaR, as it measures the average loss if a loss larger than the VaR were to occur. For example, the 95% VaR for developed market equities is 7.96%, meaning there is a 5% probability of losing 7.96% or more in a single month. In these 5% of cases, the average monthly loss was 10.7%, which corresponds to the 95% expected tail loss.

Serial correlation measures the correlation between returns and lagged returns: we use a one-month lag in Table 13.1. Serial correlation can be an indication of return smoothing due to the illiquid nature of the underlying investments. The serial correlations reported in Table 13.1 are all reasonably low, suggesting that it is not a major concern for global macro and managed futures strategies.[5]

Table 13.2 exhibits correlations across various asset classes and

Table 13.2 Correlations across various asset classes

	Developed market equities	Emerging market equities	Commodities	Fixed income	Global macro	Managed futures
Developed market equities	1					
Emerging market equities	0.81	1				
Commodities	0.41	0.45	1			
Fixed income	0.02	–0.02	0.04	1		
Global macro	0.23	0.28	0.25	0.28	1	
Managed futures	–0.03	0.01	0.25	0.18	0.30	1

macro strategies shown in Figure 13.1. Global macro strategies and managed futures exhibit relatively low correlations to equity and commodity markets, partially explaining their appeal as candidates for improving portfolio diversification.

Correlations can vary significantly over time, however, and Figure 13.3 shows correlations of different hedge fund strategies with developed market equities on a 36-month rolling basis. While correlations of global macro and managed futures with developed market equities vary significantly over time (from negative to positive), the correlations are significantly lower than those of equity long/short and event-driven strategies with developed market equities.

Figure 13.3 Correlation of various hedge fund strategies with developed market equities (36-month rolling window)

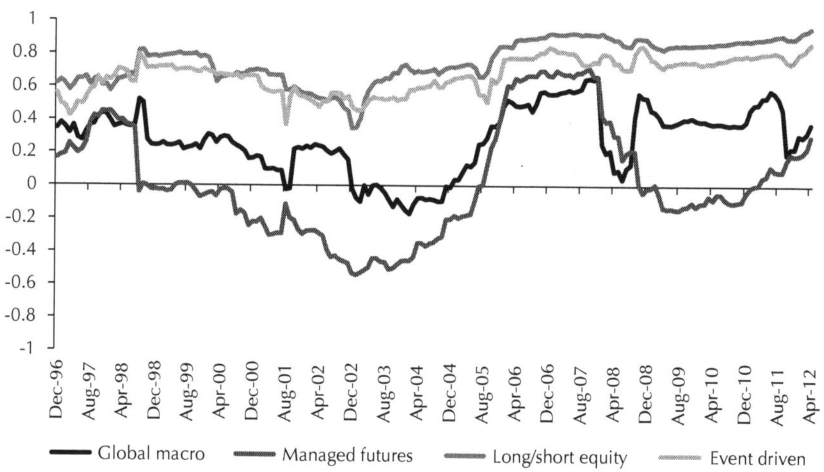

In summary, global macro and managed futures have performed well over these 20 years, with global macro strategies being rather exceptional, and have historically provided investors with significant diversification benefits. In the next section, we consider how global macro would fit into an overall asset allocation.

HOW DO GLOBAL MACRO STRATEGIES FIT IN THE OVERALL ASSET ALLOCATION?

In this section, we consider how global macro strategies fit into an overall asset allocation plan using a portfolio optimisation framework. We make a couple of adjustments to the hedge fund return series before running them through the portfolio optimisation procedure. First, we adjust hedge fund returns for serial correlation (ie, we unsmooth the return series to eliminate any effects of illiquidity that may artificially dampen volatilities and correlations). We refer to Conner (2003) and Getmansky, Lo and Makarov (2004) for details on the methodology to unsmooth hedge fund returns that we employ.[6]

Second, we use a mean/expected tail loss optimisation framework to account for any skewness and kurtosis in hedge fund returns that are not captured by simply focusing on volatility as a measure of risk, and compare the results to the standard mean/variance optimisation approach.[7] Finally, as we are mostly interested in the diversification properties of global macro strategies, we adjust the mean return of all asset classes so as to equalise their Sharpe ratios, instead of simply using historical average returns that would heavily bias the results in favour of global macro strategies given their strong historical performance. We arbitrarily set the Sharpe ratio equal to 0.3 for all asset classes.[8]

Figure 13.4 shows both the mean/variance efficient frontier and the mean/expected tail loss (using a 95% confidence level) efficient frontier. Figure 13.5 shows 20 optimal portfolios along those two frontiers. While the optimal portfolios look very similar – particularly at the shorter end of the risk spectrum – there are some notable differences. The mean/expected tail loss optimisation framework calls for a lower allocation to commodities and global macro in favour of managed futures/CTAs. This is mostly explained by the better tail risk mitigation properties of managed futures/CTAs. Even in the case of mean/variance efficient portfolios, the optimiser prefers managed futures/CTAs compared to discretionary global macro strategies due to their stronger diversification properties versus equity and commodities markets (see Table 13.2). It is worth pointing out that we heavily penalised discretionary global macro strategies relative to other asset classes due to the much lower Sharpe ratio assumed in the optimisation compared to historical experience. If we were to assume a higher Sharpe ratio for discretionary global

Figure 13.4 Efficient frontiers and random portfolios

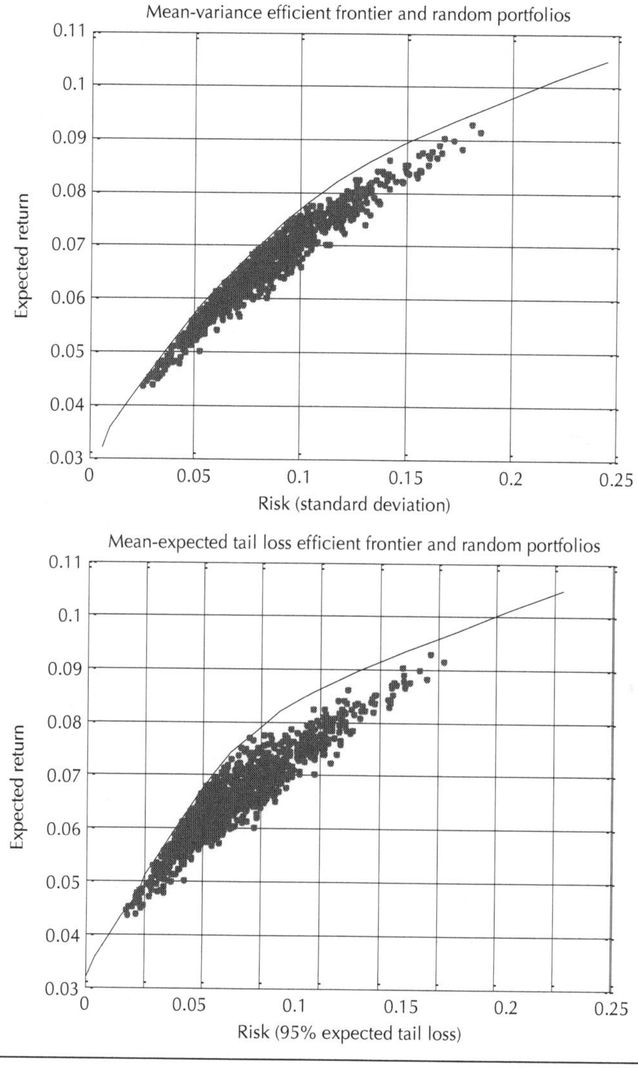

Figure 13.5 Efficient portfolios

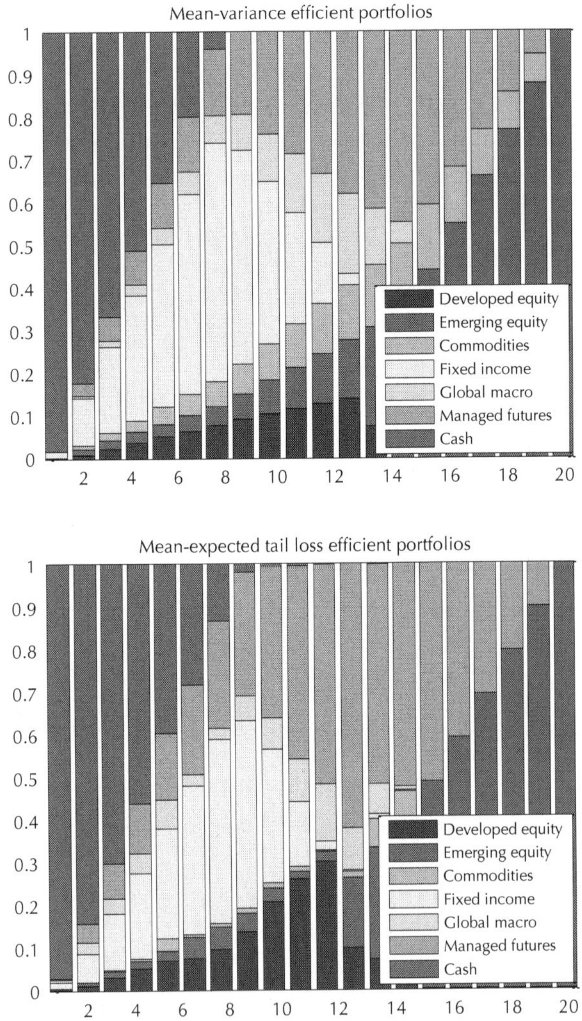

macro strategies going forward, the optimiser would allocate a substantial part of the portfolio to such strategies.

The allocation to managed futures is quite significant in both the mean/variance and mean/expected tail loss efficient portfolios. In practice, investors typically impose constraints on such optimisation exercises, but the unconstrained optimisation illustrates the potential attractiveness of managed futures as a diversifier against traditionally equity-heavy institutional portfolios.

HOW DO GLOBAL MACRO STRATEGIES FIT IN A HEDGE FUND PORTFOLIO?

In the previous section, we looked at the role of global macro strategies in an overall asset allocation framework. In this section, we consider how global macro strategies might fit in a hedge fund portfolio. We use the DJCS hedge fund indexes over the period January 1994 to April 2012, with the exception of equity market neutral, where we use the HFRI equity market neutral index because of a data issue with the DJCS Equity Market Neutral index.[9] Again, we unsmooth the hedge fund return series to adjust for serial correlation in returns. We adjust the expected return of the various hedge fund strategies by assuming that the Sharpe ratio is identical across strategies (we use a Sharpe ratio of 0.5).[10]

Figure 13.6 shows both mean/variance and mean/expected tail loss (at a 95% confidence level) efficient portfolios. Note that the mean/expected tail loss framework allocates more to global macro, managed futures and equity long/short strategies and less to fixed income arbitrage, distressed and multi-strategy hedge funds. Figure 13.7 shows two portfolios that both target an expected return of Libor + 500 basis points. The portfolio at the top minimises volatility while achieving the target return, whereas the portfolio in the bottom minimises the 95% expected tail loss. It is worth noting that the mean/expected tail loss optimal portfolio is more diversified across different hedge fund strategies and has a higher allocation to global macro strategies, managed futures, equity long/short and event-driven, and a lower allocation to fixed income arbitrage, distressed and multi-strategy hedge funds. Even in the case of the mean/variance optimal portfolio, there is a significant allocation to global macro strategies and in particular to managed futures/CTAs (38% combined, versus 47% for the mean/expected tail loss optimal portfolio). Managed futures/CTAs not only provide good diversification against broad asset classes, they also provide good diversification against other hedge fund strategies.

DO GLOBAL MACRO STRATEGIES MITIGATE TAIL RISK?

In the last two sections, we found that global macro strategies in general, and managed futures or CTAs in particular, provide useful diversification against major asset classes and other hedge fund strategies. In this section, we consider whether global macro strate-

Figure 13.6 Efficient hedge fund portfolios

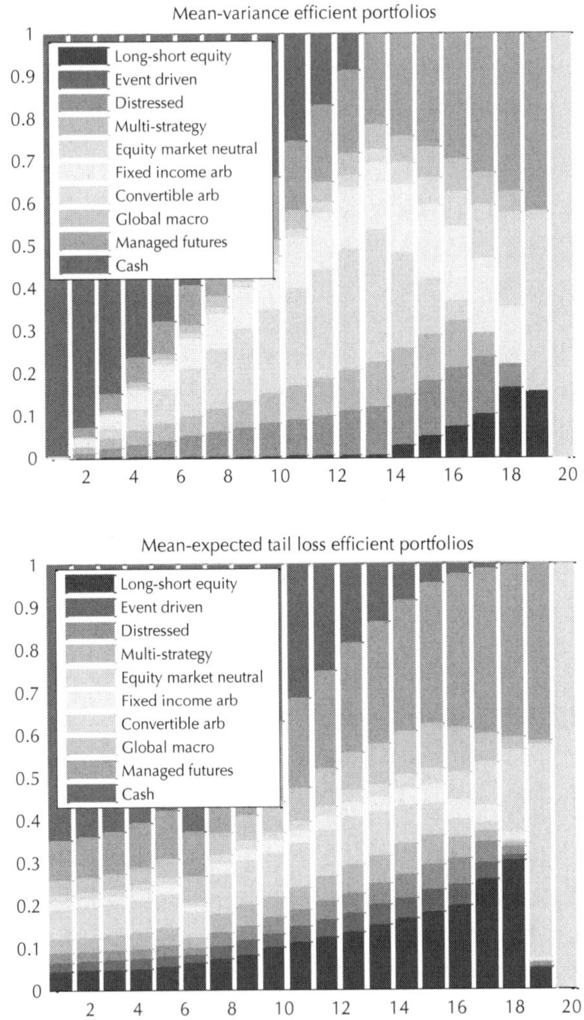

gies can be helpful in a tail risk event. Correlations only tell part of the story. Investors typically allocate to hedge funds in the expectation that these strategies will do better during periods of significant market turmoil when their equity portfolio is performing very poorly. Figure 13.8 shows how different asset classes and macro strategies performed during periods in which equity markets sold off significantly. As is clear from Figure 13.8, global macro strategies

Figure 13.7 Efficient hedge fund portfolios with a target expected return of Libor + 500 bps

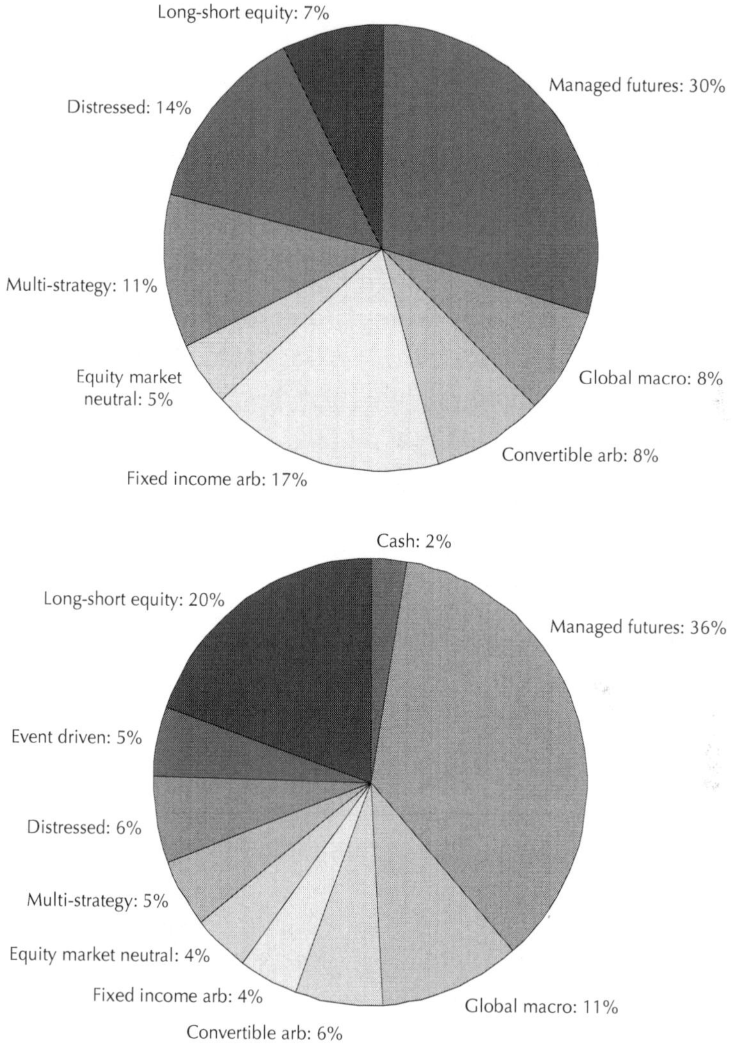

and managed futures, as well as standard fixed income portfolios, have held up relatively well during those periods. The periods in Figure 13.8 were chosen as distinct time periods where either developed market equities or emerging market equities fell by more than 15%.[11]

Figure 13.8 Performance during market turmoil

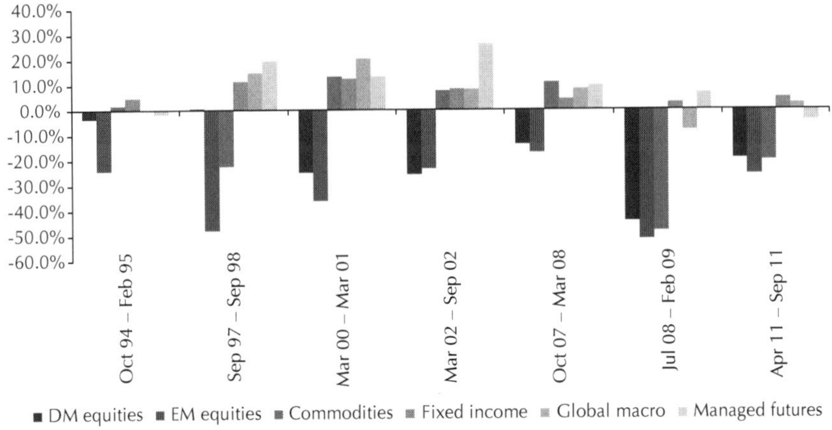

Figure 13.9 confirms this picture when we look at the average return of different asset classes during periods when equities were down and periods when equities were up. The returns shown in Figure 13.9 are average annualised returns computed for all the months in which equities posted a negative return and for all the months in which equities posted a positive return. A large part of the appeal of global macro and managed futures strategies is that they have historically provided some level of diversification during periods of poor equity performance.

Figure 13.10 shows scatter plots of the returns of both global macro and managed futures against developed market equities. We fitted a polynomial function to these relationships. The result for global macro is pretty typical of other hedge fund strategies: a concave relationship between hedge fund returns and equity market returns – implying that these strategies have a higher exposure to equities in falling equity markets than in rising equity markets. The result for managed futures, however, stands in contrast to the typical relationship, as these strategies seem to have better performance when equities are falling. This is the type of tail risk mitigation that many investors are looking for. As can be seen from Figure 13.10, however, the R-squared statistics of these regressions are quite low, so we should be careful in interpreting the results, as the concavity and convexity of these returns are driven by only a few extreme

Figure 13.9 Performance during equity-up and equity-down markets

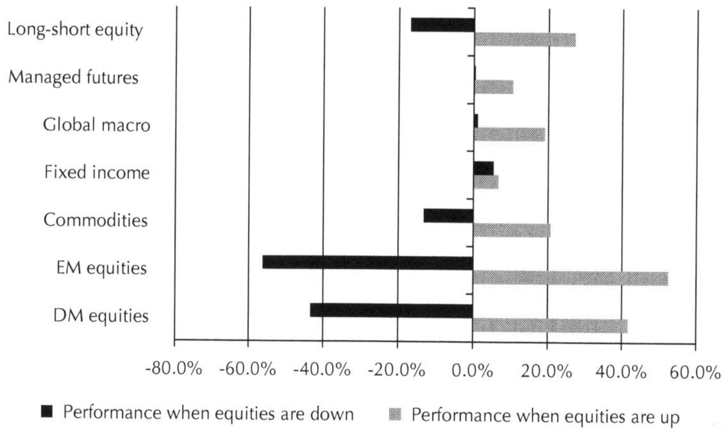

observations and we cannot assign a high confidence to this phenomenon repeating in the future.

RISK FACTOR EXPOSURES IN GLOBAL MACRO STRATEGIES

Global macro strategies in general, and managed futures in particular, offer diversification benefits and should be included in a hedge fund portfolio. In this section, we analyse the risk factor exposures embedded in global macro strategies. The goal of the risk factor analysis is to uncover what exposures global macro and CTA strategies offer that investors may not yet be exposed to through other asset classes or hedge fund strategies in their portfolio.

We use two sets of risk factors. The first uses the MSCI Barra[12] equity risk factors augmented with two fixed income risk factors: an interest rate risk factor (excess return of 10-year government bonds versus three-month bills) and a credit risk factor (excess return of US investment-grade corporate bonds versus US government bonds on a duration-adjusted basis). The second risk-factor set uses the Fama–French equity risk factors[13] – ie, the equity risk premium, the value premium (high book-to-price minus low book-to-price) and the small cap premium (small cap minus large cap). The Fama–French three-factor model was developed by Fama and French (2003) to describe stock returns. The traditional asset-pricing model, the capital asset pricing model (CAPM), uses only one variable, equity

Figure 13.10 Global macro and managed futures returns versus developed market equity returns

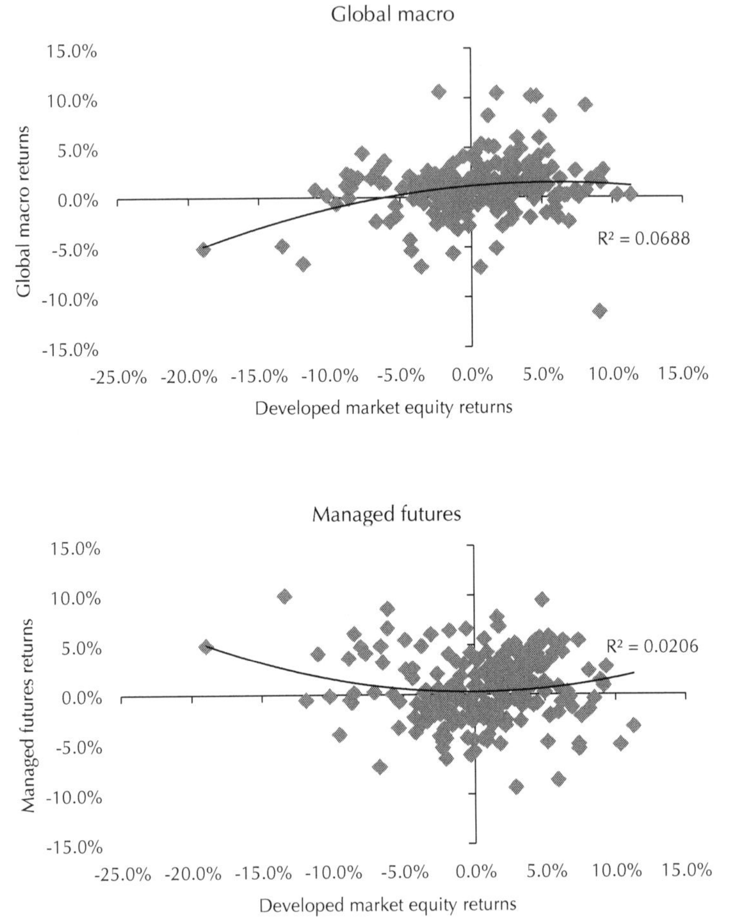

beta, to describe stock returns using the overall market return as the factor. The Fama–French model extends the CAPM to include two additional factors: a value premium and a small cap premium. Fama and French found that the three-factor model does a better job of explaining stock returns compared to the single-factor CAPM. In addition to the three Fama–French factors, we use another eight factors: an equity momentum risk factor, changes in the 10-year US Treasury constant maturity yield, changes in the credit spread (measured as the difference between Moody's BAA corporate yield and the 10-year US Treasury constant maturity yield), and five trend-following risk factors from Fung and Hsieh[14] for bonds, currencies, commodities, interest rates and equities.

These five trend-following factors were developed by Fung and Hsieh (2001) to better explain hedge fund returns. Many hedge fund strategies typically generate option-like return streams that are difficult to capture with standard risk factors. Fung and Hsieh model the trend-following factors using look-back straddles. The trend-following factors can be particularly useful in trying to explain the return streams of CTAs, as such funds typically employ a variety of momentum-based strategies.

For the first set of risk factors, we regress returns to various hedge fund strategies on the risk factors using monthly data for the period January 1998 to April 2012.[15] Table 13.3 shows the regression results (we only show the statistically significant factors). Note that global macro and managed futures strategies have the lowest explanatory power of all hedge fund strategies analysed, meaning that a large part of the return variation is unexplained by standard risk factors. Global macro strategies have some exposure to the equity risk premium (a beta of 0.26), momentum, value premium and a negative exposure to size and liquidity.

Managed futures are only exposed to the value premium and the term premium (interest rate risk). We should not make too much of these findings, however, as the R-squared statistics of the regressions are quite low for global macro (25.4%) and particularly for managed futures (7.7%). A more important take-away from the results in Table 13.3 is that the returns of many other hedge fund strategies can be explained to a much larger degree by standard risk factors, with R-squared typically above 50% and even as high as almost 80% for equity long/short funds. This suggests that global macro and managed futures strategies are quite distinct from other types of hedge fund strategies.

For the second set of risk factors, we regress returns to various hedge fund strategies on the risk factors using monthly data from January 1994 to June 2011.[16] Table 13.4 shows the regression results (again, we only show the statistically significant factors).

As was the case with the first factor set, global macro and managed futures strategies have the lowest explanatory power of all hedge fund strategies analysed. The explanatory power of global macro is

Table 13.3 Risk factor exposures of various hedge fund strategies using factor set 1

	Long-short equity	Event driven	Distressed	Multi-strategy	Equity market neutral	Fixed income arb	Convertible arb	Global macro	Managed futures
Intercept		0.48%	0.66%	0.61%			0.42%		
World equities	0.50	0.25	0.20		0.09			0.26	
Momentum	0.68	0.19		0.18	0.38			0.50	
Volatility						–0.26	–0.23		
Value					0.52			0.79	1.11
Size	–0.82	–0.68	–0.66					–1.04	
Growth						0.73			
Liquidity	0.73							–0.84	
Leverage	–0.84	0.77	1.21	0.69		1.39	0.70		
Rates		–0.13	–0.13						0.41
Credit	0.25			0.54		0.49	0.99		
Adjusted R2	**78.6%**	**67.2%**	**64.8%**	**55.3%**	**41.8%**	**49.7%**	**58.6%**	**25.4%**	**7.7%**

Table 13.4 Risk factor exposures of various hedge fund strategies using factor set 2

	Long-short equity	Event driven	Distressed	Multi-strategy	Equity market neutral	Fixed income arb	Convertible arb	Global macro	Managed futures
Intercept	0.62%	0.64%	0.70%	0.72%	0.41%	0.51%	0.67%	1.01%	0.70%
Equity risk premium	0.51	0.25	0.24	0.10	0.09	0.06	0.09	0.16	0.14
Small minus large	0.20	0.12	0.12						
High minus low	–0.11	0.09	0.09		0.09				0.32
Momentum	0.27	0.06			0.11			0.19	0.18
Change in 10yr UST						–1.45	–2.01		
Change in credit spread		–1.79	–2.11	–3.29		–5.42	–5.48	–3.78	
Bond trend following		–0.02	–0.02						0.05
FX trend following						–0.01			0.04
Commodity trend following									0.04
Interest rate trend following				–0.01		–0.01	–0.01		
Stock trend following	0.02			0.02	0.01				0.06
Adjusted R2	**78.8%**	**60.9%**	**51.0%**	**38.7%**	**33.3%**	**52.1%**	**45.2%**	**14.9%**	**26.0%**

lower with the second risk-factor set (15% versus 25%), while the explanatory power of managed futures increases (26% versus 8%). Managed futures are, not surprisingly, mostly exposed to the trend-following factors from Fung and Hsieh, which is why the explanatory power goes up when using these factors. Still, the explanatory power is relatively low, implying that global macro strategies in general offer investors unique characteristics not captured by other hedge fund strategies or asset classes in the portfolio.

The risk factor analysis supports earlier conclusions that global macro strategies, and managed futures in particular, offer diversification benefits by exposing investors to other sources of risk not typically captured by the standard risk factors that drive returns for most asset classes and many other hedge fund strategies.

CONCLUSIONS

In this chapter, we have studied the risk and return characteristics and diversification benefits of global macro strategies – both discretionary global macro and managed futures or CTAs. Discretionary global macro strategies have historically offered very solid returns with low risk and reasonable diversification benefits in traditional portfolios. Managed futures strategies, on the other hand, have historically offered lower returns and lower Sharpe ratios compared to discretionary global macro, but appear to offer much stronger diversification benefits in traditional portfolios. Managed futures strategies can be especially attractive as a means of mitigating tail risk in a portfolio with a large exposure to equity risk. It is not surprising, therefore, that global macro strategies have attracted strong investor interest in the past few years.

While we have made the case in this chapter for global macro strategies from a quantitative perspective, there are also important qualitative factors that need to be taken into account before embarking on a search for global macro managers.

First, because global macro strategies tend to be more opaque compared to other hedge fund strategies such as equity long/short, the due diligence process is even more important. For discretionary macro funds, it is important to understand the manager's macroeconomic outlook, how the macro view translates into trade ideas, how individual strategies are implemented in the portfolio and how the manager manages and controls risk. For systematic strategies, it is important to understand the theoretical basis of the algorithms, the history of the development of these algorithms, and the manager's background and experience in developing and evaluating complex quantitative models. For systematic strategies, risk management is typically embedded in the models and investors should understand the various risk management tools that are integrated into the systems. Historically, many endowments have shied away from investing in global macro strategies due to the perceived lack of transparency compared to other hedge fund strategies, such as equity long/short. While it can be more challenging to evaluate the skill of global macro managers, this does not strike us as a compelling enough reason to shun global macro strategies in principle.

Second, it is important to build a diversified portfolio of global macro managers. While many hedge fund strategies tend to be limited to specific asset classes, global macro hedge funds can invest across the broad investment landscape and switch asset classes, sectors and instruments when economic and market disequilibria present opportunities. While this flexibility allows global macro managers to perform well in a range of different economic environments, it also leads to wide dispersion of returns between the best and the worst performing global macro funds. Given the typical lack of performance persistence in the hedge fund industry more generally, it is best to create a diversified portfolio of global macro managers and combine both discretionary and systematic macro funds.

Finally, as discretionary macro managers typically invest based on a relatively small number of big bets driven by their fundamental forward-looking views, they can experience significant volatility and potentially large drawdowns. Consequently, investors should have patience and take a long-term view when investing in discretionary global macro. Endowments are better suited to have such a longer-term view and can be more patient compared to pension funds. In addition, endowments tend to be more tactical compared to pension funds, and a few strategic relationships with global macro managers could help strengthen their own internal processes for tactical shifts and the development of forward-looking top-down views.

1 We use the following indexes for the asset classes shown in Figure 13.1: for developed market equities we use the MSCI World index, for emerging market equities we use the MSCI Emerging Markets Free index, for fixed income we use the Barclays US Aggregate

index, for commodities we use the Dow Jones–UBS commodities index. For both global macro and managed futures, we use the Dow Jones Credit Suisse Broad indexes.

2 We use the following Dow Jones Credit Suisse Broad hedge fund sub-indexes: Global Macro Hedge Fund Index, Managed Futures Hedge Fund Index, Long/Short Equity Hedge Fund Index and the Event Driven Hedge Fund Index.

3 For calculating the Sharpe ratio, we used the average annualised return on three-month US Treasury bills as the risk-free rate, which over the period in question was 3.15%.

4 Kurtosis is measured as excess kurtosis relative to a normal distribution, ie, if returns are normally distributed the kurtosis shown in Table 13.1 should be equal to zero. A positive number indicates that the returns have fatter tails compared to a normal distribution, while a negative number indicates that the returns have thinner tails compared to a normal distribution.

5 If we were to measure the same statistic for fixed income arbitrage or multi-strategy hedge funds, we would find significantly higher numbers due to illiquidity. Over the period December 1993 to April 2012, for example, the one-month serial correlation of the DJCS Fixed Income Arbitrage Index is 0.55 and the one-month serial correlation of the DJCS Multi-Strategy Index is 0.51. In the presence of significant positive serial correlation, annualised volatilities tend be underestimated, while Sharpe ratios tend to be overestimated. Also, when returns are serially correlated, we can no longer annualise monthly volatilities by multiplying with the square root of 12. An extensive discussion on the effect of serial correlation on Sharpe ratios can be found in Lo (2002).

6 As discussed earlier, hedge fund strategies may exhibit positive serial correlation that reflects stale pricing due to the presence of illiquid instruments in their portfolios. The idea behind unsmoothing returns is to remove this positive serial correlation by adjusting the observed returns. Both Conner (2003) and Getmansky, Lo and Makarov (2004) assume that observed hedge fund returns are a weighted average of their "true" economic return and provide algorithms to back it out. The resulting "true" returns have the same sample average as the observed returns, but typically exhibit higher volatility and higher correlation with equities.

7 Another reason for relying on expected tail loss instead of the more traditional VaR is that the latter has several weaknesses that make it a poor risk measure, not least the fact it is not sub-additive (see Artzner *et al*, 1999). This means that diversification may, in fact, increase the VaR of a portfolio, which is counterintuitive. Expected tail loss does not suffer from this problem. It is worth mentioning that the Basel Committee on Banking Supervision proposed on May 3, 2012, to use expected tail loss (or expected shortfall) instead of value-at-risk in market risk management. The main advantage of using expected tail loss in portfolio construction is that mean/expected tail loss optimisation can be reformulated as a linear optimisation problem, as was shown by Rockafellar and Uryasev (2000), that can easily be solved with most statistics packages even in the case of non-normal return distributions.

8 A Sharpe ratio of 0.3 seems reasonable in light of the long-term historical experience of equities, commodities and fixed income. Table 13.1 shows that over the past 20 years the Sharpe ratio of equities, commodities and managed futures has been close to about 0.3. Fixed income and global macro strategies, on the other hand, have registered much higher Sharpe ratios over this 20-year period. This high Sharpe ratio for fixed income can be explained by falling interest rates over the past 20 years. Over a longer history of 60 years (from 1952 to 2012), the Sharpe ratio of fixed income is closer to 0.3. The important point here is not the actual Sharpe ratio that we use, but the fact that we equalise Sharpe ratios for all asset classes. This makes all asset classes equally attractive on a stand-alone, risk-adjusted basis, and the optimal portfolios will therefore solely be driven by correlation effects and tail risk, as measured by the 95% expected tail loss.

9 The DJCS Equity Market Neutral index posted an abnormal –40% return during the month of November 2008, while the HFRI Equity Market Neutral index only posted a –0.02% return in the same month.

10 This is higher than the Sharpe ratio of 0.3 that we used in the previous section, but still quite conservative compared to the historical experience of most hedge fund strategies. Again, the actual level of the Sharpe ratio is irrelevant for the results, what matters is that we make all hedge fund strategies equally attractive in terms of risk-adjusted returns and let the optimiser choose portfolios on the basis of correlations and tail risk properties only.

11 The period from October 1994 to February 1995 coincides with the Mexican Tequila Crisis. The period from September 1997 to September 1998 coincides with the Asian financial crisis and Russian default, culminating with the collapse of LTCM. The period from March 2000 to March 2001 coincides with the collapse of the tech bubble. The period from March 2002 to September 2002 coincides with a range of US accounting scandals coming to light post the collapse of Enron. The period from October 2007 to March 2008 coincides with the first leg of what was initially called the subprime crisis and later became the global financial crisis, culminating with the downfall of Bear Stearns. The period from July 2008 to February 2009 captures the nadir of the global financial crisis, and finally the period from April 2011 to September 2011 coincides with rising problems and uncertainty in the eurozone.

12 MSCI Barra provides risk management solutions for institutional investors, and its equity risk factors are widely used in the asset management industry.

13 The Fama–French risk factors and the equity momentum risk factor can be obtained from: http://mba.tuck.dartmouth.edu/pages/faculty/ken.french/data_library.html. We use the global factors, not the US factors.

14 See Fung and Hsieh (2001). The factors can be downloaded from: http://faculty.fuqua.duke.edu/~dah7/HFRFData.htm.

15 The reason for using a shorter time period compared to the analysis in the previous sections is that we only have data for the MSCI Barra risk factors from January 1998 onwards.

16 As the data for the second risk-factor set goes back to January 1994, we use a slightly longer timeframe compared to the previous factor regressions. The sample ends, however, in June 2011, as data for the Fung and Hsieh trend-following risk factors are only updated through June 2011.

REFERENCES

Artzner, P, F. Delbaen, J. M. Eber and D. Heath, 1999, "Coherent Measures of Risk," *Mathematical Finance*, **9**, pp 203–28.

Conner, A., 2003, "Asset Allocation Effects of Adjusting Alternative Assets for Stale Pricing," *Journal of Alternative Investments*, **6(3)**, pp 42–52.

Fama, Eugene F. and Kenneth R. French, 1993, "Common Risk Factors in the Returns on Stocks and Bonds," *Journal of Financial Economics*, **33(1)**, pp 3–56.

Fung, William and David A. Hsieh, 2001, "The Risk in Hedge Fund Strategies: Theory and Evidence from Trend Followers," *Review of Financial Studies*, **14**, pp 313–41.

Getmansky, M., A. W. Lo and I. Makarov, 2004, "An Econometric Model of Serial Correlation and Illiquidity in Hedge Fund Returns," *Journal of Financial Economics*, **74**, pp 529–609.

Lo, A. W., 2002, "The Statistics of Sharpe Ratios", *Financial Analyst Journal*, July/August, pp 36–52.

Rockafellar, R. Tyrrell and Stanislav Uryasev, 2000, "Optimization of Conditional Value-at-Risk," *Journal of Risk*, **2**, pp 21–41.

14

GTAA and Global Macro for Long-term Institutional Investors

Gerlof de Vrij, Roy Hoevenaars and Pieter Jelle van der Sluis

Blenheim Capital Management BV

INSTITUTIONAL PORTFOLIO MANAGEMENT

Financial markets occasionally go through severe boom–bust phases. Based on their experience since the 1980s, investors have increasingly begun to realise that expectations of long-term risk premia are conditional on the current state of markets, and as such cannot be applied in strategic investment plans unconditionally. Furthermore, during the global financial crisis of 2007–09, institutional portfolios were subjected to unprecedented real-life stress tests, reinforcing the quest to build more robust portfolios.

Investors often overreact in their search for peace of mind by adopting short-term investment horizons and pro-cyclical risk management practices, which typically results in them paying an excessive insurance premium. Investors can be prone to overreaction on both sides: searching too desperately for yield on the upswings and hunkering down and buying too much expensive protection in the troughs. Long-term investors looking for robust all-weather solutions and confronted with high cyclicality and regime-switching behaviour of markets should bear in mind the following wise words:[1]

> It is not the strongest of the species that survives,
> nor the most intelligent that survives.
> It is the one that is the most adaptable to change.

This poses the question whether long-term investors should focus on allocation to *static* and *illiquid* assets or whether there should be a much bigger role for *dynamic* allocation using *liquid* asset classes, factors and instruments.

Investment professionals have pursued different approaches to managing institutional portfolios. Traditional equity/bond allocations are commonly extended to include alternative investments – such as real estate, hedge funds, private equity, infrastructure and commodities. Some asset managers focus on liquid asset classes and expect to reap beta returns from long-term risk premia, while others expect to harvest illiquidity premia. On top of that, active management tries to add alpha through security selection.[2] Differences between the objectives of funds, their risk and return preferences, and future cashflow dynamics make sure that there is no such thing as a single universally applicable blueprint for long-term investors. Investment objectives may vary considerably among sovereign wealth funds, university endowments, family offices and pension plans. Strategic investment policy is often unique and tailored to the specific abilities and preferences of each individual fund and its stakeholders.

Nevertheless, what most long-term investors seem to share is a low tolerance for large drawdowns. To avoid them, some institutions try to make their asset mix more adaptable to change. This implies a paradigm shift from a static to a dynamic approach to return and risk. We believe our past experience in global tactical asset allocation (GTAA) and global macro investing at one of the largest and most advanced pension funds in the world, and our current involvement and affiliation with a renowned global macro firm, may help to unveil some interesting and useful insights for institutional investors seeking to pursue a more dynamic approach.

The pyramid in Figure 14.1 displays the typical layers of an institutional investment process: asset and liability management (ALM), strategic asset allocation (SAA), dynamic asset allocation and overlay, GTAA and active management. Although the most important and value-adding part of the pyramid is at the top, typically most resources are allocated disproportionately to the bottom.

We strongly believe that there needs to be an interaction between the different layers in the pyramid. Bottom-up market intelligence and investment technology can be very beneficial in opening up the "ivory tower" of SAA by introducing dynamic asset allocation and overlay strategies. In turn, top-down risk management and portfolio

Figure 14.1 Taxonomy of a top-down investment process

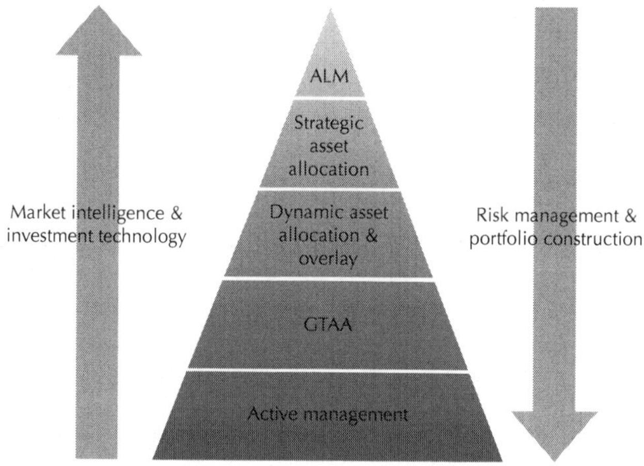

construction discipline can add value to certain areas of active management, where: investors tend to hold *collections* of assets rather than *portfolios* of assets; investments are compartmentalised within their asset class and geographical silos; and sometimes the difference between alphas and (alternative) betas is blurred. Top-down and bottom-up insights from global macro should be translated to the top of the institutional pyramid, thereby going full circle.

The classic tactical asset allocation (TAA) model was based on medium-term asset class views. The first TAA programme is thought to have started in the 1970s. With the disappointing performance of stock markets in 1973–74, investors believed some value could be added by actively monitoring and managing their asset allocations. The introduction of liquid futures markets further spurred investor interest and participation in TAA strategies. In the 1980s, academics started to distinguish between different sources of fund returns by attributing them to asset allocation, market timing and security selection. These studies showed that asset allocation determined almost 95% of the variation in fund returns.[3]

Although such tactical allocation between asset classes is easy to implement in practice, it has important limitations.[4] First, traditional TAA programmes only exploit investment opportunities in a limited number of asset classes, and most of the time they tend to use cash instruments. Both aspects reduce the capability to exploit investment opportunities. The low frequency of tactical decisions – typically monthly – further limits the breadth of TAA strategies. Furthermore, risk management of traditional TAA strategies is often inadequate. A decision to tactically overweight stocks requires an opposite position in another asset class, such as bonds. However, equities are typically riskier than bonds, and therefore the new portfolio can be unbalanced and inefficient from a risk perspective. Finally, a disproportionately large part of the active risk budget of a pension fund is spent on the tactical decision. Its impact can easily dwarf bottom-up alpha from security selection.

This chapter will describe our experiences with GTAA and global macro investing in an institutional setting.[5] We will discuss various factors that are critical for the successful implementation of a global macro mandate. In doing so, we describe a blueprint for such a mandate based on how we would advise its construction in an ideal world. We acknowledge the heterogeneity in global macro approaches, which range from fundamental to quantitative, technical to valuation-based and discretionary to systematic. (Of course, there is a lot of room for discretion when building and implementing any global macro mandate, for the simple reason that it is a "people business.") We believe that GTAA and global macro, as it is now understood and implemented, is the natural successor to the more traditional TAA strategies of yesteryear, and we advocate the translation and application of global macro insights gained through this process to the top layers of the institutional asset management pyramid.

The approach described below aims to achieve attractive risk-adjusted absolute returns. Through a structured and disciplined investment process, we propose a mandate that aims to produce robust returns in different market conditions. Our top-down strategy builds on the investment philosophy of dynamic time-varying returns on risky assets within and across asset classes. Our global macro approach aims to extract alpha from macro markets and blends insights from global macro investing and global asset allocation. In contrast to bottom-up investment managers, who decide which individual securities to buy and sell, we invest long and short in various asset classes – such as equities, fixed income, currencies, commodities, inflation and volatility. The reach is global, and within these asset classes the focus is on sectors and countries. Next to diversification across asset classes, we diversify across investment styles, strategies and time horizons. Most positions are directional in nature and are implemented via liquid derivative instruments. The ability to be net short global markets safeguards low correlation with the underlying markets over the long haul. The mandate has an absolute return target to outperform cash within a given risk budget.

The next section will discuss the role of global macro in institutional portfolios from a return and risk perspective, before we elaborate on the distinctive elements and sources of return not easily accessible to institutional investors otherwise. The following section describes practical implementation of the proposed global macro mandate in an institutional context. We discuss portfolio construction and the role of internally versus externally managed global macro programmes. We also elaborate on the risk management for the mandate, leverage and governance structure.

THE ROLE OF GLOBAL MACRO IN INSTITUTIONAL PORTFOLIOS

There are at least three ways in which a global macro mandate might fit into an institutional investor's portfolio:

1. as a distinct alternative investment strategy within the overall hedge fund portfolio or absolute return allocation (ie, as part of the "alternatives" risk budget);
2. as a source of portable alpha on top of a specific asset class or as an alpha overlay on the entire portfolio, potentially boosting returns while keeping the strategic asset mix intact; and
3. as an innovative, better diversified and more robust successor to traditional TAA for capturing active returns in asset allocation space.

In addition to these different approaches, large benefits can potentially be derived from the successful translation and application of global macro insights in the top-down management of institutional portfolios. We stress that this should be considered irrespective of which of the three approaches listed above is used.

A global macro or GTAA mandate enables access to risk and return sources not easily accessible for institutions otherwise. A typical GTAA programme[6] comprises four sleeves: asset class timing, equity country selection, fixed income country selection and currency selection. Apart from asset class timing, which is closest to the original TAA philosophy, GTAA benefits from time-varying returns on risky assets and relative mispricing across and within asset classes, which are motivated by relative value across geographical regions. The ability to go net short markets and to position the portfolio based on relative investment opportunities rather than absolute mispricing assures low correlation with the underlying markets and asset classes.

Even more investment opportunities can (and should) be added to further enhance the breadth of the strategy. For instance, currencies can be seen as an asset class on their own, thus providing an additional source of active returns and an extra layer of diversification to an investor's portfolio. Other useful additions include commodity markets, emerging equity and bond markets, and credit markets. In addition, dividends, volatility and correlation have become tradable, both within and across asset classes. We focus on combining uncorrelated return sources and stand-alone investment strategies into a multi-strategy approach that has the potential to enhance the information ratio of the composite significantly. These enhancements can lead to a well-diversified programme that is capable of harvesting time-varying returns on risky assets across the globe and exploiting global mispricing.

There are three main reasons why an investor might want to allocate part of their risk budget to global macro strategies. First, while it cannot be guaranteed, a good macro programme can be expected to generate positive returns on a stand-alone basis, with low systematic correlation to the underlying asset mix. To achieve an attractive return per unit of risk, it combines fundamental/discretionary and systematic/quantitative investment strategies, as well as diversification across time horizons and investment processes. Simultaneously, risk is controlled in multiple dimensions within the portfolio: from the composite fund level, via investment strategies, all the way down to individual position level. In this way, the mandate provides investors with a series of exposures that may not otherwise be present in their portfolios. Managing these exposures provides an opportunity for the generation of returns that have low correlations with other sources of active returns, and as such they can be expected to lead to more reliable added value.

Second, global macro provides excellent diversification benefits to the overall investment portfolio. It strives to achieve absolute returns, independent of market conditions. The flexibility to allocate across global asset classes and the broadening of the investment universe significantly enhance the diversification profile of the overall portfolio. Figure 14.2 illustrates the risk–return characteristics of a global macro mandate, both as a stand-alone strategy and in the context of an institutional portfolio, during the turbulent times of January 2007 to December 2010.[7] The investment mandate is based on the investment beliefs described in this chapter.

In Figure 14.2, graph (A) illustrates how a dynamic approach enables the distinction between good and bad correlations. The 12-month rolling pair-wise correlations between the excess returns of GTAA and equity markets (S&P 500), bonds (10-year US Treasuries) and a hedge fund mix[8] show that GTAA exposures turned bearish via short equity and long bonds in 2008, which contributed positively to the performance during the start of the recession. The overall portfolio exposure became more bullish again in 2009 and 2010 when equity markets started to recover.

Whereas graph (A) illustrates the correlation between GTAA and various market indexes, the following one, graph (B), displays the average correlation within the assets classes in a standard institutional asset mix, a hypothetical fund of hedge funds portfolio, and the positions in the GTAA portfolio.[9] In other words, for each category we display the degree of diversification that is obtained from the various building blocks. While diversification benefits deteriorated in 2008 within a typical fund of hedge funds portfolio and within a typical pension fund portfolio, correlations decreased – and thus diversification benefits increased – between the constituents of the GTAA fund.

Graph (C) displays the correlation between a generic pension fund asset mix and a standard hedge fund mix (grey line) and GTAA (black line). It clearly indicates the deteriorating diversification benefits of the average hedge fund portfolio in 2008, and the improved diversification benefits of GTAA to an institutional investor. To illustrate one of the sources of diversification, we focus on the CTA strategy as part of the GTAA mandate in graph (D). Here we plot the 21-day CTA returns for each asset on the y-axis and the corresponding long-only returns on that asset on the x-axis. The resulting straddle-like payout structure indicates how the ability to go short

Figure 14.2 Risk–return characteristics of a global macro mandate in an institutional portfolio

(A) Good and bad correlations

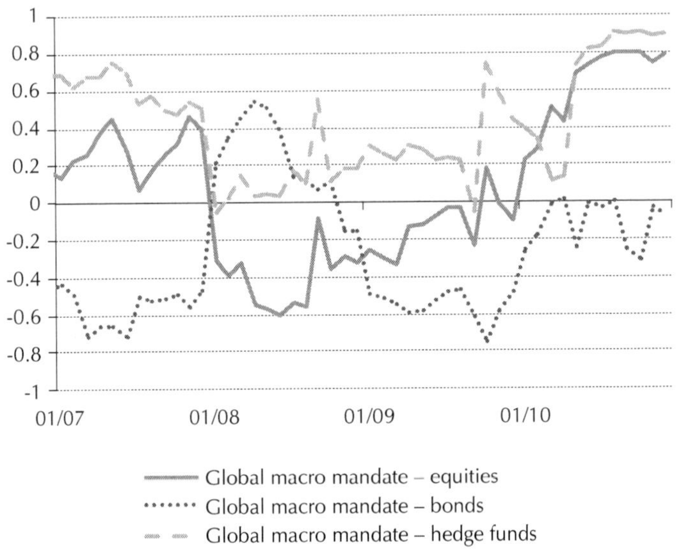

(B) Average correlations

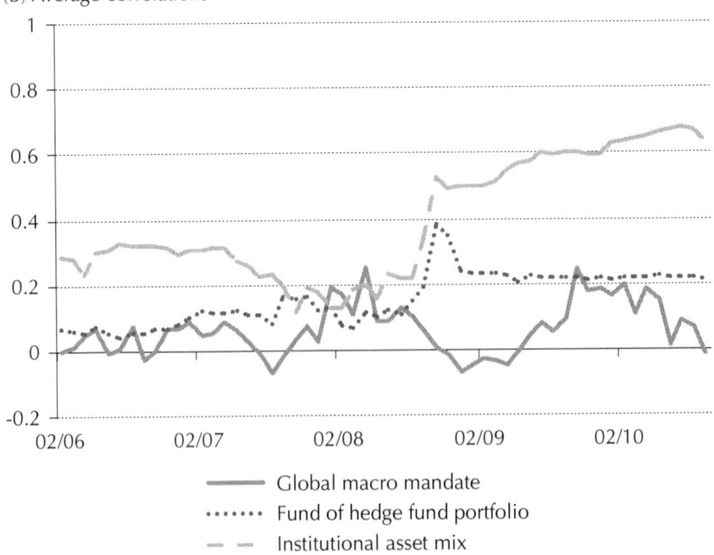

(C) Time-varying correlations

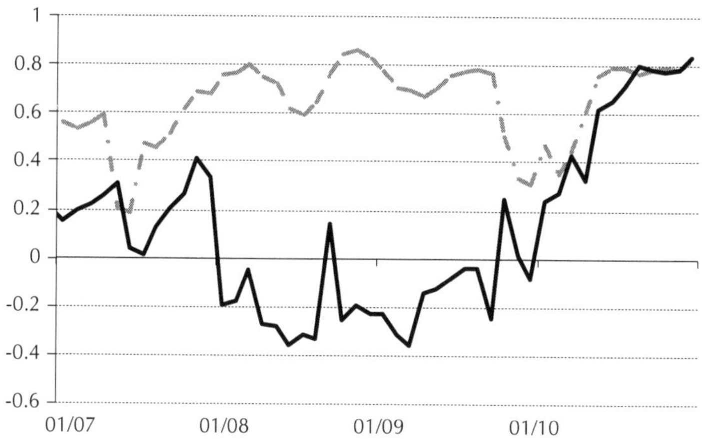

(D) CTA returns versus underlying returns (21 days)

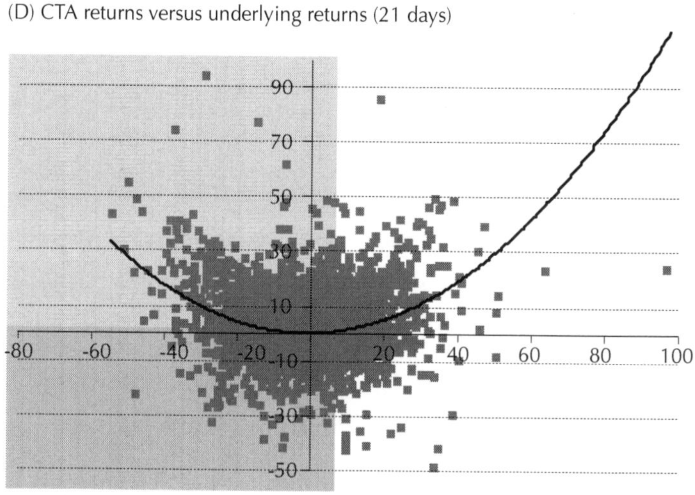

Note: Graph (A) displays the 12 month rolling pair-wise correlations between the excess returns of GTAA and equity markets (S&P 500), bonds (10-year US government bonds) and a hedge funds mix. Graph (B) displays the average correlation within the assets classes in a standard institutional asset mix, a hypothetical fund of hedge fund portfolio and the positions in the GTAA portfolio. Graph (C) displays the correlation between a generic pension fund asset mix and a standard hedge fund mix and GTAA. Graph (D) has the 21-day CTA returns for each asset on the y-axis and the corresponding long-only returns on that asset on the x-axis.

enables a CTA strategy to generate positive returns if the underlying markets plummet. The dynamics of the strategy also yield a very beneficial non-linear correlations pattern – ie, positive correlations to the asset mix in good times and negative correlations during bad times. Overall, the graph illustrates how dynamic positioning within a broadly diversified global macro mandate can lead to diversification benefits within an institutional asset mix and a fund of hedge funds portfolio.

Finally, top-down macro insights and longer-term investment positions can be translated into strategic asset allocation decisions at the top of the pyramid. A GTAA mandate introduces elements of dynamic allocation, risk parity, valuation and innovation to the overall investment process. Within a broadly diversified GTAA programme, there is room to allocate part of the risk budget to a strategy that closely resembles medium-term dynamic strategic asset allocation. Such a strategy applies longer-term valuation models to all relevant asset classes, currencies and factors. Longer-term valuation-driven positions can then be translated into tilts in strategic asset allocation, overlay management, rebalancing policies, benchmark choice and risk management.

From our own GTAA experience, we recall that in the heyday of the leveraged finance market in 2006 and 2007, investors held large leveraged positions to squeeze the last juice out of tiny credit spreads. In contrast to a benchmark-hugging approach, our valuation-based process in 2007 resulted in short credit, short carry, long volatility and long undervalued Asian currency positions. Such tilts can easily be translated and applied to the overall institutional asset mix. Another example from our experience relates to currency hedging strategies. During 2008, based on valuation arguments, we advised the setting up of a defensive currency hedging strategy for the non-euro-denominated part of the overall portfolio.

Direct access to market intelligence, day-to-day portfolio management activity and in-depth market knowledge enable a GTAA/global macro group to help manage overlay strategies at the strategic level. These events have also reinforced our view that a contrarian mindset requires a rigorous stop-loss and take-profit discipline, not only because it is hard to go against the crowd, but also because profits must be harvested in timely fashion, as markets do not correct by going sideways.

UNIQUE SOURCES OF RETURN

To an institutional investor, the attractiveness of a global macro approach comes from several sources. Performance differentials across asset classes are frequently substantial, but most of the investment community still tends to focus more on within-asset-class security selection. Global macro therefore tends to be a less-crowded space. Furthermore, the type of analysis and decision-making practices carried out by global macro specialists are focused on cross-market comparisons, which is very different from the analysis required for comparison and selection of individual securities within given markets. An interesting feature is that the strategy is primarily implemented via derivatives instruments, which are, for the most part, highly liquid and efficient in terms of transaction costs. A global macro mandate can rebalance positions on a daily basis, which enables the fund to benefit from different investment horizons. Most of the strategies have a foundation in academic research.

Although a uniform classification of the sources of active returns in global macro is difficult, below we present and discuss some of the more feasible candidates:

- time-varying returns on risky assets;
- a broader universe of eligible investments;
- more efficient portfolio construction;
- inefficiencies from *home bias* and asset class silos; and
- differing objectives of non-profit-maximising agents.

There is a growing consensus in academic circles that expected returns on stocks and bonds exhibit *time variation* with the business cycle.[10] Expected returns are higher when economic conditions are weak and lower when economic conditions are strong. Yet, by sticking to a calendar-based portfolio rebalancing approach, investors typically do not exploit the time variation in expected asset class returns. Based on macroeconomic fundamentals and valuation, a well-designed GTAA/global macro programme can exploit these opportunities. Furthermore, the ability to net short markets enables global macro to generate positive returns when expected returns turn negative at certain points in time.

A *broader instrument base* enables a GTAA/global macro manager to widen the universe of return sources. There is no restriction on asset classes. Within GTAA there is also room to harvest time-varying returns from risk factors, different investment strategies and opportunistic investment themes. Monetary policy targets inflation and uses interest rates as its policy tools. Multiple risk premia, such as the equity risk premium, the term premium, swap and credit spreads, vary over the business cycle, as do volatilities and correlations. The prudent use of derivatives enables pure positioning in swap spreads, credit spreads and term spreads to time-varying economic fundamentals. Both the traditional asset classes, such as equities and fixed income, and the alternative less-liquid asset classes, are exposed to a mixture of macroeconomic variables and idiosyncratic risks. It is important to identify exposures to common risk factors, such as equity beta, duration exposure, credit beta, inflation, volatility and illiquidity. On top of that, there is value to be added by broadening the investment universe to include timing of investment styles and strategies, such as value, size, carry, momentum, etc.

Portfolio construction can also be a source of alpha and a key ingredient to preserve a fund's staying power in times of adversity. Traditionally, most institutional investors have pursued a calendar-based rebalancing approach, a buy-and-hold strategy or a portfolio insurance-type rebalancing methodology.[11] Academics have studied alternative utility functions to the Markowitz approach for portfolio optimisation. From the practitioner's perspective, investors have considered fundamental indexation and minimum volatility investing as alternative portfolio construction techniques.

Despite all this machinery, when an asset mix is based on capital allocation subject to a return target and risk constraint, the resulting portfolio is not necessarily well diversified in terms of risk. This is typically the case if the return target increases and the asset allocation therefore shifts into risky or illiquid assets to meet the expected target return. For example, consider a standard 60/40 allocation to stocks (with a standard deviation of 15% and a Sharpe ratio of 0.35) and bonds (with a standard deviation of 5% and a Sharpe ratio of 0.35). If we assume a correlation of 0.20, the asset allocation is far from balanced in risk terms. If risk is represented by the standard deviation, stocks contribute 92% to the risk of the asset mix. It is often questionable whether expected returns are robust enough to warrant disproportionate risk allocations or common loadings to risk factors.

It is essential to construct a portfolio that is balanced from several different risk perspectives. Risk allocation rather than asset allocation provides a partial solution to this.[12] Nevertheless, it remains important to fully understand the benefits and pitfalls of different portfolio construction techniques and to adjust the portfolio accordingly. In particular, for risk allocation, the appropriate forward-looking risk measures may differ by trade and strategy type. Furthermore, the degree of leverage applied within the fund will need to take into account how crowded a trade may have become, as well as the validity of risk premia going forward. It is very important to adopt an active, forward-looking, risk- and valuation-based absolute return approach to portfolio construction rather than a passive, mechanistic, benchmark-driven relative return approach.

In the same category, the dynamic nature of global macro and the ability to construct trades with an asymmetric payout profile are other examples of how "smart" portfolio construction can generate alpha in macro markets. In this way, an asymmetric option-like return profile can be achieved with a larger upside than downside and with low correlation to the underlying markets and risk factors.[13]

Some of the opportunities in global markets arise from *inefficiencies, barriers and impediments* that the various market participants face. The asset management industry is traditionally organised along asset class silos: stocks, bonds and alternative investments. These units typically operate with a significant degree of autonomy, which makes investors reluctant to trade on drifts in cross-asset valuations. Global macro does exploit these opportunities. Another source is the "home bias" phenomenon, whereby investors are either restricted or just reluctant to trade outside their home market. This gives rise to segmentation of global markets, which may lead to differences in returns on risky assets.

Other investment opportunities arise due to the fact that not all market participants try to maximise their expected risk-adjusted returns, because they may have *differing objectives*. In commodities markets, for example, natural resource producers may offer a risk premium to investors to take on some of their exposure to future commodity price fluctuations. Their demand is driven by insurance motives rather than profit-maximisation objectives. Central bank intervention in currency markets is another example of such non-profit-maximising behaviour.

IMPLEMENTING GTAA/GLOBAL MACRO IN AN INSTITUTIONAL PORTFOLIO

Combining internal and external macro programmes

In our experience, a team of a dozen seasoned investment professionals is quite capable of successfully running a multi-billion dollar institutional GTAA/global macro portfolio at 15% target risk. The mandate would have a *cash-plus* performance target rather than an index benchmark. The focus is therefore on generating absolute returns in all market circumstances, and managing total risk rather than relative risk. In this case study, the fund comprises external macro managers as well as internally managed portfolios. In a full-fledged set-up, the mandate is centered on three competences:

1. external manager selection competence;
2. internal fundamental-discretionary competence; and
3. internal quantitative-systematic competence.

There is diversification within and across these groups in terms of investment process, horizon and strategy. The synergy and cooperation within the whole team is central to the investment process. On a regular basis, the allocation committee decides on the allocation between the mandates, navigating the overall fund through turbulent markets and preserving its staying power for longer-term oriented valuation-based trades. This is a discretionary process, which accounts for the time-varying nature of the various underlying return drivers and risk factors in a constantly changing macro environment.

External asset managers can be a considerable part of the overall risk allocation. It should be an explicit goal of the fund to diversify the portfolio across strategy, investment process, horizon and manager skill. In addition to strategies that focus on the long investment horizon typical of institutional investors, some of the underlying strategies will benefit from shorter investment horizons. The allocation to internal versus external managers depends on a number of factors, not least the size of the overall portfolio, but also the available expertise, resources and infrastructure. This applies to both internal portfolio management and external manager selection. Another important aspect in determining the allocation between internal and external managers is the ability to reduce the fee load paid.

Combining a portfolio of best-in-class external managers with internal teams can be beneficial to both. Chinese walls must be in place between the external management team and the managers of internal portfolios with respect to sensitive information. Internal mandates can help strengthen discussions with external managers on "non-sensitive" topics such as macroeconomics, market knowledge, derivatives and system developments. This form of strategic partnership is able to create synergy and win–win on both sides. External managers are only selected if they are differentiated enough from the internally managed portfolios. For example, this can be due to their specialist expertise in certain areas (eg, emerging markets or volatility) or because their strategy has high barriers to entry (eg, large and costly infrastructure).

The external manager selection team aims to select the best-of-breed managers in the GTAA and global macro universe, which ranges from TAA, currency overlay and global macro style to related macro styles such as CTA and volatility. The external manager portfolio is diversified across four investment quadrants: one dimension is systematic versus discretionary and the other is technical versus fundamental. Furthermore, there is diversification over investment horizons and strategies, including pure-play GTAA, volatility, currencies- or commodities-centred managers. The external competence is a team of dedicated investment professionals focusing on the selection and monitoring of external managers. The due diligence process is robust and focuses on the investment process, risk management team and company, operational process and the overall fit within the existing portfolio. The monitoring process is robust and supported by state-of-the-art risk and performance attribution reports. When selecting the right managers for the portfolio, they negotiate bespoke terms and conditions for fee structures and liquidity terms, thus embedding an institutional mindset in their dealings with all external managers.

Investments tend to start as small risk allocations, but grow as confidence in the manager grows. There is a constant dialogue with external managers about their strategy and views, as they need to remain different from the internal portfolios. In addition, return-based style analysis is used as a powerful monitoring tool to ensure the manager is indeed generating genuine alpha and is not simply loading on betas. In the global macro universe, betas are often time varying. To cope with time variation, it is advisable to use techniques that adapt to changing betas (such as described in Posthuma and Van der Sluis, 2005).[14] The fund may establish strategic partnerships with their external managers. This gives rise to unique thought-sharing opportunities for issues like portfolio construction, trading and macroeconomic outlook. Turnover in the external manager portfolio is expected to be very low.

The *internal fundamental-discretionary team* implements two approaches: one with a shorter-term horizon of three to six months and the other with a longer-term horizon of three years and longer. Each trade in the shorter-term approach is motivated by concepts like fundamental macro, cycle, sentiment and thematic analysis. In the longer-term approach, positions are established only if the asset in question is significantly under- or overvalued with respect to its fair value. By exploiting an institutional investor's long-term investment horizon, this approach will be able to target a relatively unexplored source of genuine alpha in a less-crowded space of long-term positioning with liquid instruments.

Although many financial institutions engage in asset allocation, it is typically implemented either from the strategic perspective mentioned earlier or from a shorter-term tactical perspective. When the timing of a normalisation in valuations is either unclear or takes longer than originally thought, not many investors can afford to step in or stay in the trade. Clients and senior management often evaluate and reward investment managers on short-term performance track records. This short-term evaluation horizon will dissuade most investors from taking investment decisions based on longer-term drivers such as valuation, when the trend or sentiment temporarily goes against them. Therefore, exploiting this investment horizon segment is potentially a powerful source of both beta and alpha generation, although it requires firm belief in your long-term forecasts, a discipline to stick to them and stay in a potentially losing trade at times when momentum and market sentiment run strongly against you.

The processes are discretionary, although models are used as an input in the decision-making process. The portfolios will typically consist of a diverse set of different investment themes or trades. An investment theme can often be represented by different assets and instruments. To limit portfolio risks and ensure diversification, the marginal risk contribution of each theme is limited. To avoid unintended effects, themes should be implemented in as pure a format as possible.

Through a diversified combination of systematic, dynamic and efficient top-down investment strategies, the *internal quantitative-systematic team* aims to earn (alternative) time-varying returns and profit from behavioural biases in global macro markets. By its dynamic nature, these strategies generate returns that are by design virtually uncorrelated to the underlying asset classes. The systematic model-based approach provides return, breadth and capacity to the overall fund and differentiates itself from the internal discretionary global macro strategies. The systematic investment style is an objective and repeatable investment strategy with the ability to cope with large investment universes, quantify exposures, risks and costs. All of the above characterisations of the systematic investment style carry a portion of genuine alpha. One of the sources of alpha from the systematic approach is the emotional detachment – ie, the exploitation of investors' emotional involvement, behavioural biases and cognitive errors. The models are simple, robust and transparent, and well-rooted in economic fundamentals. The portfolio incorporates internally developed proprietary models. The investment horizon of strategies in the portfolio will range roughly from one day to three years. However, through the dynamic nature of the portfolio, the positions can be rebalanced on a daily basis if needed.

Leverage and risk management

The public debate on leverage occasionally seems to confuse the use of leverage and risk. The key question here is: which weighs more – a pound of feathers or a pound of lead? The misconception is that a levered asset is always riskier than an unlevered asset, even if the levered asset has lower risk. Put differently, the actual economic risks of a levered asset are often incorrectly perceived to be larger than the actual economic risks of an unlevered asset. However, all depends on the market risk of the underlying assets. Leverage is not risk, and it does not always lead to more risk – it can actually reduce risk on the portfolio level. Let us consider some potential benefits of using it in an investment portfolio.

First, leverage allows investors to construct a larger investment position and thus achieve higher exposure to certain risks. Different degrees of leverage can turn investments in assets with different risk profiles into investments with comparable risk. Take the example of stocks and bonds: it may turn the risk of investments that typically have a low risk profile (eg, bonds) into a risk profile that is comparable to equities. Second, leverage can enable investors to exploit diversification benefits more fully. Equity risk typically dominates unlevered institutional portfolios during periods of market turmoil. Often the return on a bond allocation does not compensate for the drawdowns experienced on a capital allocation to the stock market of the same size. By smart and judicious use of leverage, drawdowns in one asset can be balanced more with profits in another asset. Third, the trade-off between return and diversification no longer exists once leverage is used. Investors often demand a high capital allocation to risky assets to meet their return constraints. This comes at the cost of an unbalanced risk profile. Fourth, another important application of leverage is to control the overall risk level of the portfolio. Dynamic leverage may create a risk profile that is more constant over time than a portfolio that is based on capital allocation only. Compared to unlevered portfolios, these features enable investors to construct portfolios that target a particular risk profile, are more diversified with respect to different risk factors and robust to a variety of market conditions.

Obviously, risk management, risk control and portfolio construction will be different for a levered portfolio. Not only is there an increased focus on liquidity and counterparty risk, there are also a host of different risk measures, such as capital-at-risk, conditional value-at-risk, concentration risk, tail risks and stress tests.[15] Portfolio construction builds on drawdown control, contribution-to-risk and diversification in tail events. As discussed, leverage allows investors to redistribute risks between a broader set of risk factors in a more balanced way. Proper risk management, risk control and portfolio construction may actually result in a portfolio that has lower economic capital at risk than a similar unlevered portfolio. In other words, from a risk management and risk control perspective, leverage does not automatically lead to more financial risk. Instead, it requires a different risk management approach. We stress that leverage may be properly used for controlled risk management, disciplined portfolio construction and the implementation of a richer investment opportunity set. The focus should be on drawdown controls and the availability of capital to absorb real losses at times when it is needed most, rather than focusing on potentially misleading accounting-based measures.

Our investment philosophy is that risk premia vary through time, and that forward-looking downside risks are highest when risky assets are rich and volatility levels are low. Therefore, volatility – as it is traditionally used in the industry – is an improper measure of downside risk. Markets tend to over-extrapolate past trends, and periods of capitulation are followed by periods of complacency. Markets are most vulnerable in a state of complacency, when they are easily caught off-guard: risk premia tend to be very low and markets tend to be in a search-for-yield mode, thereby compressing future returns even further. Applying pro-cyclical leverage at this stage to squeeze more yield out of tiny spreads is very dangerous. It is much wiser, albeit unfashionable, to de-risk or buy protection in order to preserve capital in such an environment.

Since the global financial crisis of 2007–09, the number of genuinely long-term oriented investors has shrunk considerably, and as simulations of tail-risk protection strategies – with the benefit of hindsight – appeared to do well in 2008, their popularity has increased commensurately. However, the very act of considering hedging or insurance on an asset should be construed as a strong warning signal to re-evaluate the holdings of that particular asset in the portfolio in the first place. Risk management is the backbone of portfolio management and risk cannot be managed in isolation. Risk management and risk allocation can be seen as a source of alpha: risk is driving asset returns. Portfolios should be balanced in terms of multiple risk perspectives.

In our investment philosophy, short-termism is a real danger for risk management. Specifically, it is dangerous for a contrarian investment style to use short-term risk parameters. Risk management should lead to a better understanding of risk, and not necessarily to higher risk aversion. It is better to look at a measure like downside deviation or, better still, valuation-based forward-looking measures of risk. Formulated in the context of equity markets, it makes a huge difference for the underlying risk, not reflected in volatility, whether equities are rich or cheap. A backward-looking risk system would have allocated more to equity in 2007 (with the S&P 500 at 1500) than in 2003 (with the S&P 500 at 1000), whereas a valuation-based approach would have lowered the allocation in 2007 and increased it in 2003. Using internal risk systems in combination with the best off-the-shelf third-party products provides not only the flexibility to determine what the relevant risk measures are, but also an awareness of their potential pitfalls. It is impossible to capture risk in just one number. Multiple risk measures, approaches and systems should be used in parallel. Looking in the rear view mirror is simply not enough.

By definition, internal portfolios are fully transparent: there is full position transparency at every point in time. Daily valuation of the managed accounts is carried out by an external administrator using price information from independent vendors. Furthermore, all positions are input into the best practice off-the-shelf risk management systems with a broad coverage of instruments. Independent risk controllers use those risk management systems to perform disciplined risk analysis (eg, short-, medium- and long-term risk measures, risk exposures, stress tests, warning signals, top 10 positions). This information is then disseminated to the fund and portfolio managers on a daily basis.

There is a continuous dialogue between the risk controllers and the portfolio managers. The two teams discuss the risk reports on a regular basis and take action if and when needed. Furthermore, internal mandates allocate risk to different investment opportunities. Off-the-shelf risk management systems are complemented with internally developed proprietary risk management and portfolio construction systems. Obviously, there is a central role for stress tests, tail-risk analyses and risk attribution. During the implementation phase, portfolio managers select investment instruments to implement their views in as pure a way as possible, while at the same time controlling for tail risks. The tail dependencies between assets and strategies are measured through quantitative tools, but also assessed on a commonsense level with a healthy dose of paranoia. Internal portfolio managers are first and foremost managers of risk, as they are actively allocating it. In addition, the above-mentioned risk controllers are independent from the fund. This set-up ensures proper risk management governance of the internal portfolios and the fund as a whole.

Liquidity and cash management are two other important aspects of risk management. In addition to initial margins and collateral requirements, a portion of the notional of the underlying portfolios is reserved for variation margins to adapt to fluctuations in the markets. The actual positioning, choice of derivatives, stress-test results and the nature of the underlying strategies are all important factors in determining a sufficiently conservative cash buffer. Leverage is moderate and determined by the above cash requirements. Leverage is a tool to mitigate risks and not a control variable. After using quantitative and qualitative analyses to stress test the portfolio with different degrees of leverage, the appropriate cash buffer levels are then determined.

Significant use of derivatives increases the importance of managing counterparty risk. This is mitigated by the fact that, in GTAA and global macro programmes, most derivatives are typically linear instruments – such as futures, forwards and swaps. Moreover, in the futures market, counterparty risk is limited to a one-day jump risk because the exchange requires daily margin adjustments from all counterparties. Also, the exchange can change the capital requirements at any time, and because of relatively liquid markets, it can sell a party out of positions quickly if necessary. In the over-the-counter (OTC) market, counterparty risk is a bigger issue because there is only one counterparty per trade. But in an interest rate swap, the principal is not exchanged. So, if the counterparty shuts down, the only risk is to the gain or loss on that contract. Paradoxically, risk is mitigated by the fact that it is a derivative. In addition, daily collateral management further mitigates counterparty risk. However, it is important to monitor the quality of the counterparties and make changes to the exposures when needed.

Governance and operations

Governance structure and operational set-up are key ingredients for the successful implementation of a global macro mandate. The governance structure must aim at minimising principal-agent conflicts and should embody independent oversight, accountability and clear responsibilities. In theory, principal-agent problems arise in asset management whenever there is incomplete or asymmetric information between the principal stakeholders and the agents who are hired to run parts of the portfolio under potentially conflicting terms of interest. Discrepancies may arise from differences in investment horizons, career risks, irrational preferences for specific asset classes and a focus on a bottom-up rather than a top-down approach, as well as lack of ownership, dedication and responsibilities.[16] For example, governance of traditional TAA committees is often sub-optimal. Too often, inefficient committee structures have resulted in dismal decisions and poor performance. Low frequency of meetings and lack of accountability can lead to slow and inefficient implementation. In contrast, in the global macro set-up described above a dedicated and accountable full-time portfolio management team with timely access to market intelligence assures clear delineation of responsibilities and fast implementation. It also ensures a top-down cross-market focus rather than a bottom-up silo orientation. Of course, there should be independent lines for risk management, valuation and compliance to guarantee independent oversight and control.

CONCLUSION

In our experience, a global macro mandate tailored to an institutional setting enables long-term investors to access unique and attractive risk–return signatures not easily accessible otherwise. A well-diversified global macro programme is capable of harvesting investment opportunities from inefficiencies, time-varying returns, a broader investment and instrument universe, and risk-controlled portfolio construction. The blueprint described in this chapter builds on our investment philosophy and experience managing an absolute return mandate in an institutional context. It aims to achieve attractive risk-adjusted absolute returns through a structured and disciplined investment approach. The mandate achieves diversification via dynamic risk allocation to a diverse set of return sources, risk factors, investment strategies and styles. It builds up exposures in different liquid global asset markets, such as equities, fixed income, currencies, commodities, inflation and volatility.

Besides internally managed portfolios, the mandate may also allocate to externally managed global macro mandates. We believe that institutional investors can benefit from cross-fertilisation between externally and internally managed global macro funds, especially if resources are not available internally or if the external manager invests in a niche market. The optimal allocation between external and internal managers depends on assets under management, costs, expertise, technological infrastructure and resources. Evidently, a proper governance structure and solid operational infrastructure, including in-depth risk management, are key ingredients for success. As such, the described mandate is very different from traditional TAA programmes, as it represents a blend with the global macro hedge fund style. As a consequence, the global macro mandate can fit within an institutional portfolio in a number of ways: as part of a hedge fund allocation, as a portable alpha overlay or as a successor to a traditional TAA programme.

Moreover, on a regular basis, financial markets are likely to be subjected to serious exogenous shocks, ranging from natural disasters and terrorist attacks to political unrest and fears of large sovereign defaults. Based on a combination of quantitative triggers and qualitative assessments, *ad hoc* committee meetings can be called to assess whether protective measures need to be taken to adjust the overall portfolio exposures to the new reality. Real-time insights in market dynamics and interconnections can be very useful as an input for such responses. A well-designed global macro programme can add considerable value in this regard.

Finally, by building strategic partnerships with their external managers, institutional investors can benefit from translating insights from a properly constructed global macro mandate into their own strategic investment decisions. Strategic and dynamic asset allocation, benchmark choice, rebalancing policy, overlay structures, derivatives knowledge and top-down risk management are just some of the areas that would have a natural fit with the global macro mandate in question.

1 Leon C. Megginson, paraphrasing one of the key tenets of Charles Darwin's work on evolution.

2 See Lerner, Josh, Antoinette Schoar and Jialan Wang, 2008, "Secrets of the Academy: The Drivers of University Endowment Success," *Journal of Economic Perspectives*, **22**(3), pp 207–22, for an evaluation of asset allocations of university endowment funds. See Chambers, David, Elroy Dimson and Antti Ilmanen, 2012, "The Norway Model," *Journal of Portfolio Management*, **38**(2), pp 67–81, for a comparison of the investment approaches of the Norwegian Government Pension Fund Global and the Yale endowment fund, and Ambachtsheer, Keith, 2012, "Norway vs. Yale...Or vs. Canada? A Comparison of Investment Models," March, for a comparison of those funds to the investment approaches of the Canadian pension plans.

3 See the seminal article on the determinants of portfolio performance: Brinson, Gary P., Randolph Hood and Gilbert L. Beebower, 1986, "Determinants of Portfolio Performance," *Financial Analysts Journal*, **42**(4), July/August, pp 39–44.

4 See the article: Clarke, Roger, Harindra de Silva and Steven Thorley, 2006, "The Fundamental Law of Active Portfolio Management', *Journal of Investment Management*, **4**(3), third quarter, pp 54–72.

5 We use the concepts "GTAA" and "global macro" interchangeably as we think of them as one and the same. We are cognisant that other market participants operating in different settings will often make a distinction between the two.

6 See Carhart, M, "Global Tactical Asset Allocation," in Bob Litterman (ed), 2003, *Modern Investment Management: An Equilibrium Approach* (Hoboken, NJ: John Wiley).

7 It is based on the excess performance of the absolute return GTAA fund the authors managed at a very large pension fund during this period.

8 The hedge fund mix consists of Dow Jones Credit Suisse sub-strategies (convertible arbitrage, distressed/restructuring, emerging markets, equity-neutral, event-driven, fixed income arbitrage, global macro, long-short equity and managed futures).

9 We back out the correlation within GTAA, the pension fund asset mix and the hedge fund portfolio by comparing the aggregate portfolio risk to the stand-alone risk of the underlying composites.

10 See, among others, Dahlquist, Magnus and Cambpbell R. Harvey, 2001, "Global Tactical Asset Allocation," *Journal of Global Capital Markets*, Spring; and Fama E. F. and K. R. French, 1989, "Business Conditions and Expected Returns on Stock and Bonds," *Journal of Financial Economics*, 25; and Ilmanen, Antti, 2011, *Expected Returns: An Investor's Guide to Harvesting Market Rewards* (Chichester, England: Wiley), for an excellent and comprehensive read on time-varying risk premia.

11 Perold, Andre F. and William F. Sharpe, 1988, "Dynamic Strategies for Asset Allocation," *Financial Analysts Journal*, **44**(1), (January–February), pp 16–27.

12 Inker, Ben. 2011, "The Dangers of Risk Parity", *Journal of Investing*, **20**(1), pp 90–8.

13 See, for instance, graph D in Figure 14.2.

14 Posthuma, N. and P. J. Van der Sluis, "Analyzing Style Drift in Hedge Funds," in Gregoriou, Greg N., Nicolas Papageorgiou, Georges Hübner and Fabrice Rouah (eds), 2005, *Hedge Funds: Insights in Performance Measurement, Risk Analysis, and Portfolio Allocation* (Hoboken, NJ: John Wiley).

15 See Jorion, P., 2000, "Risk Management Lessons for Long-Term Capital Management," *European Financial Management*, **6**(3), pp 277–300, for a lively admonition of how leverage as a pure return enhancer can lead to disastrous events.

16 See Ang, A. and K. Kjaer, 2011, "Investing for the Long Run," working paper, Columbia Business School, for a discussion on how the potential misalignment between asset owners and asset managers hinders long-term asset allocation.

Index

(page numbers in italic type refer to figures and tables)